Grace Paley's Life Stories

Grace Paley's Life Stories

A Literary Biography

Judith Arcana

University of Illinois Press
Urbana and Chicago

© 1993 by Judith Arcana
Manufactured in the United States of America
C 5 4 3 2 1

This book is printed on acid-free paper.

Library of Congress Cataloging-in-Publication Data

Arcana, Judith.
  Grace Paley's life stories : a literary biography / Judith Arcana.
        p.   cm.
    Includes bibliographical references and index.
    ISBN 0-252-01945-8 (cl)
      1. Paley, Grace—Biography.   2. Authors, American—20th century—
  Biography.   3. Women and literature—United States—History—20th
  century.   I. Title.
  PS3566.A46Z54   1993
  813'.54—dc20
    [B]   92-5884
                                                                               CIP

This book is dedicated with affection and gratitude to Grace Paley and Joyce P. Wexler, both of whom gave me a good deal of what I needed to write it.

All sorts of American cultural workers were invited. Some laughed to hear themselves described in this way. They were accustomed to being called "dreamer poet realist postmodernist." They might have liked being called "cultural dreamer," but no one had thought of that yet.

— Grace Paley, "The Expensive Moment"

Contents

Illustrations following pp. 34 and 160.

Preface

We often read and write to discover what is unknown to us and apparently different from ourselves, but just as often we seek familiarity, similarity, a kind of homeground. As readers—Dorothy Parker's "constant" readers, Virginia Woolf's "common" readers—and as scholars and writers, we ask, what about me? Where in literature are reflections of my experience, my sensibilities, my world view, my politics? When I read and write about John Keats, or D. H. Lawrence, or *Beowulf,* I am ranging far off, studying the history and possibilities of a distant "other." But when I study she-who-is-most-like-me, I learn what has been—and might be—possible for myself.[1]

Since 1985 I have visited with Grace Paley many times, a Boswell to her Johnson at readings, meetings, and kitchen tables. Though we drank more tea than coffee and probably will never tour the Hebrides, we have managed to walk, talk, and eat together in New York, Washington, D.C., Vermont, New Hampshire, and Illinois. Like our gentlemen predecessors, we have grown into mutual respect and affection, but we have gone beyond Boswell's memory and stenography by taping many hours of formal interviews as well.

A great pleasure to me, a source of satisfaction, a delight, and an education, my work has also been a struggle. My struggle has been a self-conscious one because, in coming to know Grace Paley, I had access to sources of otherwise unobtainable information and exceptionally privileged insight. She has afforded me the opportunity, over several years, to be in her life, and she came into my life as well; I now know her in ways that I could never know subjects studied only in the library or classroom. But there was—as my readers must realize—a limit to the use I made of that information and insight.[2] That limit was defined primarily by Grace[3] herself and other of my informants, who said, "Don't quote me on this," or "Please don't use this in your book." Knowledge beyond that limit has indeed informed my analysis and my writing, but I came to see that even some of what was not censored by Grace, her family, her friends, and her colleagues was inappropriate for me to discuss in these pages.[4] On one occasion only, when this text was complete, Grace asked me to remove a sentence, a line I had quoted from an interview with someone else; she made the request because she was concerned about its impact on the person being described. I took it out.

Occasionally, I disagreed with Grace Paley about the construction of meaning or purpose in her stories and even about interpretations of her behavior and personal history. Other biographically inclined scholars and writers have dealt with this issue; their work supports and encourages mine. Sandra Whipple Spanier, for instance, in her work on Kay Boyle, discusses her struggle with the question of how we can determinedly disagree with an author's view of her own work—when that author is right there in front of us, telling us we are wrong. Claudia Tate, in her work with Black women writers, took some pains in her initial commentary and various introductory notes to discuss the intricate relationship between a writer's life and a writer's text, especially when dealing with writers who deny that any such relationship exists. Gloria T. Hull, in her work with Alice Dunbar-Nelson's niece, Pauline A. Young, encountered—and explored with her readers—several of the questions, problems, and issues that dealing with real live people must always present. Carol Ascher, Louise DeSalvo, and Sara Ruddick, themselves involved in such endeavors, edited a collection of essays by women whose lives and work are concentrated on the lives and work of other women; all of those essays, which include expressions of doubt and anxiety about exploitation of our "subjects," as well as fear and resentment of their censorship, reveal the excitement and intense pleasure of this delicate intimate enterprise.[5]

When she learned to drive—around the age of fifty—Grace

Paley loved driving so much she thought she would become a New York City taxi driver. Probably the only reason she didn't was that her schedule couldn't accommodate another commitment. Her daily mail looks like the postal carrier's load for a whole route, her calendar like an intricate puzzle with no clues. Her schedule might prompt an observer to ask what the major commitments and priorities are, in all that flurry of variegated action. And she would answer, "When you say 'major things, important things'—and ask where most of my thought and energy is now—there's such a strong connection [among them all] that you really can't separate" one issue from another. And if the observer should remonstrate, "But you can't *do* it all, really," Grace Paley says,

> Well, you *can*. . . . You can do a great deal of it. There's no reason why you can't think about several things and work on several things.
>
> Some people *are* totally interested in Central American work now, and that's real good. First of all, all of our money is going there. When we pay taxes, that's where the money is going: Central American [or Middle Eastern] militarization. . . . Then in some states, like Vermont, there's ERA stuff still. And all the stuff about women's reproductive rights. That's absolutely key. There's nothing that isn't terribly important. I mean, how can a woman think that their attack on our bodies is not a real attack? For me, my feminism is getting stronger all the time.

To get a sense of how she does what she does, I asked her to tell me her work schedule for the coming week. Teaching wasn't on the list that week, and she didn't include sweeping and laundry, or cooking, grocery shopping, and washing dishes, or attending meetings and visiting with friends and family. She also didn't specify time for writing stories. That week she had three major commitments: "The writing that I get done will be nonfiction, so to speak. I have to give a talk on Monday on Mary E. Wilkins Freeman, in our local library. It'll be a small group of people probably, and I could have taken Edith Wharton. But I chose Freeman because I figured everybody reads Edith Wharton."

"And this way they'll have to read Freeman," I say, and she says, "Yeah, if they *want* to. If they want to talk to me on Monday, they'll have to read Freeman. So I use my local reputation to get people to read Freeman. Okay, so I have to give that little literary talk. No big deal, not too many people." I ask her to tell me, in each case, what her purpose is, what it's *for.* "My purpose?" she echoes, and I think she's indignant. "They asked me." I point out that a lot of people ask her to do things.

> And I do them. First of all, I relate to this community. It's very local. I mean, it's the library down at the·corner. It's my way of being part of this community. And I agreed to do it when they asked me to do it because it's my line of work, literature. And the second thing that I have to do is on Wednesday, to speak at the local women's network, which is a dinner for which people will pay $15 or something like that. It ain't Chicago or New York, but they'll pay. It's called, 'Can Women Save the World?' But the truth is, it's going to be, it's surely gonna be, about militarism and about reproductive rights, and about what they're trying to do to women now. And I'll probably drag in some literature. And on Saturday I'm going to talk in Burlington at a conference. It's Disarmament Day, and I'm gonna talk at a General Electric plant where they make Gatling guns that they use in helicopters over Nicaragua. Okay. So you have my whole life there, next week. I can't tell it to you better than that.

But you can't really hear that conversation, can't really know what went on between us, unless you know that it took place in her kitchen/sitting room, in late Vermont autumn, and that while we talked—for hours, with tapes and recorder and microphone and wires all over the table, amidst the tea and creamed herring and bread crumbs and jelly—her husband Bob and his son Duncan were hammering repairs all over the outside walls of the house. Also the chimney sweep, a young musician named Steve, was working about eight feet away from us on the wood stove. So Bob and Duncan are banging while Steve sounds like he's scraping pieces of metal to-gether, vigorously brushing bunches of thick wires across various rough surfaces. The noise is finally so much bigger, so much *more* than our conversation, that we stop talking and then burst out laughing. Then we make more tea.

A twentieth-century Boswell, I have all the appropriate elec-tronic devices, but somehow that doesn't lessen the difficulty of getting my subject's words onto paper. Unlike Dr. Johnson, Grace Paley is uncomfortable being the center of attention for hours at a time. So until we had been working together for nearly eighteen months, we never had an uninterrupted set, an interview without other people or phone calls (the record is nine calls in two hours). She would often invite people to join us, partly because she wanted me to meet them and thought we would all enjoy each other—but mostly because then she wouldn't have to talk exclusively and extensively about herself.

Once, in New York, an unexpected large package was delivered while we were taping. We set it aside, trying to be businesslike, but within half an hour we had set aside the microphone instead, to open what turned out to be a hotshot camera with all imaginable attachments—sent to Grace as a "gift" from the manufacturer, "in recognition of" her "contributions." Maybe they want her to go on TV and say how nifty it is—but no, there were no strings attached; I read the letter twice. They just gave it to her.

During that same session, one of the longest phone conversations was with a young woman who calls Grace every few weeks for sustenance; she's been in and out of serious depressions for many months, and Grace is one of her lifelines. Another call was from her son Danny, making arrangements to meet her for a trip to the park with his daughter Laura; another was from her sister; two were from close friends; and others were from folks who want her to read, speak, petition, or otherwise join them in their efforts to raise the general consciousness of New York, New England, and the world.

Once in New York we went for a walk around her neighborhood, and she bought a pair of shell earrings for her daughter-in-law Debbie's birthday. The merchant was a congenial woman who had spread her wares—from Morocco, Bolivia, Nepal, and Kenya—over a rug on the sidewalk. We both were certainly as interested in her as in each other. Another time, when I arrived in New York for an appointment we had made long before, she explained that she had to leave for a couple hours in the middle of our session "to go to a meeting." This turned out to be—I discovered later—an awards dinner at which she received one of the PEN/Faulkner prizes. She came back home after the "couple hours" without mentioning it, and since I hadn't eaten, we went out for Chinese food.

My sentimental favorite is the time we drove around the back roads of central Vermont in her little car: I'm strapped in with the tape recorder between my knees, my folder of notes and questions across my lap, a pen in my right hand and the microphone in my left—pointed at her mouth as she answers my questions in a mostly thoughtful, soft voice. But sometimes she says, in a much louder voice, "Look at these fields. I want you to look at these fields." And, "There's lots of cows up here. I'll tell Bob; he'll be surprised. He thinks they're almost all gone already, but look, the farmers up here on these hill roads still have their cows."

The next day I listen to my tapes and find that—after all our talk about Broner, Ozick and Olsen, Malamud, Bellow, and Roth—only the Vermont hills commentary is really audible over the sound of the tires on hard dirt and loose gravel. So I say to her, "Grace, no more interviewing while driving around in the car. I listened to those tapes and they're crazy; it's impossible." She says, "No. You didn't have the mike close enough." Later, when I'm not exasperated at the failed promise of technology—and my own lapse of judgment—I realize she's probably right. I think maybe I didn't have the mike close enough.

Acknowledgments

I am immeasurably grateful to Grace Paley for her generosity and candor and for the many hours and days she gave me during the years spent researching and writing this book. Joyce P. Wexler supported and encouraged me in this project from the beginning, in the fall of 1984, when I originally conceived of a biographical study and then went to meet Grace at a symposium at Northwestern University. Joyce's criticism and advice, her careful editing and persuasive argument, have been a gift.

Friends, colleagues, and relatives of Grace Paley have given me not only their time, memories, photographs, judgments, and musings, but also their extraordinary hospitality. They cleared out their calendars, kitchens, and sitting rooms for me and my tape recorder. We ate vegetables pulled right out of the ground in Vermont and ice cream in cut-glass dishes in New York. Danny Paley took me for a walk along the river, where we viewed the skyline of lower Manhattan from Brooklyn's edge; Jeanne Tenenbaum offered me her couch for a nap and drove me across Manhattan in rush-hour traffic; Jane Cooper took me to a delicious Greek restaurant in a basement on the Upper West Side; Karl Bissinger gave me a perfect hibiscus blossom from a bush in his late summer rooftop garden. I got a walking tour of Greenwich Village—east and west—a new batch of information about bodywork and good medicinal herbs, a truck ride over miles of Vermont and New Hampshire countryside, a preprint manuscript copy of the commemorative journal for Grace's sixty-fifth birthday celebration, lots of tea and cookies, rides to train stations, extremely interesting and well-told personal histories, and an enormous amount of essential information from Karl Bissinger, Sybil Claiborne, Jane Cooper, Victor Goodside, Bob Nichols, Danny Paley, Debbie Paley, Jess Paley, Laura Paley, Nora Paley, and Jeanne Tenenbaum. I can never really thank them enough, but I do indeed thank them.

Many people who were at Loyola University of Chicago while I was there gave me support, encouragement, praise, and assistance throughout the research and writing of the first drafts of this text. They include Jane Cocalis, Gloria Conforti, Allen J. Frantzen, Suzanne S. Gossett, Carole Hayes, Paul Jay, Patricia Lorimer Lundberg, Janice Mouton, Lorna Newman, Jill N. Reich, James E. Rocks, Judith Wittner, and Nancy Workman.

Additionally, the women of Northwestern University Library's Special Collections were of great help, and Sarah Lawrence College librarians assisted me with their archives. Ruth Benn of the War Resisters League helped me with archival research. Loyola University and the Arthur Schmitt Foundation granted much-needed assistantships and a fellowship during my years of formal graduate study.

On the home front, Jonathan Arlook provided extraordinary support of almost every conceivable kind, from emotional sustenance through financial aid to technical instruction. In the years devoted to this project I also received support, assistance, and criticism from Cathryn Adamsky, Daniel Arcana-Pildes, Peaches Blessington, Pat Cramer, Arlene Kaplan Daniels, Omie Daniels, Flora Faraci, Susan Koppelman, Susan Korn, Donna Lachman, Stuart Leven, Lois Nowicki, the late Nan Nowik, Stephanie Riger, Edna Rosenberg, and Jody Speckman.

And of course this book, like so many others, would not exist if there were not hundreds of thousands of women—in the United States and all over the world—who work, make their art, and live their lives consciously in struggle toward liberation, peace, and justice.

Note on Abbreviations and Interviews

Throughout this book, Grace Paley's story and poetry collections will be abbreviated as follows:

LDM   *The Little Disturbances of Man: Stories of Women and Men at Love.* New York: Doubleday, 1959.

ECLM   *Enormous Changes at the Last Minute.* New York: Dell, 1975.

LSD   *Later the Same Day.* New York: Farrar Straus Giroux, 1985.

LF   *Leaning Forward.* Penobscot: Granite Press, 1985.

Quoted dialogue not otherwise cited is taken from audiotaped interviews done in person by Judith Arcana over several hours (except in the case of Bob Nichols and Jess Paley, when notes were made during conversation). Interviews with Grace Paley were done over a period of years, as indicated.

Karl Bissinger	1987	Manhattan
Sybil Claiborne	1987	Manhattan
Jane Cooper	1987	Manhattan
Victor Goodside	1987	Mount Vernon, N.Y.
Bob Nichols	1987	Vermont and New Hampshire
Danny Paley	1987	Brooklyn
Debbie Paley	1987	Brooklyn

Grace Paley	1985–89	Manhattan, Vermont, Chicago
Jess Paley	1987	Manhattan
Laura Paley	1987	Brooklyn
Nora Paley	1987	Vermont
Jeanne Tenenbaum	1987	Manhattan

Grace Paley's Life Stories

Introduction

By translating her life into art, a writer not only "saves"—in Grace Paley's terms—her own life, but offers others the revelation of meaning in that life. That offering and its integral revelation are at the core of this work, which is a biographical reading of a strongly autobiographical writer. A separation of "the work" from "the life" of an artist in biographical study is always artificial and arbitrary, performed with difficulty and resulting in necessarily false distinctions. We usually make that separation for ease of handling, accepting the partition as appropriate to academic and marketing enterprises. Grace Paley is a writer whose life and work resist separation, demanding an integrated analysis of her family, her political work, and her writing.

Other critics have focused on Grace Paley as a Jew and as a woman.[1] Building on their work, asserting the value of biographical scholarship, examining the relationship between biographical critic and autobiographical writer, I read Grace Paley's work as the art of a contemporary American author who is a woman, a mother, a Jew, and a political activist; my work seeks an understanding of the relationships among these categories. I benefit from the focused studies of other readers in my placement of the individual artist within a matrix comprised of many categories and definitions. This matrix is enriched by recent Paley scholarship, which often concentrates on yet another single dimension, her use of language.[2]

This study is undertaken with the knowledge that the ability of readers to "know" the lives or determine the intentions of authors, like the ability of readers to distinguish fiction from nonfiction or autobiography, is debatable, to say the least. Critical debate notwithstanding, we can see that much of Grace Paley's work is what we have traditionally considered autobiographical; often her stories and characters are drawn directly from her own life. On the other hand, her work frequently includes *apparent* autobiography that is either disproved by the facts of her life or denied by her.

What are the relationships among these transformations and mistaken identities? Where are the writer's choices made, and why? I suggest we can understand that transition—from life into fiction—when we "read" both Grace Paley and her texts. We cannot read the texts as if they were the life; nor can we sever the life from the texts. We can, however, study the relationship between the life and the texts by examining the transitional space—that peculiar set of personal, sociohistorical circumstances—in which the author chooses to render an actual room or boy or woman or tree *into* the room or boy or woman or tree in a story.

This book is a telling of stories about Grace Paley's life and work; it examines and comments on both, developing an analysis through the evolution of her career. In the earliest chapters, when Grace Goodside Paley is not yet a writer, there are references to stories (written later) and connections noted between the facts of her life and the "facts" of her stories, but there is little overt discussion of her literary work. As she develops into a working writer over time, a critical analysis develops in this book; fuller commentary is then interwoven throughout the biographical text.

Literary scholars consider Grace Paley a writer's writer; they are impressed with her craft, her characterization, and the extraordinary presence she projects in her prose.[3] That presence—the *apparent* presence of the author in the work—is no doubt responsible for the widespread assumption among Paley readers that in her stories the characters, narrators, and author are all one—and that the reader, by knowing the fiction, also knows the writer. Even various personae, differing in gender, race, class, and age from their author, still seem to represent her; they convince their readers that they are "real," that the writer is "really" speaking to them.

In her early stories, Grace Paley did create one female character —as did Katherine Anne Porter, Mary McCarthy, and Hortense

Calisher, among others—whom several critics refer to as the author's "alter ego." Introduced in "The Used-Boy Raisers" in *The Little Disturbances of Man* (1959), Faith Darwin Asbury has become a touchstone, a central figure who appears in at least thirteen—fifteen or sixteen, if we count honorable mentions and unnamed narrators who replicate her—of the forty-five collected stories, as well as at least three short pieces published separately.[4] By 1985, with the publication of Grace Paley's third story collection, despite certain clear and specific differences, Faith's personal history, politics, and relationships still seem to mirror her author's.[5]

By creating Faith and her parents, her children and friends, her history and community, and by having them move through what theater people call "real time"—aging and changing as the world does—Grace Paley has constructed an ongoing story cycle. Stories in a cycle are "linked" so that the reader has "successive experience on various levels of the pattern," which "modifies . . . experience of . . . [its] parts." In a story cycle, protagonists are "realized through recurrence, repetition with variation, association, and so on" (Ingram, 19–22).[6] As in the classic example of the story cycle in twentieth-century literature in the United States, *Winesburg, Ohio*, each story may be read, understood, and valued individually, but it is through their cumulative impact that the power of the writer's vision is most fully experienced. Each of Grace Paley's forty-five collected stories is a scene in the cycle, a story from the spatial and chronological neighborhood that covers more than one country and nearly one century, from memories of her family's last years in Russia to the present, located most often in New York City—"in all [her] places of paying attention—the park, the school, our street" ("Friends," LSD, 72–73).[7]

So powerful is the identification of this author with her characters that some readers—including a few scholars, who have lodged personal complaints with me—are surprised, even resentful, when they discover that Grace Paley is not, and has not ever been, the single mother of two sons. They feel that they have been tricked because the author has been so good at making up Faith; readers believe in her and seem to count on her. Certainly "Faith" and "Grace," two proper nouns that name spiritual or religious abstractions, refer to each other in their obvious association.[8] Perhaps a central point here is that for women who identify strongly with

Faith, she becomes a kind of role model. Can readers, like Faith, "with one hand typing behind [our] back[s] to earn a living," get enough peanut butter and jelly sandwiches onto the table, love our kids, be with our friends, and stay sane and funny? Women read about Faith and think, well, if she can do it, I can do it.

Addressing the issue these readers raise, Grace Paley says, "The only thing you can say is that Faith *is* a real person. . . . Every story I write is a story of what I think happened. Even if I invented it. I made up the story and here's what I think happened in the story. . . . I think this is what might have happened, or this is what *could* have happened—you know, a person like Faith could have existed—that's important. That woman could have existed, and she could have been one of my best friends." This is essentially the answer made by the narrator in "A Conversation with My Father" in *Enormous Changes at the Last Minute* (1974). She says to the reader, about a character she has created and has to defend against her father's criticism, "That woman lives across the street. She's my knowledge and my invention" (167).

About the insistence that Grace Paley *is* her characters or the resentment that she's misled us because she is *not*, the writer says, "That's just a false view of fiction; you can't say what these people are saying." She believes that the difference between "fiction" and "nonfiction" is an artificial thing and that "it's created partly for selling purposes," for merchandising, maybe even for ease of shelving. She uses the example of Maxine Hong Kingston's *The Woman Warrior*. That book, "for instance, was sold as nonfiction. And it's obviously fiction. Well, maybe every mother in it might be her mother, like with my father," in the collected stories. "But it's obviously fiction. If anything is a piece of fiction, it's that. . . . This is like an argument that's not real. It's an argument that's created but has no reality."

We read the stories of Grace Paley and find out about Faith, her neighborhood, her work, her people, and her politics. Then we "read" Grace Paley and find out about her neighborhood, her work, her people, and her politics. And in the transitional space between the written life and the lived life, we try to see the relationship between them as she transforms one into the other.[9] Asked about her childhood in the Bronx, she says, "Oh, it's in the stories, it's all in the stories." Is she saying that these stories are autobiography?

"No. I'm not saying that. I'm saying that I wrote my life *into* the stories; don't you see the difference?" To make that difference clear, she explains that the first few lines of the first Faith story ("The Used-Boy Raisers," LDM) describe a scene she personally witnessed in the fifties. She went to visit a close friend and found her there in her kitchen with her two husbands: "So I was thinking about her in my first paragraph. . . . But all the rest I made up. . . . after that first paragraph, none of it is real, none of it." She put words in the mouth and ideas in the head of that character that her friend "would never say, or isn't even interested in."

The reader wonders then: aren't they still the words and ideas of Grace Paley? Was George Willard "really" Sherwood Anderson? Or in that even more complicated case, in which memoir is fiction and memory is talking-story, is the voice of the narrator in *The Woman Warrior* "really" Maxine Hong Kingston? The answer here must be "sometimes" or "sort of" or "in a way—yes." But the text is not the life.[10] The crafting of fiction, in taking "real life" as its material, is like the craft of the artist who takes the sculpture out of the stone or sees a figure in the newly sanded wood.

That craft, invisible as we read—carried along by the story— appears under the light of analysis. For instance, Grace Paley's stories produce the effect of "reality" while they call traditional literary definitions and categories into question. They often lack conventional literary direction, so that readers must follow a story's movement from one voice, one year, or one scene to another, out of order and without the usual markers—those hints and guides that literature used to offer before the radical postmodern rulebreakers got our attention. In Grace Paley's texts, there is no apparent line, no formal, defined separation between fictions, between fiction and nonfiction—or between life and art.

Certainly her frequent use of the I-narrator and the style of her dialogue—now almost always without quotation marks—produce a spoken quality in tone and language, encouraging readers to feel they are being addressed directly and personally or are overhearing an actual exchange. The occasional direct address of earlier writers, such as the nineteenth century's classic "Reader, . . . ," was suddenly and strikingly at odds with its surrounding text, but Grace Paley's conversational engagement of her reader is wholly integrated with her narrative. One of the principal devices she employs—

producing the immediacy of an apparently live presence—is the *overheard narrator:* characters respond in dialogue to what narrators say—as if they had been reading along with us and have "heard" the narrative voice.

Moreover, in her most apparently autobiographical work, characters reflect her well-known political stance, including her struggle to be responsible for her own consciousness: what she learns is learned by those characters. Faith is revealed as less than lovable when the erstwhile racist and sexist Zagrowsky "tells" and when Cassie angrily points out that she—and all other lesbians—have been "left out" of Faith's stories. Appearing at the end of *Later the Same Day* in 1985, Cassie's words echo the equally educational and disciplinary conclusion of *Enormous Changes at the Last Minute* in 1974, when the younger Faith lives "for about three weeks" with Mrs. Luddy, who tells her more than once, "Girl, you don't know nothing" (192). In the story called "Anxiety," the first-person narrator is a verbal and political ringer for Grace Paley; she leans out her window and chides a young father who refuses to see himself as the power-wielder his little daughter knows him to be. "Of course it never really happened," the writer says. "I mean, I do have a window, and they're in the school next door, and. . . . I *was* looking out my window. . . . "

That narrator lives where Grace Paley lives, maybe even in Grace Paley's apartment, where her own children finished their growing up. That narrator sees and hears the children go in and out of PS 41 every day and, in the voice of Grace Paley, radical activist and wise woman, she admonishes the young father: "Son, I must tell you that madmen intend to destroy this beautifully made planet. That the murder of our children by these men has got to become a terror and a sorrow to you, and starting now, it had better interfere with any daily pleasure" (LSD, 101). Grace Paley absolutely intends to effect social change—if not revolution—in her work. She is trying to save the world, or at least to "save a few lives," as one of her narrators asserts.

Scholars have begun to analyze the intimate and overtly personal translation of the family life of women and children into art, and they have defined autobiography as a frequent and major subject—acting as both cause and effect of sociopolitical consciousness—in the literature of women and (other) despised groups. Autobiography in fiction offers a telling of stories that have been untold or ghettoized, stories that have been buried, warped, or shunted aside. Ironically, their telling *realizes* them in a world that has defined them as fantasy or denied them into nonexistence. Grace Paley's stories constitute and provide such realization. Indeed, her life's work is defined by its internal coalition of political action and literary production.

1
The Immigrant Story

Grace Paley believes that we are all creatures of our time, born and formed in history. Her stories always carry the past within their present, even as both turn amazingly into the future. Every story, she has said, is at least two stories, and her own often include more than two plots, more than two sets of characters, more than two "central" themes. This is one of the ways in which her work is most true and most autobiographical, for the stories of our lives never do separate and line up neatly into diagrammable, chronological plots. Instead, our stories weave in and out erratically, absorbing and eclipsing each other in turn, moving back and forth through history, which contains them all.

The stories of Grace Paley's own life begin before she was born, early in the twentieth century, maybe on a wagon piled with straw covering hidden trunks and boxes, or in a train rushing through the night of eastern Europe, carrying hundreds of immigrants to the crowded North Sea ports, where they boarded ships that would take them to America. Grace Paley's mother and father, Manya Ridnyik and Isaac Gutseit, came to the United States in 1906, when they were both twenty-one years old, he a few months younger than she. In photographs from the old country, the young bride is comely, dark, serious, and direct in her gaze; her groom seems milder, but no less attractive, with his thick moustache and carved cheekbones. They had lived in the Ukraine, in a town then called Vzovka—later Stalino, still later, Donetz. Jewish socialists, they had both been exiled—he to Siberia and she to Germany—by edict of Czar Nicholas II but then suddenly released in an amnesty declared in honor of the birth of that czar's son.

Manya and Isaac were part of the swelling revolution, members of a growing network organizing resistance to oppressive feudal monarchy. One of Isaac's brothers, Russya, was killed in a workers' demonstration in 1905, during the season Jews came to call "bloody Easter."[1] Russya's niece Grace keeps a framed photo of him in her New York apartment: there he is always a sweet-faced Russian boy, almost a man. She memorialized him nearly eighty years after his death, explaining in the story called "In This Country, But in Another Language, My Aunt Refuses to Marry the Men Everyone Wants Her To" the grief her family hoped to leave behind in the old country: "He was a wonderful boy, only seventeen. All by herself, your grandmother picked him up from the street—he was dead—she took him home in the wagon" (LSD, 108).

In the wake of that death, probably spurred by the retaliatory wave of pogroms, the family decided to leave Russia. Knowing the unpredictability of royal whim, Natasha Gutseit, Isaac's widowed mother, sent the young couple to America before the czar could change his mind and snatch them back again. Manya was pregnant when they arrived, and Victor, her first child, was born in December 1906. The young people were ignorant in many ways when they came here; Victor Goodside says the immigration authorities were the first to know his mother was pregnant.

They lived at various addresses in lower Manhattan and then moved up to West 116th Street. The rest of the Gutseit family followed; Isaac's mother and two sisters soon came to New York, and they all lived together. The family spoke Russian at home, and Russian was the first language of the children, all born in New York. Victor still recognizes Russian colloquialisms, which he calls "shades of language," heard in passing. Yiddish was also spoken in the house, primarily by his grandmother, and most of the family soon became fluent in their heavily accented English. That fluency, enriched by those accents and by Victor's "shades," is the root of Grace Paley's fictional "voices"—the voices of her family, taught and inspired by sources beyond their conscious knowledge, speaking in tongues even as they spoke American English. In fiction, the author's sensibility extends well beyond her family, into the full community of voices she grew up into. Grace Paley's most autobiographical figure in her first two story collections, Faith Darwin Asbury, relishes the sound of language: "I like your speech, I said [to a group of Black people in the Bronx, in "The Long-Distance Runner"]. Metaphor and all. . . . Yes my people also had a way of speech. And don't forget the Irish. The gift of gab" (ECLM, 181).

Actually, Isaac Gutseit's first "American" language was Italian, which he learned while working in a photography studio. He had been a photographer in the old country and found similar work when he came to the States. In the same profession, Manya worked at home with glass plates, retouching photographs. Her first daughter, Jeanne, born in December 1908, says that her mother would sit in front of a window with a black hood over her head, working—"I remember she did that for years." Like most of the immigrant population of New York City, the Gutseits had little money and struggled toward the American dream. Sheltered on the North American continent but untouched by the economic boom that accompanied World War I, such families painstakingly created new patterns for their lives. Victor says that they "must have had a tough time," for they were themselves still young, "saddled with two kids practically immediately. They were twenty-three years old and they [already] had me and they had Jeanne. I remember apartments that were crummy, and winters that were cold, and clothes that were inadequate."

Isaac's mother took care of Jeanne and Victor while the young parents and aunts were working. In the summers she would take them off to a *kuchelane* in the country, usually in the Catskills. No forerunner of the giant summer resorts now scattered over those mountains, the *kuchelane* was a large collective house in which everybody shared the kitchen. Each woman was assigned a burner on the stove, and the Gutseit children's grandmother, whose sweetness made her everyone's friend, was one of the few cooks whose pots and pans were never pushed aside. The children and Natasha spent summers in those cooperative homes in the years that their mother was working and their father was going to school. Manya Gutseit believed that time out of the city was necessary for her children's health and spirit, and she worked to make sure they could go away each year, to lie on their backs in tall grass and look through green leaves into blue skies.

The family lore is that though Isaac Gutseit learned to speak Italian in his photography work, he taught himself English by reading Dickens's novels. Although Manya did not attend high school, he finished in six months. Soon enough his name, as well as his language, was Americanized. By 1914 he was facile enough in English to enter medical school, from which he graduated four years later, providing a model for Alexandra's father in the story "Enormous Changes at the Last Minute": "He remembered the first time he'd seen the American flag on wild Ellis Island. Under its protection and working like a horse, he'd read Dickens, gone to medical school, and shot like a surface-to-air missile right into the middle class" (ECLM, 122). Isaac Goodside first had an office in Little Italy in Manhattan, opened on the premise that since he knew Italian he could develop a practice. But that lasted only a short time, and then the whole family moved to the Bronx, where he was immediately busy and successful. It was 1918—the year of the great flu epidemic—and everybody was sick. His son remembers that he made forty or fifty calls a day in his first season as a doctor. "And for a young man, this was a bonanza. He did very well."

It's a good thing he did, for his daughter Jeanne says they "were very poor, very poor." She remembers that when they first moved to the Bronx, they moved in the middle of the night so none of their new neighbors would see their "horrible furniture." When Jeanne went out to meet the other children on the block, the family's fears were realized; the furniture was all inside, but Jeanne's clothes were clearly visible in daylight, and the other children mocked her. She ran home and told her mother what happened, and, like a character in one of her husband's Dickens novels, Manya spent the night cutting up and tailoring one of Isaac's coats for Jeanne, so she could go back out the next day. "That's how poor we were."

Manya assisted Isaac in his work for several years, giving up her job as a retoucher; the husband and wife worked together at creating the middle-class family into which their youngest child would be born. Jeanne recalls their mother taking on several jobs, as nurse, technician, "receptionist," and medical assistant, and working long hours. In addition, when their financial situation improved, she had the responsibility of running their new house, which held both Isaac's office and their home. By the time Grace was born, however, Mrs. Goodside no longer worked directly with her husband, as she had done in the earlier years of his practice; she was a housewife and took care of the business of administering a large household. Grace remembers her father's accounting methods: "It was a poor neighborhood. He got paid a dollar or two dollars for going somewhere to see a patient. At night he took his pants off, turned them upside down, and all these dollar bills fell out."

The Goodside family—and their house—was a kind of way station for people coming to the United States from Russia. People would come over with no jobs, no money, and of course no homes of their own, and they would stay at the Goodsides' for weeks or months at a time. First, second, third, and even more distant cousins would sail into New York harbor and land on the Goodsides' front steps; they would stay for a while with Isaac, Manya, Luba, Mira, Natasha, and the children and then move on. Every Friday or Saturday night, there was company, mostly family; they would all sit at a big round table in the dining room, talking about events in the old country or American politics. When only the immediate family was home—young Jeanne and Victor, their parents, their aunts, and grandmother—they would read. Almost every evening, seated on those scratchy old overstuffed sofas and chairs, by the light of low table lamps and tall torchieres, the whole family would read. Jeanne points out that "of course there was no television at the time, and very little radio. And it was only when we moved up to the Bronx that *we* had radio."

The family was, as their politics might suggest, rather irreligious. Only the elder Mrs. Goodside practiced Judaism; Grace remembers that when she was a young child, on holidays she would walk her grandmother down the block a few doors to the synagogue, which was a house just like their own. She herself did not attend more than a few Sunday school classes. Jeanne recalls that their father's mother went to temple on the holiest days, and Manya would always spread a special tablecloth for her mother-in-law during Pesach. Grandma Goodside's husband, the grandfather they never knew, had been violently antireligious, and in the old country, there was serious disagreement between father and son over this issue. Notwithstanding those fights with his father, Isaac Goodside eventually gave up religious observance entirely; he and his wife did not even make Victor a bar mitzvah. As an old man in the Bronx, Dr. Goodside would spit on the street when he saw religious Jews and when he passed a synagogue.

So what would he think if he knew that his daughter Grace has begun to attend services for Rosh Hashanah and Yom Kippur? Would he, who lived in a culturally Jewish milieu all his long life, understand her desire to locate and maintain Jewishness every autumn in Christian Vermont? He could never have experienced such a need, for his family was strongly identified as Jewish, and he lived surrounded by Jews all his years in the United States. Unlike Judaism, *Jewishness*, Jeanne says, "was a given" and was never given up. The Goodside family was not unconsciously seduced by the insidious force of American assimilation. They chose to live as the kind of secular Jewish thinkers—intellectually, philosophically, and politically inclined—they had already become in Russia. They believed, as Grace's character Misha Abramowitz explains in "The Loudest Voice," that "after all, history teaches everyone. . . . What belongs to history, belongs to all" (LDM, 59), and they maintained a secular perspective, adapting those elements of the religious tradition that suited their convictions without the trappings of belief.[2] When Grace Paley recently composed some ruminations on one woman's pleasures in this imperfect world, she produced a piece that is not a poem and not quite a story but rather, in the rabbinical tradition, something Anglo-American critics might be inclined to call a "meditation." In the tradition of her people, she calls it a "midrash."[3]

The judgment of the patriarch of the Goodside clan might continue to be a consideration in his daughter's decisions about religious observance and ceremony. "My father was wonderful," Grace says. "He was humorous, he was brilliant, he was sophisticated . . ." (Perry, 42). Dr. Goodside held an enviable, even an exalted, position in his family. Victor too, himself now "Dr. Goodside," says that while he and Jeanne were growing up, they felt their father "could do no wrong." They believed then that he was always right about everything. Victor respected him and thought he was "wonderful"—and he thought everyone else thought so too. Isaac was, his son acknowledges, a fine doctor, a competent and responsible family practitioner, with "a knack for dealing with people"; he was hardworking, successful, and well respected.

But as they grew older, both Jeanne and Victor began to think differently about their parents and their parents' marriage. They recognized that their mother had suffered a certain unhappiness in her home and had gotten less satisfaction than her husband and children had from family life as the extended family lived it. A small round woman whose peasant features were strong in her maturity, Manya got little recognition compared with the steady flow of praise and admiration her still-handsome husband received. Victor says he and his sister have realized their mother was "little noticed," though she was definitely at the heart of the family—always present but rarely prominent. He points out that even though his grandmother and aunts could easily have lived elsewhere—the aunts always worked and made a decent living—they continued to live with his parents, despite his mother's unhappiness about that situation. The family was "made up of women who were all busy adoring my father—while my poor mother was out in left field."

Jeanne remembers her grandmother as "very lovable" and as a woman whose influence in the family circle was strong. But Jeanne's dear grandma was, after all, Manya's mother-in-law, the mother of a man whose children all describe him as busy to the point of preoccupation, apparently oblivious to the emotional dynamics within his family. Whatever homage Isaac Goodside may have offered to his mother, his children recollect little attention or deference to their mother. Though Jeanne knew that her mother was the one who made many of the decisions—in the background—and that they were generally carried through, her father was regarded as "the kingpin." She explains that he was "in many ways a very rigid man, and a big egoist. Though he was short, he was attractive—and everyone liked him, because he would flaunt his personality. All his patients loved him. But in many ways he was a selfish man, because he put himself first in almost everything. He would often bring up the fact that my mother was a few months older than he [supposedly as a joke but] he was very caustic."

Grace, the baby born so much later, understood perhaps even sooner and better than her older siblings that her mother wasn't satisfied with life in the large family. After all, by the time Grace was old enough to know what was going on around her, Manya had been in that position for more than twenty years. One aunt, Luba, had married and moved out, but Manya's sister-in-law, Mira, and her mother-in-law remained in the house. "You know," Grace says now, "extended families are really good for children . . . [but] they're not very good for anybody else."

Like Jeanne, she thinks that her father was essentially unconscious of her mother's problems. She saw another dimension to that marriage too: "He admired her, but one felt that she really was crazy about him. He was a very attractive man, you know, people talked of him as very attractive. And my mother was less so, less physically attractive than he. . . . I didn't think my father was, until one of my girlfriends told me, 'Gee, your father is so goodlooking.' I said, 'My father!?' I mean, I loved him, I was crazy about him, but I didn't think he was so good-looking." By the time she was fifteen years old, however, Grace Goodside realized that her mother was a woman married to a man generally acknowledged to be better looking than she "and more exciting."

Isaac Goodside, though he was no despot, lived with a harem. Even in the years when Grace was growing up, "In that house, when my father would say, 'Pass the salt,' three women would jump over each other to give him the salt." Her analysis of her own response to her father is very like that of other literary daughters whose fathers' energetic and demanding charisma has drawn its power from women—sisters, mothers, wives, and daughters who devoted their lives to the character and success of the patriarch. Virginia Woolf—whose father's domination of his family went far beyond that of Grace Paley's father, to the point of abuse—wrote of her father after his death, "His life would have entirely ended mine. What would have happened? No writing, no books;—inconceivable" (Woolf, *Writer's Diary*, 135). In a similar—but fortunately lesser—vein, Grace Paley said of Dr. Isaac Goodside after his death, "In some ways he was very good, but in some ways I could never have done anything until I got away from him" (Perry, 42).

The fathers of Anzia Yezierska and Gertrude Stein, Jewish women writers closer to the tradition into which Grace Paley would develop, were also domineering, even forbidding, in their attempt to impose control over their daughters from their positions of power within two widely separated social and economic classes. Indeed, it must have been her father's position in his family—far more than the behavior of any of the other men in Grace Paley's life—that gave rise to her question in the early story "A Subject of Childhood": "What is man, that woman lies down to adore him?" (LDM, 143).

When they bought the two-story house where Grace was born and grew up, at 1538 Hoe Street between 172nd and 173rd streets in the Bronx, there was a comfortable, quiet living room where Isaac and Manya would sit together, listening to music and reading. Dr. Goodside bought one of the first victrolas—Grace says they had "one of the best record players in the Bronx"—and developed an enormous classical record library, including 78s of all the famous singers. They held "musicales" in the house; friends and neighbors would come in every week and listen to recordings of classical music. He loved music "passionately," Jeanne says. "My mother liked music, but she never followed through on her perfect pitch. She could play any instrument, but she never followed through on that." In "Mother," Grace Paley describes the scene in that room and the emotional dynamic between the couple who most often occupied it:

> She sat beside him. They owned an expensive record player. They were listening to Bach. She said to him, Talk to me a little. We don't talk so much anymore.
>
> I'm tired, he said. Can't you see? I saw maybe thirty people today. All sick, all talk talk talk talk. Listen to the music, he said. I believe you once had perfect pitch. I'm tired, he said. (LSD, 112)

Grace's birth, on December 11, 1922, was a surprise to Jeanne and Victor; old as they were at the time (fourteen and sixteen respectively), neither one had understood their mother was pregnant. The family—including Grace herself—attributes this to the fact that Manya Ridnyik Goodside was by then a fat little woman who "just seemed a little fatter." Victor explains that she tended, like her husband, toward "an old world prudishness" that prevented her from mentioning her pregnancy to her children. He says he knew that "something was going on" that day, but his mother was "rather quiet than outgoing," and "this was something that one didn't discuss freely." Jeanne says, "I was so naive at the time. I mean, at my age we were all naive. We didn't know. I never knew my mother was pregnant, all the time she was pregnant. And the day that Gracie was born—she was born in the house—I was the most shocked girl in the world."

Just as there are multiple versions of many of the stories in

Grace Paley's collected fiction, there are at least two different stories about the coming of this baby. Jeanne says, "Here's a funny story about how Gracie came to be born. My father had mellowed [over the years] and so I finally asked him, 'How come you and Mama had Gracie fourteen years after I was born?' And he said, 'Well, I was by that time fairly well fixed, I was well off, and I said to mother, How about having a baby? And she said, Why not?' And so they had the baby." Grace says her father told *her*, "Mama came to me and she said, 'You know, I think it would be nice to have another child.' And I said to her, 'All right.' And so they did."

Given the "puritanism" all three of the Goodside children ascribe to both of their parents, the cultural atmosphere of the time, the traditional marriage in which this pregnancy occurred, and the passage of so many years, we can only speculate about what Manya and Isaac might have said to each other in March or April of 1922. Such speculation need not be prurient; in fact, adding a few more years to their ages, Grace Paley considered some of the possibilities in "The Story Hearer" and "Listening," both written in the eighties:

> Jack, I want to have a baby.
>
> Ha ha, he said. You can't. Too late. A couple of years too late, he said, and fell asleep. (LSD, 143)

> Faith, have you decided not to have a baby?
>
> No, I've just decided to think about it, but I haven't given it up. . . . My dear, he said, perhaps you only wish that you were young again. So do I. . . .
>
> I doubt it, I said. Besides, I'm busy, you know. I have an awful lot to do. . . .
>
> But Jack said, Oh come on. . . . Come on, kid, he said, touching my knee, my thigh, breast, all the outsides of love. So we lay down beside one another to make a child, with the modesty of later-in-life, which has so much history and erotic knowledge but doesn't always use it. (LSD, 203–6)

A thirty-eight-year-old mother of two teenagers and the busy wife of a successful family doctor whose mother and sister lived with them and doted on him, the pregnant Mrs. Goodside could easily have been of several minds about the situation herself.

The year before Grace Goodside was born, her aunt Luba had married and moved out of the family home. When Grace was two or three years old, her brother Victor also left the household to go off to school. When she was seven, her sister Jeanne married and moved out as well. From her earliest memories until her own marriage in 1942 at the age of nineteen and a half, Grace was the beloved little one in a family of grown-ups.

Her earliest memory, of getting lost in the beach town of Belmar, New Jersey, could only be the recollection of a child who was loved. "I think I must have been two and a half years old." She wandered into the basement of a neighbor's house, which resembled her family's rented summer place, "and I remember my little rubber beach shoes, little bathing shoes. Those little shoes always got full of water or sand or both." She remembers "standing there [in the neighbor's basement] for a while and being perplexed and crying a little. . . . I remember being lost, which must have been very impressive, but I don't remember being found, which must have seemed very natural." Being discovered and then held and caressed by loving adults was "very natural" for the Goodside baby, who had "a wonderful life for a child. . . . nobody was not good to me. Really, nobody. I had three women all caring for me—not even counting my sister," who was "really always half a mother to me. Except for quarrels I had with her in my early teens when she seemed to me to always be agreeing with my mother, she's really been as much a mother to me as anybody."

Being essentially an only child in a household full of middle-aged adults had two effects. "On the one hand, they were more relaxed, they knew a lot." Little Gracie could stay out late on the street in the warm weather with the neighborhood children; they weren't worried about her. On the other hand, "I was more protected. I wore long stockings very late into the season, much later than the other girls—because they were old-fashioned. So I was let alone a lot, *and* I was over-cared for."

In her memory, her family seems to have been "very cultured, but at the same time very down-to-earth. And utterly unsnobbish. [Though] the women on the block, I think, did see my mother as snobbish." They thought of Mrs. Goodside as "the doctor's wife." Grace insists that this was "mainly because she was terribly shy"—and because her mother had perfect posture. "She cared a lot about her posture, and worked at it.... I can still see her fat little figure walking along with a perfectly straight back. And having good posture is one of the things that makes other people think you're a snob. My family," she says decisively, "had very good characteristics."

When Grace Goodside was a young girl, she was a tomboy, wearing pants much of the time and sporting very short hair. In recollection, Grace says she thought she was a boy—well, she knew she really wasn't, but like lots of tough little girls, she kept up the fantasy until it became physiologically impossible to sustain. Her brother recalls that she was "a real personality around the block." Even when he no longer lived there, he knew her reputation: "What a delight she was; everybody was so delighted with her goings on—she was rambunctious. She was up and down the block; everybody knew Gracie. My father had a chauffeur, a Black man by the name of Saunders, and he took her under his wing in a way." Saunders taught young Grace to drive and let her drive the car—up and down the block—when she was only seven years old. Even at that age, she had a social conscience. The family says that she would take children from the block into the house for baths, "with my mother's approval," Victor says. "Even so young, she knew that dirty kids should be able to have a bath."

Grace sometimes says that she was a fierce tomboy; at Northwestern University in 1984, she explained to a symposium audience that "when I was a little girl, I was a boy—like a lot of little girls who like to get into things and want to be where the action is, which is up the corner someplace, where the boys are.... I could hardly wait to continue being a boy so that I could go to war and do all the other exciting boys' things" (Gibbons, 231). She remembers clearly, however, that she also loved babies and had dolls. "There were both those things struggling inside of me. No, they weren't really struggling. They were both just there, in me." In "Ruthy and Edie" (LSD), two little girls embody those not-really-struggling elements for their author. Ruthy reads about Roland's Horn at Roncevaux; Edie reads about the Bobbsey twins and Honeybunch. Ruthy wants to be brave and fight for her country when she grows up; Edie doesn't want to go to war because she hates to be separated from her mother. Despite what might seem to be irreconcilable differences (or a source of conflict within Grace Goodside), in their story, these two have remained intimate friends all through their lives.

Though Jeanne says otherwise, Grace believes that the family didn't consider their tomboy a pretty child. "Not especially," she says. Besides, she says, "I had a very cute cousin." She feels, like so many women, that "it was not thought that *I* was pretty. There was a little plainness in our family," she says, implying that she was the embodiment of that plainness. Yet we have only to look at photographs of the young Grace Goodside as she entered her teens to find not only that she was not "plain," but that her appeal was in her almost palpable eagerness, her visible energy and liveliness.

In one photograph from the thirties, the family is lined up on the summer grass, and she, right in the front row, is practically leaping out of the picture. She's so *ready:* she wants to be a woman—not a girl, not a child—she wants passionately to be adult, to be *grown*, like everyone closest to her. Her urgency explains the longing of those adolescent characters—Josephine and Cindy Anne—in the early stories, who want desperately to get older faster and push out of childhood by means of their just-born sexuality.

These stories by a woman writer unfortunately appear to justify the pop-Freudian insistence that young girls are seductive nymphets, flaunting their pubescent bodies that "ain't even quite done" (LDM, 32). But the fact that Grace Paley herself is the source here—for these young girls are autobiographical characters—can become part of our understanding of the stories. Grace explains that her straining at the leash of childhood, while it certainly included the adolescent's traditional yearning for sexual maturity, was a full-throttle acceleration "to be grown." The baby among elders for so long, Grace attributes not only her mood in that old photo, but also the interplay between Josephine's youthful hetero-sexuality and her strong woman-identification in "A Woman, Young and Old" (LDM), and the repressive patriarchal circumstances of the equally aggressive but slightly older Cindy Anne in "An Irrevocable Diameter" (LDM), to the strength of her own desire to grow up fast—very fast. "That's exactly it," she says, "You know—I was the youngest, and I wanted to be grown."

Though as a little girl she liked to play with boys and says that later she was "boy-crazy," Grace always had girlfriends who were important to her. "I always had a best friend. Always. My girlfriend

Evvie, who lived right across the street, she was very important to me. My friend Bea, and my friend Barbara—Oh yes, I always had girlfriends. . . . Well, who do you talk to about the boys if you don't hang onto your female friends?" she says with a laugh. "I had very dear friends, very dear friends." Referring to "Ruthy and Edie" (LSD), which, along with at least a dozen more stories, features women's friendship, she says that several of her stories are autobiographical "to some extent" and suggests that they be considered resources for study of her lifework: "You can go to those, you can go to those stories" for information about their author.

Though she, like her characters, was surrounded by women and girls while she was growing up, Grace Paley preferred her father to her mother. A daddy's girl in the classic tradition, she was one whose family situation provided both the patriarchal structure that encouraged such identification and a quasi-matriarchal substructure that supported her and provided her with models, who serve her well as she dismantles the male-centered form in her fiction. "In the family it was always said that I was like him, that I was very like him. And it was sort of pushed on me in that way. People do that; they push it on kids. They say, 'Oh, you're just like your father.' " The primary example of this, in her immediate memory, is one she has used in her stories. "You see, he had a sense of humor, and I was considered funny. I was a funny one." Like her strongly autobiographical character Faith, another recovering daddy's girl in "Dreamer in a Dead Language," Grace might have been called "a constant entertainment to us. She could take jokes right out of the air. . . . She had us in stitches . . ." (LSD, 18).

Grace suggests that her own mother resented the identification of young Grace with Isaac, and she recalls too that no one ever told her she was like her mother or grandmother: "I wish I could have been like my grandmother; I still wish I could be like my grandmother was. She was very dignified, she was very smart. I loved her very much. . . . She loved all of us, and as the youngest, I was cherished."

Like most daddy's girls, Grace Goodside preferred her father for the traditional complex of reasons[4] as well as the specific circumstances and dynamics of her family. Isaac was the more apparently intellectual of the two parents, better educated and possessed of more personal power than his wife, both at home and in the world beyond the family. True, his wife and sister had always done productive work in and out of their home; Manya had been an independent worker in the early years, his coworker in the development of his medical practice, and certainly the director of that large family household in the Bronx. Mira was a charter member of the International Ladies' Garment Workers' Union and worked in the shops and at home for years. But Dr. Goodside, possessing a title and a reputation, was obviously the source of their material comfort as well as their community standing. His life as a man was more interesting and more exciting than Manya's life as a mother and wife. Moreover, all the women in the house deferred to him, loving him to a fault. His youngest child learned and understood quickly, as all children do, the relative importance and status of women and men in society, and she saw that pattern played out with emphasis in her home.

Her own parents were, of course, not the only models available for her scrutiny as Grace Goodside grew up. Their friends, immigrant families in the Jewish Bronx neighborhood—no longer "socialist" but certainly "social democrats"—were almost always egalitarian in their ideas, but rarely in their daily lives. She grew up thinking "that . . . the excitement was with the men. . . . with the boys in the street and with the men in their talk, men's talk." Though she ultimately preferred to listen to the women talk, she always found the men alluring; where the women's talk was understood to be trivial by definition—"bobbeh meisehs," "just gossip"—the men were "mysterious." Considering the differences, she says that the men would play pinochle while the women would sit around a table and talk. The women would talk about what seemed to the listening girl to be "the real things" of their lives; strikingly, the men would not. "Sometimes the men would talk politics, and occasionally they would quarrel. But the women's talk was about what actually happened in life."

That male mystique—if all they did was grumble or yell at each other over the cardtable, why were they so much more important and powerful?—continued to fascinate her for many years and gave rise to the first two of her extraordinarily realistic male narrators, Frederick P. Sims in "The Contest" and Charles C. Charley in "An Irrevocable Diameter" (both LDM). But almost all of her stories, from the first ones published in the mid-fifties to those published in the eighties, are devoted to a revelation of the lives of women and children. Her changed attitude toward the subject of those stories, which she used to sometimes self-consciously call "this crap," is plainly inscribed decades later at the end of *Later the Same Day* in "Listening" (202–3), where we find Jack pleading with Faith to tell him her stories of women—after he has told his own "woman stories" at the beginning of the book. Faith—unlike her author—won't tell. Faith retaliates for more women writers and readers than Grace Paley alone when she leaves Jack—even temporarily—in the world of men and men's voices.

With the exception of her relatively brief sojourns in army camps with her first husband, the world of women's voices has always been Grace Paley's environment. Beyond the immediate household, Mrs. Goodside had many women friends, many people around her all the time. "Lots of people came up to the house to see my mother," Grace says. "Lots of women." She says that they were "half-relatives; everybody around was related and sort of related and nearly related. And you have to realize that [any] person might turn out to be somebody who was from their village in Russia who might even *be* family. It's not the same thing as now," when we make definite distinctions between family and nonfamily on the basis of a blood relationship. "There were always women around who I called my aunt this, my aunt that."

This familial warmth might seem to be at odds with the "puritanism" their children attribute to the elder Goodsides, but the general atmosphere in their home was hardly repressive. Dr. Goodside would often say "goddamnit!" and then Manya would say, "Ah, Zenia!" using his family name to remonstrate with him at his outbursts. "He thought he was very risqué, saying that, and he would tell a terrible joke every now and then which was as mild as soap, but he didn't think so." Mindful of the many contradictions of family life, Grace wishes to have it understood that her father respected her mother: "He never didn't think well of her. They would yell and scream, but he always thought well of her. They would holler and holler and holler (and to this day I can't stand anyone hollering)." And they "weren't terrible about lying. Mostly it was, 'Oh, don't tell the real truth, don't tell how it really is because you'll hurt the person's feelings.' . . . It wasn't to the extent of harm, or anything like that." She laughs and says, "After all . . . you could [operate] like [some people], who tell the truth out of sheer malice. . . . so it goes both ways."

All the adults in the family wanted the children to hear and understand what they were saying. They didn't use their other languages for secrets, to shut out the children from adult conversation, as parents in so many immigrant families have done—perhaps in retaliation against the relentless assimilation, the "Americanization," of their children. Grace has remained fluent enough in Russian to speak to and understand her colleagues when she traveled to the World Peace Conference in Moscow in 1973. There was always the very strong desire that the children should be knowledgeable, as well as educated. They should be smart, and they should be competent; they should make a living and succeed in America.

When Grace was seven years old, Jeanne married Sam Tenenbaum, a psychologist, and he took the child for testing. She was "very bright" and scored "very high" on tests at City College of New York. Grace may no longer remember the specific events and feelings of that experience, but the experience—and what it meant to those who fostered her development—is clearly delineated in the pharmacist Zagrowsky's pride in his grandson: "he was just five, he can already read a whole book by himself. . . . My other ones . . . were also very smart, but they don't hold a candle to this character. Soon as I get a chance, I'm gonna bring him to the city to Hunter for gifted children; he should get a test" (LSD, 152).

As if she had been part of the earlier family reading circle, Grace was a voracious reader from the age of three, when Jeanne taught her to read and encouraged her to write as well. Jeanne still hasn't forgotten her little sister's sounding out the word "*ssss uh nnn*, and when I said, 'Faster, faster, say it faster,' she got the word *sun*, and from there, she learned to read." Her little sister wrote that encouragement into a story about mothering: "The sister-mother is the one who is always encouraging. You can do this, you can get an *A*, you can dance, you can eat squash without vomiting, you can write a poem" ("Mom," 86).

Grace spent a lot of time at the library when she was still quite small and remembers reading *The Secret Garden* and two books called *Nobody's Boy* and *Nobody's Girl*. She wrote poetry as a child, a small book of which Jeanne Tenenbaum has kept all these years. In fact, with the exception of one or two experiments that have survived only in her memory,[5] Grace Paley wrote only poetry until she was over thirty—though she didn't publish a poetry collection until the fall of 1985 (*Leaning Forward*).

"But the [childhood] poems, they were really nothing. Really nothing. Your average kid now could write rings around 'em."[6] Whether these juvenilia are prizewinners or not, the point is that we have them because Grace Paley's childhood writings were valued, praised, and encouraged by her family. "They were a typical Jewish family; they were very verbal; they expected me to be very verbal. I talked a lot; they liked it." They might have occasionally made her be quiet, she recalls, but they mostly liked it when she wasn't.

Schooling, however, was different from learning, and Grace Goodside's report cards would no doubt demonstrate the distinction. "Well, I think I liked [school] when I was small. But you know, I don't seem to remember a hell of a lot. I remember being very good at school, very smart, you know, and liking *that*. And I remember also *not* liking school, so that when my glasses broke I'd be happy to say, 'Oh, I can't go, my glasses are broken.'" The family, delighted with their smart little girl—and with her high test scores—simply assumed she would always get the grades to match those scores, but they didn't apply any pressure she could feel until several years later.

2

The Story
Hearer

Encouraged to grow and develop in every direction, young Grace Goodside did just that. She wrote, she read, she talked, and she listened. As she grew into adolescence, her political views became more radical than those of her parents—who had grown in the other direction as they settled into middle-class life—and her social life provoked family antipathies unknown in the lives of Jeanne and Victor. Her mother was worried, and her father was angry; both were disappointed. A young poet who was often in love but rarely in school, a blooming anarchist and a confirmed romantic, Grace was a constant frustration to her surprised and anxious parents.

In the summer of 1933 the whole family was at Long Pond in Mahopac, New York, where they had purchased a vacation home. Dr. Goodside had become president of the community organization there, and he remained president until he died, many years later. The family was welcomed and appreciated at Long Pond, and its youngest member was soon a popular figure. Grace, however, was getting "very wild," Jeanne remembers. Manya was unable to control her and asked Jeanne to find something to interest the child. So that summer Grace became the editor of a newspaper her sister started in the vacation community, "and she ran that paper for a number of years, and was damn good at it."

Success as a journalist did not solve the problem, however. That eleventh summer, when she entered adolescence, she "imme-

diately went into conflict with [her] family, which was—remember—
very puritanical, and I mean *very* puritanical." Those first years of
her adolescent rebellion strained her relationship with her mother
and unfortunately coincided with the discovery of Manya Goodside's
breast cancer, the beginning of her long illness. "Her illness didn't
change anything for me," Grace says, speaking of her youthful
refusal to accept the meaning of her mother's disease. "Being in
love with a boy changed everything more for me than my mother's
illness." Her mother's hospitalization and intermittent semi-invalid
status did not result in the loss of a strong maternal presence in the
girl's life, as it might have in a strictly nuclear family. "You know,
there were other people around all the time, my aunt, my grandmother, my sister, my father; I was very dear to my father."[1]

When Grace was thirteen, Manya Goodside became seriously
ill, and most of the family's attention focused on that illness. For
years, Manya had done her husband's X rays, taking the pictures
and developing them. In 1935 she discovered a small lump on her
breast; Isaac examined it and rushed her to the hospital. Her breast
was removed that day, and she was told that if she lived for five
years she would probably be cured. In the period between that
operation and the recurrence of malignancy, Mrs. Goodside suffered
from pain and lessening mobility in her arm and was hospitalized on
several occasions. "I didn't want to know about her illness. I hid it
from myself." The family hid it too. They didn't talk about it with
Grace; no one actually told her what was happening, so she found it
relatively easy to practice her childhood denial, as she has described
in her writing: "One evening I hear the people in the dining room
say that my mother is going to die. I remain in the coat closet,
listening. . . . [after some debate] I am not told. Thereafter I devote
myself to not having received that knowledge" ("Mom," 86).

Grace remembers her obstinate autonomy. "And whatever I
wanted to do, I would do. I was very headstrong. No matter what
they would say—if they would say, Oh, you're killing Mama, I would
do it anyway." Even in her *early* teens, she stayed out late at night
and ignored her schoolwork, so that she got poor marks. Though
hospitalized occasionally over the years, Manya Goodside was home
much of the time during her illness, aware of—and increasingly
frustrated by—her adolescent daughter's behavior. She was conva-
lescent and relatively active, but she was never completely healthy

again before her death in 1944. The family's threats were false as well as cruel: her younger daughter's wildness did not kill Manya Goodside; she died of cancer. But she worried because she knew she wasn't strong enough—nor would she live long enough—to take care of Grace. Her fictional counterpart in "Mother" says, "You never finish your lunch. You run around senselessly. What will become of you?" (LSD, 111–12).

According to Grace's memory, when she was considered a real problem in the family, she was sent to her brother Victor and his wife, who lived in upstate New York, where he had begun his own medical practice. She can't remember what the exact infractions were that merited her exile, but she thinks that when she "just got to be too much" for her mother, she would be sent to stay with them. These banishments, however, were actually never more than a week or two and often seem to have coincided with school holidays.

Grace Goodside was not regarded as a delinquent, nor was she punished with anger or violence. Hurt, puzzled, confused, and frustrated as her parents must have been, they never abused her. "When something really bad happened, my father would grab me by the arm and say, 'What's going on here? What is this?' " No one ever struck her. Indeed, they were a physically affectionate family— "very huggy"—"to the extent that I was brought up to kiss everybody goodnight around the table before I would go to sleep, kiss the company and whoever was there." This family tradition held intact for adult children, and it appears in her fiction, with the addition of irony; in "Faith in the Afternoon," "Faith . . . kissed Mrs. Hegel-Shtein, because they had been brought up that way, not to hurt anyone's feelings, particularly if they loathed them, and they were much older" (ECLM, 45).

Despite all those kisses—and a highly cultured family circle— there was no talk about sex and bodies, not even physiology. The Goodsides, who fought and argued and wrangled over international, domestic, and personal politics, who were themselves medically knowledgeable, were just as reluctant to discuss sex and reproduction as most parents of their generation and culture. "The Russian-born mother has said on several occasions that there are no such words in Russian" ("Mom," 86). That reticence is probably the reason Mrs. Goodside never actually voiced her fears and concerns— and they were strong—about Grace's developing sexuality. She did share her anxiety with her elder daughter, who was by then in her twenties and married ("What's going to happen to Gracie? All she does is like the boys!"), but she never joined the majority of American girls' mothers in their overt warnings, never told Grace to beware of boys because *they only want one thing.*

"In that kind of puritan socialist atmosphere my mother would never say such a thing. Men were supposed to be comrades, so she would not speak of them that way," Grace says. Nevertheless, her mother made herself clear: "I understood. My mother didn't like me to play with boys, she didn't like me to go see boys, she didn't even want me to go to bar mitzvahs. . . . I was in real conflict with her." Throughout her teen years, Grace knew—as daughters do—that her mother didn't want her to run around with boys because it was dangerous, and she knew that pregnancy was the danger. The message was not that boys were bad by definition, but that association with them was dangerous for a young girl.

Though she probably saw more of her father than did most children since he worked at home, she didn't actually spend much time with him. Sometimes, though, she would accompany Dr. Goodside on his rounds. "He'd say, 'Get in the car. Come on in the car with me.' " And she would go with him to pay a house call and would sit in the car and wait until he was done. "Then we would have these conversations. Who remembers what we talked about? We talked about anything. Babble, babble, babble. He was a very smart guy, a very intelligent guy. It was no problem for me to see my father. I saw him all the time. My friends' fathers went away in the morning and they came home for supper. But when I came home for lunch from school, there he would be."

Of course, "I didn't expect [to spend more time with him]. It never occurred to me. My father didn't come to my high school graduation. It was nothing to me. I never thought to complain about it. It didn't bother me. (It bothered my sister, though.) It seemed to me he was very very busy. I mean he had patients day and night. And it seemed to me the graduation was pretty boring. I never was bothered by stuff like that."

Some fathers try to encourage their daughters to be closer to their mothers, to treat their mothers better. Many, as baffled as their wives by the adolescent behavior of formerly adorable daughters, try to negotiate treaties between the two, acting as go-betweens and trying to re-create or rearrange the family's dynamics.[2] "My father was so busy he would never even notice. He wouldn't even be there. Besides, I was mad at my father *too* in my teenage years. I was angry at him too. He'd yell at me for his own sake, not just about my mother."

He disapproved of her attitude about school, for instance, and was certainly disturbed by the change in her academic behavior and accomplishment. She had breezed through the lower grades with no trouble, she recalls. "I don't seem to have had to do a minute of work until later on. And the minute that I had to do work, I got into trouble.... [because] I thought if I had to do any work [that meant] I was stupid. I never had to do anything before. So between the pressure to do well and the idea that to do a lot of work would show me at my stupidest," she began to feel "bad" about herself by the middle of junior high school.

This situation was further aggravated in senior high:

> In high school all that really interested me was literature and love.... I started to work less and less and less in everything except English. I always did very well in English because of course I always read a lot. I never didn't read. And I loved writing.... essay questions on an exam would make me very happy. But other than that, I began to go downhill. And I *speedily* went downhill.... I really did poorly in most subjects. I studied very little and I was very lazy. I thought about boys constantly and I was mostly in love.

Her nonscholastic attitude notwithstanding, in high school Grace was "serious, very serious" about her writing. Even as a boy-crazy teenager, she kept reading and writing; she wrote love poems. If she did think about what she would be when she grew up, "I thought I was a writer," she says. Her sister Jeanne's understanding of the school situation may take into account all those love poems, but it stands in strong contrast to Grace's own perception: "Like grade school, in high school she never had to work; she was very popular. She had a lot of boys hanging around her. She was very pretty; slim, very pretty."

Grace's memory of high school is somewhat different. Her "bad" feelings continued to develop out of that private belief that she wasn't as smart as everyone thought after all, and they were exacerbated by the gulf between her intense interests and the standard academic curriculum and practice. Perhaps when Grace remembers herself as "boy-crazy," she is, like many women, accepting the popular description of our institutionalized discouragement of intellectual growth in adolescent girls, which often creates a dammed-up emotional pool into which their disappointment flows in the wake of hormonal chaos.[3]

Grace Paley is not the first artist to have suffered through the approved schedule of intellectual and aesthetic progress that is formal schooling; but as a girl and woman, she is one of those who accepted full responsibility for her "failure." "Something happened to me at school. After junior high I just sort of went inside myself. I became desperately unhappy." This was "even earlier" than ninth grade. "I was very unhappy. I finished high school when I was fifteen and a half. I did very badly at school. And I never talked [in class]. I mean, I *never* talked. I didn't write poems in school. I didn't contribute to any school magazine or paper until later, when I went to NYU for a year. And I was married already then. I was married, but I don't think I was more than twenty-one."

Though the standard curriculum and classroom discussions couldn't capture that young mind, it did not lie fallow. Through other students and extracurricular activities, Grace became aware of the Spanish Civil War, as well as the Italian bombing of Ethiopia, which remains a strong memory even now. She was in the student union in high school, and "we talked about it, we discussed it, we talked about what it meant. After all, my family always talked politics. But these particular things were things that were *happening*. And they were part of what was active among young people in our lives." Her sources of information and opinion broadened, going beyond the family circle. This experience was, she felt, quite different from her parents and their friends sitting around the table and talking about the czar and the Russian revolution. Her political perspective, which had been shaped by their memories and commentary over the years, diverged further from the now relatively comfortable liberalism of that dining room table. She moved left, criticizing the U.S. government and advocating more action for social change than her parents had taken in decades.

She feels that she was "just normally political, no big deal. . . . In New York at that time, if you lived in that kind of neighborhood, it was normal to go to student union meetings and things like that; it was no big deal" (Endor and Thiers, 5). Her sister Jeanne recalls the impact of this "normal" involvement: Grace "and my father and mother were on two sides of the fence. My parents were social democrats; she was very much to the left of them. And they used to have terrible fights, political arguments. And she was very active politically. There was always literature about the left side—all this material piled high in her room—and my mother would go crazy. Because she, my mother, was on the right of the left, you see. She wasn't right, but she was on the right side of the left." These arguments figure prominently in Grace's third story collection, as in this excerpt from "Mother": "I had just issued a political manifesto attacking the family's position on the Soviet Union. She said, Go to sleep for godsakes, you damn fool, you and your Communist ideas. We saw them already, Papa and me, in 1905. We guessed it all" (LSD, 111–12).

"Gracie gave them trouble," Jeanne assumes, "because she was so different from me. . . . They didn't know what to think of her. But she went along in her own way. Nothing stopped her. They didn't try to punish her or keep her in." They fought and argued constantly, but "it didn't do [my parents] any good. She did exactly what she wanted." It's certainly true that young Grace did many other things that bothered her parents—there was all that running around with boys, for instance, and the fact that her room was always a mess—but Jeanne recalls they were particularly upset about the radicalism of her thinking and allegiance and the knowledge that she was politically active but never told them what was happening, where she went, or what she did.

"You brought her up like that and now you're surprised," says one mother to another in the story "Friends" (LSD, 121). Like Richard and Tonto (LDM, ECLM, LSD) and Rachel Larsen (LSD), children of radical and progressive parents often challenge those parents to live up to their ideals—as well as to accept and support the children's idealism. The disappointment and disillusionment of our children are powerful consciousness-raisers, as Faith explains after Richard yells in "Faith in a Tree"—"I hate you. I hate your stupid friends. Why didn't they just stand up to that stupid cop and say fuck you. They should of just stood up and hit him" (ECLM, 99)— and then takes action himself, as a graffiti sloganeer. His mother, much impressed, says that "that is exactly when events turned me around, changing my hairdo, my job uptown, my style of living and telling. . . . I thought more and more and every day about the world" (ECLM, 99–100).

Grace Goodside's parents, whose political theory did not translate into overt action in this country, may have felt vaguely guilty in the face of her behavior, but at the same time they were outraged. Though they never moved far to the right, they did gratefully accept the U.S. government, finding in this nation answers and solutions to the questions and problems they had faced in the old country. Members of the generation that revered Franklin Roosevelt and Fiorello La Guardia, they made a favorable comparison between even the grimmest of New York streets and the bloody roads through shtetl and ghetto. Their daughter, born into the safety they had risked their lives for, couldn't share their gratitude: "She was leaning against their bedroom wall. She was about fourteen. Fifteen? A lot you care, she said. A giant war is coming out of Germany and all you say is Russia. Bad old Russia. I'm the one that's gonna get killed. You? he answered. Ha ha! A little girl sitting in safe America is going to be killed. Ha ha!" (LSD, 186).

As illustrated here in "The Expensive Moment," Grace Paley's political heritage was not just familial; the history she grew up in was global as well as local. The Great Depression had begun just when she was old enough to notice class and money distinctions. Though she never thought of her family as "rich" when she was a child, she "knew that we had comforts. We had a house. In a poor neighborhood, we had a house—a big house. No one talked about money in the family; it wasn't something you talked about. But I lived in a neighborhood where a majority of the people were suffering." The neighborhood was "hit very hard by the depression. Into a neighborhood that had at one time been lower-middle class, a working-class neighborhood—you know, mostly garment workers, people like that—into that neighborhood came this great unemployment; a tremendous number were unemployed, and a lot of people were already on relief. They were on relief for ten years in some cases, and they suffered terribly from that time."

"I was very aware of that, and very aware of myself as a privileged person. Yes, I . . . felt very privileged; a lot of my friends were from families that" suffered in ways the Goodsides never did.

Grace Paley's parents, Manya Ridnyik and Isaac Gutseit, in Russia, circa 1903–5. They changed the family name to Goodside when they came to the United States. Goodside and Paley family photos used by permission.

Grace Goodside on Hoe
Street in the Bronx, circa
1926-29.

Jeanne Goodside Tenenbaum, Grace's sister; Manya Ridnyik Goodside, Grace's mother; and Grace, probably at
their summer home in Mahopac, circa 1930.

Grace; her father, Dr. Isaac Goodside; and her sister, Jeanne
Goodside Tenenbaum, on the porch in Mahopac, circa 1932–33.

Grace Goodside at
Long Pond in Mahopac,
circa 1934–36.

Grace Goodside,
circa 1939–41.

Grace Goodside with Jess Paley, circa 1939–42, before Jess was in the Signal Corps.

"And I would take these girls with me for rides in the car or out to Pelham Bay or City Island or things like that." Unwilling to play the role of Lady Bountiful even in her childhood, Grace says she "didn't feel like I was doing them favors, but I did know that their families were in pretty bad straits." This comment about "favors" is spoken out of the concern that never disappears from the mind of a woman of conscience who has also been a woman of privilege. She wants to be understood as having seen and felt her community's need and loss, having understood that need and loss when she was quite young.

"By the time I was eight or nine years old the depression was very deep. People were being thrown out of apartments all the time. I saw whole households out in the streets under blankets. . . . Everyday I saw this, and I felt it strongly, very strongly. I felt lucky. Very sorry for everybody else and very lucky myself. I was conscious of it and even a little embarrassed. . . . I had my own room, which clearly was incredible to the other kids. My family didn't suffer at all!" Her fortunate position—economic and familial—is shared by Faith in the story collections, and, as in this excerpt from "The Immigrant Story," she sometimes takes a little heat during spasms of resentment or envy from her friends: "One Hundred and Seventy-Second Street was a pile of shit. . . . Everyone was on relief except you. Thirty people had t.b. Citizens and non-citizens alike starving until the war. Thank God capitalism has a war it can pull out of the old feed bag every now and then or we'd all be dead" (ECLM, 173).

Grace's best friend lived with her mother, father, and brother "in . . . a tiny, tiny apartment. I can still see it quite clearly." The reason it's so clear, she says sarcastically, is that "I lived in an apartment just like it with my kids on Fifteenth Street when I was in my period of downward mobility. You know, somebody slept in the dining room. . . . nobody had room of any kind at that time. And my friend's father was out of work; everyone was out of work. It came to a point where half the people I knew were on welfare." When she went to visit her friend, there was a special signal, a secret way she would ring the bell so they would know she wasn't the social worker or someone else who was going to give them grief. "By the time I was in my teens, the parents of most of my best friends—with the exception of my friend Evvie, whose father had a hardware store, a paint store—were in really very very bad shape."

Grace talks about the fact that the depression took the heart out of people, people who had struggled, often desperately, and had worked their whole lives. "There was the sense that they had worked very hard, you know? It was that whole immigrant generation. My parents were of that generation." They worked steadily and constantly, and they willingly took the burden of that work onto themselves—even those with luck, who rose above their earlier poverty and pain.

Grace describes her father's day, in the years of his success: "He would have a small breakfast. Then he would see patients. Then he would have his main meal at midday. Then he would see more patients. Then in the evening he would drive all over the Bronx to see other patients, people who had not come to the office in his home. He would often have office hours again, after he returned. He would have his supper late, and then later on in the evening he would look over X rays. And that was his life. That was what he did every day. My father worked harder than any human being I've ever seen. He was burdened, and he was determined to support his life." The economic and social reality at the base of Dr. Goodside's sense of responsibility is clearly stated in his daughter's story "The Burdened Man": "The man has the burden of the money. It's needed day after day. More and more of it. For ordinary things and for life" (ECLM, 109).

Her mother worked "just as hard" as her father, tending that big house with its twelve rooms and suite of offices, always filled with people. In "Mom," Grace explained the dynamics of the Goodsides' partnership: "Together with the aunts and grandmother she worked to make my father strong enough and educated enough so he could finally earn enough to take care of us all. She was successful" (86). Manya Goodside "enabled him to do all of this," Grace knows, and when she was dying, when they were both fifty-nine years old, he had the first of several serious heart attacks. Despite family opposition, Isaac Goodside immediately sold his twenty-five-year practice and retired from medicine when his wife died.

Grace Paley recalls a man who, before he died at the age of eighty, told her that when he had contracted pneumonia in his youth, Isaac Goodside "went and picked him up and brought him home, and my father and mother, together in their house, nursed him and took care of him until he was well. He had been far from home—another Russian Jewish immigrant. Maybe he was from their village. Maybe he just knew someone who knew someone who was their cousin." We need not romanticize urban immigrant culture in the early twentieth century in the United States to understand that generosity, which differs from the philanthropy born of noblesse oblige—or tax breaks. No matter how much money or status Isaac Goodside attained for his family, his younger daughter insists, " 'really he was just a ghetto Jew'. . . . Basically he was . . . a working-class man and he really never got over . . . [his] deference to Anglo-Saxonism. He worried a lot whether we would make fools of ourselves [among the gentiles]" (Perry, 42).

Jeanne too describes their parents' kindness; virtually institutionalized within the family, it was simply what was done, what was right. "My mother was a very principled woman, very principled. During the summertime when they . . . used to go out to Belmar for the season, they'd rent a house with a friend, a Dr. Katz. And my mother would always bring with her two children from an orphanage. And they would spend time with us there, with Gracie, with me, and with the other people who had children about our own age. . . . that was my mother's choice."

This woman, whose mothering extended to motherless children, worried more about her youngest child than about her own dying. Manya got weaker and sicker as Grace grew older and—in her mother's eyes—wilder and more reckless as well. Like Gittel Darwin in "Faith in the Afternoon," she must have asked—even if rhetorically —"When will you be a person?" (ECLM, 33). She couldn't control her daughter, and she couldn't understand her either.

Jeanne Tenenbaum, whose love for her sister is palpable when she speaks of her, says that though Grace gave the family a great deal of pleasure when she was a child—and, of course, has been a source of great satisfaction and enjoyment for many years—"she's caused us a lot of pain too. Just because she's wonderful, don't think she hasn't." When Grace went to college, right after high school, Jeanne was working as a dean in the city high schools, "sitting on one side of the desk and talking to parents who sat on the other side being miserable about their children." Mrs. Goodside had been sick for a few years by then, so when she got a letter from Hunter College saying that they wanted her to come in for a meeting with her daughter's counselor, she couldn't go. Dr. Goodside couldn't go either, so Jeanne "was elected. I went, and there I sat on the other side of the desk. And I discovered that my little sister had not been going to school, had been cutting classes."

She would intend to go to class, Grace explains, would even *want* to go to class. But on the way into the building, going up the stairs, she would hear something—maybe a scrap of conversation, a story being told—that would catch her mind and take her away, right back down the stairs and out of the building. She left school that same year, shocking her family. Victor and Jeanne had attained the education and professional careers their parents' struggle had paid for: they were a doctor and a teacher; they played the piano, and they played tennis. Grace, the golden child of their parents' later years, born of their comfort and success, had failed.

Dr. Goodside refused to allow her to drop out completely. He argued for her to study business—a stenographic and typing course—so that she would have some way to earn a living. Jeanne explains that Grace finally agreed to that, and she did get work "someplace, I don't even remember the name. . . . but of course her heart wasn't in it."

Young Grace knew that her parents were "very disappointed" and that they "really felt bad," which made her feel pretty terrible herself. "They had wanted me to do everything," she says—to go to college, be a teacher, be a social worker—to change the world. At the same time that there was much encouragement of her intellectual and social endeavors, there was also disapproval of her politics, horror at her "wildness," and fear of the results of both of these. There was also an overriding concern about marriage. Grace felt that the "whole atmosphere in the house was that if you didn't get married you were in trouble." Of course they had expected their bright, pretty, funny, strong, and determined child with her high test scores to rise to the top—sweet cream that they knew she was—and achieve wonders in the new world of America. But it never entered their minds that she wouldn't also be a wife and mother.

After all, her aunt Mira was right there in the house, a living example of what happened if a girl did not marry: bitterness, resentment, the waste of a woman's vitality. "She was a very unhappy woman, a profoundly unhappy woman. [Mira was also] very beautiful, extremely beautiful.... oh, there were many men who wanted to marry her. But," Grace eventually understood, "the only man she wanted to marry was my father." This extraordinary complication, apparently long recognized by the adults of the family, did not prevent Mira from being a bad example for her young niece, who remembered and recorded her aunt's fate in her stories. "[She was] the one who was mocked for not having married, whose beauty, as far as the family was concerned, was useless, because no husband ever used it" ("Mom," 86).[4]

The family's attitude toward Grace began to change when she did poorly in high school, and it hardened into disappointment when she left college. With no forethought to match our hindsight, they decided that intellectually she was, as she puts it, "a dud." They had thought she was a brilliant star; they had thought she would make her mark in the world—but when she married before the age of twenty, they decided she would be "just a mother," and they arranged their hopes and expectations accordingly. Little Gracie would grow up to be only a woman, after all. Her grandmother's thwarted ambition and disappointment in marriage, her aunt's ironic acceptance of life on the sidelines, and her mother's struggle toward integrity had not been lost on young Grace Goodside though; they percolated slowly through her consciousness, and they eventually rose in her stories. One of the most poignant examples is in "Lavinia: An Old Story," which the writer describes as being rooted in the lives of her grandmother, a friend,[5] and herself.

> Now see Lavinia going about improving the foolish, singing in the choir, mending the lame. Now see her ... that gal apt to be a lady preacher, a nurse, something great and have a name. Don't know what you see ... but I got in mind to be astonished. [But then, when her mother realizes that the young woman has become "just a mother" and has apparently failed—like her mother before her—to fulfill her promise] I let out a curse.... I cry out loud ... Damn you, Lavinia—for my heart is busted in a minute—damn you, Lavinia, ain't nothing gonna come of you neither. (LSD, 67–68)

Grace thinks that despite such heartfelt disappointment, her mother was enormously relieved to have her baby marry so young, because then, as she slowly and painfully died, she wouldn't have to worry about her. That maternal anxiety is recorded in "In This Country": "One reason I don't close my eyes at night is I think about you. You know it. What will be?" (LSD, 108). The belief that Grace would be taken care of by her husband led to Manya Goodside's acceptance of her daughter's leaving school and marrying—an attitude that was shared by Isaac, their daughter speculates. Though her "wildness"—both political and social—was indeed modified by the marriage and ensuing motherhood, the Goodsides' relief is ironic in view of Grace's husband's World War II duty in the South Pacific and the young couple's financial difficulties throughout the decade following the war.

Jess Paley's appearance on the scene offered no immediate foreshadowing of those difficulties, however. Like reading and politics, music was a central feature of life in the Goodside household, and when Grace Goodside married Jess Paley, she brought another passionately musical sensibility into the family. "I met him because we had a very big record collection," Grace says. Her stories, as in the following brief segments of "Faith in a Tree," are filled with references to specific works, musical terminology, musical metaphors, and music lovers like Jess.

> two men strolled past us, leaning toward one another. They were . . . music lovers inclining toward their transistor, which was playing the "Chromatic Fantasy." They paid no attention to us because of their relation to this great music. . . . "do you hear what I hear?" "Damnit yes, the over-romanticizing and the under-Baching. I can't believe it." . . .
>
> [One of them] puts his transistor into the hollow of an English elm, takes a tattered score of *The Messiah* out of his rucksack, and writes a short Elizabethan melody in among the long chorus holds. . . . (ECLM, 88–89, 92–93)

Many of her friends were guests at the every-other-Friday night musicales held at the Goodsides' in the thirties; a good number of the listeners on any given Friday night were teenagers. "Since I was very wild and they were very worried, they didn't want me running around," so her parents arranged for Grace to host their musical evenings. Her father helped her plan and arrange the first program, but after that she would do it herself; the selections were always classical music.

"So one day, in late 1939 or 1940, a couple of guys came to the house and they rang the bell and said, 'Is this the place where they play music?' " She told them they had the right house but the wrong night—it was Thursday, and Dr. Goodside was playing pinochle downstairs. The fellows pointed out that even though it was Thursday, they were standing there on the doorstep and, besides, it was raining, so couldn't they, maybe ——? Grace conferred with her father, who said she could let them in to listen to music while the family went upstairs and had tea. "So they came in, the boys, and they sat around and they listened to music, and that's how I got to know Jess."

Jess Paley, who is a few years older than Grace, says he was "enthralled with" Dr. Goodside, though he "never had much sense of" her mother. Manya Goodside knew who he was though. She told her daughter, "He's a very nice boy. He doesn't say hello and he doesn't say goodbye, but he knows the way to the icebox." His own parents were less accepting of the relationship; the Paleys may have considered Grace—and her family—not quite up to the mark. "They were very difficult people," says Grace, but then, immediately realizing that she has uttered a criticism, adds, "but not really any more difficult than anybody else. I did get close to them very quickly." During that first year, when Grace was turning eighteen, the young couple saw each other steadily, and the Paleys were openly displeased with their son's choice. After that, the charm—and the concerted effort—of their future daughter-in-law won them over to acceptance of, if not delight in, the union.

The Paleys were Jewish, but they were Latvian and spoke German in their home. Grace explains that their sense of social position in the Christian world was very different from that of her own family and neighborhood. The disparity between the two families was rooted in the traditional lack of sympathy between German Jews (who had been in the United States since colonial times and were generally more educated and wealthier) and Russian or Polish Jews (usually peasants, less educated, frequently impoverished, who began to arrive in great numbers at the end of the nineteenth century). The Paleys didn't even live in a Jewish neighborhood. Like many German Jews, they had chosen to live among Christians on a street of brownstones in the borough of Manhattan, while the Goodsides, even when they could afford to move, remained in the Bronx, in a plebeian two-story brick house; though it was a detached single house, it was among others just like it. Grace Goodside, unlike her new boyfriend, "was always surrounded by Jews; very comfortable among Jews, I was."

Nevertheless the Paleys presented an oddly familiar mirror of the Goodsides, with a mother, father, uncle, and grandmother in Jess's house as complement to the mother, father, aunt, and grandmother in her own. Moreover, the uncle was a doctor—which may have contributed to Grace's fondness for him—and Jess had an unmarried aunt as well. One striking difference was that in Jess's family, the grandmother was not only important but also powerful. Grandma Goodside was not; she was cherished—"we all loved my grandmother, we all adored her, but she was living in my mother and father's house. My father was the one who had the power."

Jess's grandmother was pious and set the tone in the Paley household. She was, Grace recalls, religious enough to take the subway all the way downtown just to get Kosher chickens. "My own grandmother was, of course, mildly religious, but she was not officious with the family." Jess's mother tried to obey her mother, and she struggled to make her family conform to what her own mother wanted. Because of that, she would say to her son, "Do this, Grossmutter wants it." He rebelled, becoming even more irreligious, or antireligious, than the atheist Dr. Goodside.

Grace now contrasts his situation with her own, explaining that she grew up with no need for such a bitter rebellion because "no one ever tried to make me do anything religious; I loved taking my grandmother to synagogue." Jess was resentful, she thinks, because of being constantly cajoled or urged to accept the forms of orthodoxy; he resisted what he considered hypocrisy. "He was angry because it was forced. He always thought [religious practice] was false because it was presented as what one does for Grand-mother, not as the thing itself." Perhaps in relief as well as appre-ciation, Jess was at ease with Grace's family and came to the Goodsides' house often. Jeanne says, "He loved my grandmother, just loved my grandmother," who seemed to return his affection.

Dr. Goodside, unlike his mother, had reservations about Jess, as he had had about Sam Tenenbaum, Jeanne's husband. But surely a man whose family of women was a constant source of praise and support to him might be expected to express something less than wholehearted acceptance of the men who took two daughters out of his house.

Victor Goodside, who sustained no such loss at the addition of his brothers-in-law, liked Jess Paley and says, "He had a peculiar kind of humor which didn't always come out just right, a wry sort of humor, kind of oddball." He recalls that Jess "just objected to the world as it was," which is also a fair description of the world view of the Goodsides' own wild girl. "In the army he was court-martialed for writing on the pavement somewhere, 'Beware, this is a salute trap!' They caught him at it. He was a constant objector to the situation as it was, and he always laughed at it." Maybe this "oddball" sense of humor was what made some of the family think that Grace's boyfriend was very strange and fear that he would not make a good husband; some thought him a difficult man.

In the years that Grace Goodside and Jess Paley were "going around together," she worked at office jobs and tried going to college again. This time she took a class with W. H. Auden, who was spending England's war years at the New School for Social Research in Manhattan. She had been reading his poems, loved them, and was strongly influenced by them. "Of course I was one of about two hundred people in the class, which met in one of these big lecture halls, but I did a very brave thing. He asked, 'Are there any poets? Are there any people here who would like me to see their work?' And I put my hand up. I still can't believe that I put my hand up, since I hadn't spoken a word for three years in high school. So he took [my poems] and then I met him for lunch and we talked."

Auden talked to her about the language she used in her poems, about her ear, and about the voices she heard and spoke in her poetry. He asked if she really "talked like that" or heard other people talk the way she was writing. "I was using words like 'trousers,' which of course I'd never actually say in conversation." Essentially, he urged her to write in her own language—to write what she actually heard and spoke—instead of the language of an upper-middle-class Englishman, which was the voice of the poetry she had been listening to in her head. "I was really writing just like Auden for a few years there. I had all these poems, and most of them were just like his, which is kind of funny. But I was young." Because he told her the truth and was kind in the telling, he was a good critic and mentor for the young American. "Just to be in the presence of someone who was writing for real was important." Her boyfriend Jess didn't care for poetry, but he never discouraged her; he thought of her as a poet. "Now and then he'd like a poem." During that year Grace sent some poems to the college newspaper, and they were accepted and published, which was "very exciting" for her.

She and Jess married when Grace was nineteen and a half years old. Her choice and its emotional outcome provided Grace with the raw material for "An Interest in Life," in which Ginny, whose fictional girlhood smacks of Grace's own youth, explains, "Once I met my husband with his winking good looks, he was my only interest. Wild as I had been with . . . others, I turned all my wildness over to him and then there was no question in my mind" (LDM, 93). Her parents made no overt objections to Jess; "they liked him. They thought he was fine. Well, maybe my father didn't like him so much." The Paley family, however, did object to the marriage. Having set aside their earlier aversion to the Goodside connection, they now opposed the timing of the wedding. Jess's parents thought their son was too young to marry, and they knew he would soon have to go into the army. He was their only child, and they were strongly invested in his future. They felt he should go through the war and come back free to make decisions, free of responsibilities. "For all I know they were right," Grace muses now. But she remembers her own father saying, "When I wanted to get married, I didn't ask my mother if I could." He thought it was "ridiculous" that Jess's parents should have anything to say about the marriage at all, and he said to them, "I'm surprised he even mentioned it to you."

Grace explains that in the Great Depression nobody got married, and then, when the war came, everybody got married; all her friends were suddenly getting married. She attributes her own decision to "peer pressure; everybody was graduating—those who went to college or were finishing high school"—and marriage was "the next thing, the next thing to do." His family wanted a synagogue wedding, but her family objected to what they considered the oppressive and unnecessary trappings of organized religion, saying, "For this we came to America?" So not in shul—but with a rabbi— Grace Goodside married Jess Paley on June 20, 1942.

3

The Expensive Moment

In the same month that he married Grace Goodside in 1942, Jess Paley took a degree in physics from City College and then joined the Signal Corps. His membership in the corps, though it wasn't "regular army," required schooling at various sites in the United States, and he soon was moved from one training camp to another. His bride traveled with him, writing poetry and working at a variety of clerical and menial jobs. Their marriage, born in World War II and growing into the Korean War of the fifties, was subject to the political and social atmosphere of the postwar and cold war periods; moreover, the definition and structure of "family" was changing for the young couple. Some of their elders grew ill and died, and they became parents themselves. Grace Paley began to develop the sense of herself as a woman in the world that soon informed—indeed suffused—her earliest stories, which were written in the fifties.

Grace traveled with Jess from Belmar, New Jersey, where they lived for three months, to a military camp in Aurora, Illinois, near Chicago, where the Signal Corps was "sort of related to" the reserves; the men were studying radar. Then Jess was shipped to Florida for basic training in Miami Beach. There was no camp in the forties resort town, and the men lived in the resort hotels. They drilled by walking up and down the stairs of the luxury hotels along Collins Avenue; the army had commandeered them all. They would also drill in the streets, in full uniform. Grace remembers that "it was very hot, and you could almost smell the platoon coming."

Grace went to Miami Beach with Jess, but she could not stay with him in the hotels or in an on-base apartment, as she had in the other cities, so she rented an efficiency apartment. Although Jess hated the army and could hardly enjoy his situation, she recalls, "I had a real good time. There I was, meeting all these people, all these boys—it was really a good time for me." She loved living among "the boys" because, as a young woman in the early years of World War II, she felt that all the excitement, all the action was with them.[1] "I adored to listen to men talk during the war. I would hang around PX's and just listen to them talk. What good fortune it [seemed]—there I was, a young girl, surrounded by these young men. I thought it was really great."

That excitement was a mixture of the thrill of the extraordinary political and historical importance of the soldiers' lives and the physical fact of being a young heterosexual woman surrounded by young men who were both radically constrained and charged with energy. The experience became a primary source for the story "A Woman, Young and Old," one of Grace Paley's first three stories, written in the mid-fifties. It was first published in one of what were then called "men's magazines," which is an intriguing commentary on this story. Grace chose to make Josephine, who is not quite fourteen, sexually aggressive in her own cause—which is to seduce and marry Corporal Brownstar, her young aunt Lizzy's boyfriend.

Both the mother and grandmother in the story make exceptionally positive statements about women's mutual affection and reliability, and they are teaching the girls in their care to mistrust the sexual opportunism of men. These feelings and teachings, however, are undercut by the grandmother's loyalty to a man who "whacked" her daughter "every day of her life" (LDM, 25) and the mother's blind romanticism and willingness to go to bed with the first man who embodies her fantasy—even if he is her younger sister's date for the evening. Like Rosie Lieber, Ginny, and Anna—who all appear in *The Little Disturbances of Man* with them—Grandma, Marvine, and Josephine are fools for men, but they aren't fools.

That is, these women and girls fall for the heterosexual romance and erotic excitement that suffuse these "stories of women and men at love," but they already carry, like Grace Paley herself when she created them, the seeds of a feminist analysis that, sometimes ironically and sometimes angrily, began to define these contradictions differently in the next decade. Grace realizes now that her perspective had shifted, from the years of the experiences themselves to the years of writing about them. "By the time I was in my thirties, it was different, and I wasn't so interested in hearing men talk—you know, like hearing remarks about Jews, and hearing the way they would talk about women." Not only do the younger women in this story appear to be learning from their elders' mistakes, but "A Woman, Young and Old" actually suggests a positive near-lesbian sensibility at its conclusion, when Josephine, having lost Browny to a failed Wasserman test and his company's relocation, is "grateful for" the companionship of her baby sister Joanna, who has "moved in with" her since their mother's remarriage. Josephine, like her aunt Lizzy before her, is neither bitter nor resentful, and she understands that her relationship with Browny represented no more than his "hope for civilian success" (LDM, 40). She is comforted by and satisfied with her sister Joanna: "She is a real cuddly girl" (LDM, 40).

Josephine, along with Cindy Anne in "An Irrevocable Diameter," which was written soon afterwards, is autobiographical in that she embodies Grace's precocious sexual and intellectual exuberance, as well as her experience in army camps. The problem here is that the author has combined the child's excitement with the young woman's experience, thus giving credence to the pornographic image of the young girl as Lolita, powerful in her effect on men, capable of and responsible for defining her own actions. A superficial reading, one that ignores the narrative's contradictions and the characters' ambivalences, offers support for that dangerous and inaccurate definition of young girls.[2] *Nugget* probably took the story for this reason. In fact, the magazine changed the title of the story from "A Woman, Young and Old" to "Rough Little Customer," which misrepresents Josephine to serve the sexual bias of its editors and readers.[3]

In her years as a young military wife, Grace Paley was lucky; her ingenuousness and exuberance protected her, just as those qualities protect the fictional Josephine. She was generally employed on the base where her husband was stationed, or at least nearby, when they moved from town to town. Miami Beach was the one place she couldn't get a job, but when they moved from there to

West Palm Beach, she became a domestic worker—taking care of children and cleaning house. "The lady taught me because I didn't really know how to do it. I made incredibly little money, but it was a very short time; I didn't mind."

In fact, her mind was elsewhere; not only the "boys" occupied her attention and imagination. Grace wrote poetry while they were in Florida; that was a rich time for the writer learning her craft. She was young, and as they traveled, she was still free of the responsibility that her motherhood and postwar commitments would bring. She "actually had a few poems published in a real magazine," called *Experiment*. She thinks, retrospectively, that "they're not bad."[4]

They moved next to North Carolina, where Grace had a good job; she was the secretary to the fire chief and "made a lot of money—relatively speaking." On this base she had the job of ringing the fire bell to mark the noon hour for the whole camp each day. After a while, Jess says, he asked her how she knew when it was exactly noon, how she timed the bell. She explained that she always set her own watch by the central clock on the base which—they suddenly realized—was set each day by the bell she rang.

This period of her life was also marked by sharp emotional upheavals and contrasts. As Grace's interesting experiences increased, Jess moved closer to combat duty. Moreover, her mother had become gravely ill; Manya was dying. Manya's arm had remained enlarged and tender, extremely swollen, on the side where her breast had been removed. The family considered her "a very stoic person," Jeanne explains, but after several years of sporadic pain, she had a recurrence of the cancer, and in the treatment her chest was severely burned. She couldn't swallow; she couldn't eat. She was fed directly through her stomach.

Jeanne was the one who "fed" Manya this way. The family could easily have hired a nurse to do so, she explains, "but at that time it was different"; families took care of their own. Manya's painful death is surely the author's source when Faith, in conflict with Ann in the story "Friends," thinks, "I decided not to describe my mother's death. I could have done so and made Ann even more miserable" (LSD, 81). Not only does the character Faith decide not to use her mother's pain and grief to make Ann feel guilty, but the author Grace has chosen, so far, not to write her mother's final suffering into fiction.

Finally, perhaps when it was absolutely clear that there would be no recovery, Jeanne wrote to Grace. "My sister wrote me a letter and said, 'It's time you came home.'" She went home immediately and stayed with her mother for three months. Of her relationship with her mother in those months, she says, "Well, it was good," and she says it in such a way that other daughters, hearing her voice, understand that Grace made certain that "it was good." Though she didn't resent having to stay at home, she began to worry about Jess. When her mother had been in a coma for many days, Grace thought about her young husband, and the fact that he could at any moment be sent overseas and killed. "I asked my father, 'Pa, how long is this going to go on?' And he said to me, 'What do you want? Do you want me to kill my wife?' I think now, in these days, maybe I would have. But then, in those days, no—we didn't think like that."

Dr. Goodside had had a severe heart attack at the same time the recurrence of his wife's cancer was discovered; they were hospitalized together. When they came home—he to convalesce and she to slowly die—Isaac Goodside announced that he intended to sell his medical practice. His daughter Jeanne tried to convince him not to do it, but she was not successful. Mrs. Goodside lingered, weakening steadily, but her husband sold the practice quickly, and they moved with his mother and sister to a new place, an apartment in the West Bronx that Grace had gotten through a friend.

Manya Goodside had always confided in her elder daughter that she "want[ed] the time to come when I can move into an apartment with your father and close the door, without anybody in the house." She never lived to see that day, but she did live to see that new apartment. She was carried around in a chair—she could no longer walk—to see all the rooms. Jeanne recalls that her father was very kind to his wife. "I remember they had very beautiful moments together before she died. I listened for a while, but I left the room; I couldn't stay. They were as though they had just met. They were talking in very endearing terms, which they never did during their life. And then she died," Jeanne says, echoing the refrain in Grace's story, "Mother" (LSD, 112). "It was a very terrible time."

Their brother Victor had been given a brief leave from his base in San Francisco—perhaps thirty-six hours—to visit his mother, but he was not allowed to leave again when she died and so was not present at her funeral. Their father stayed on in the apartment with his mother and sister. Mira Goodside also died in the forties, and her mother died in 1949, one month before the birth of Grace's daughter Nora. Isaac Goodside lived the rest of his long life in that apartment, until his own death in 1973.

Jess was finally shipped out to the South Pacific, where he was on active duty for eighteen months. All but one of the men Grace knew served in the Pacific; none of those close to her saw action in Europe; none had any suspicion of the extent of Hitler's war and his genocidal program. Like most Americans outside of the federal government, her family and friends didn't know exactly what was happening in eastern Europe until the concentration camps were opened at the end of the war. "But we knew terrible things were happening," Grace recalls. "The city was filling up with refugees; my father sponsored refugees. There were many, many people that we knew personally who had escaped from Europe, from Hitler, from the German armies, from the action there. So we knew, we knew it in other ways."

"Even when I was a kid, when the war was building up in Europe, I remember my mother saying, 'It's coming. It's coming again,' and it was like a terror, a terror that was acknowledged. We knew," because her parents had escaped, because they had lived through pogroms, because they had been put in prison. They felt it; their Jewishness was palpable. Jeanne was a dancer, and during the war she danced for the young political groups, including the anti-Nazi German socialists who met in New York City. Even though these people were anti-Nazi, "They had this long blond hair; they were all Christians." There was a feeling there that Jeanne would tell about, a feeling about who these people were, and what that meant to the Jews—to be close to them, to work with them. Even those who were allies could arouse the terror.

While Jess was overseas, Grace continued to move around. She spent a month in Texas with her high school friend Gloria Miller, who had a job there as an occupational therapist. Then she came back to New York and lived a few months with another friend from Evander Childs High School—Bea Loren, who got letters from her husband three times a week. "From India, from Australia. Those guys were really traveling. Jess didn't write much. He wasn't a writer, but he had this little camera and he took pictures. He sent pictures from everywhere." Grace Paley, like almost all young wives in wartime, experienced contradictory emotions about her husband's absence. Even though she got a few "sweet letters" and many photographs in the mail, "I still worried about him; I really worried about him. [At the same time] I was optimistic though; I always felt that he'd be all right. I missed him a lot—well, I did a lot in that time, so I can't say 'missed,' but I was very glad to see him when he came home. I was very happy to see him."

She worked "somewhere downtown" and went back to school for a while, this time at New York University. Going back to school, she says, was quite consciously "another try. I thought I'd try it again. I studied mostly English literature. Again, I couldn't do it, I really couldn't do it. But I did write. And remember, I had taken that one course with Auden when I was seventeen, and that was very important. It influenced me a lot." In that period she also lived in the Bronx with her father, aunt, and grandmother.

Her mother was dead, and her father had retired from medicine; he was painting. Visitors to Grace Paley's New York apartment can view his work there, including a still life of a finely detailed set of kitchen shelves on which rest some utterly edible carrots; Grace explains that this painting drew so much covetous praise that her father offered to replicate it for admirers. In Jeanne's dining room hangs a portrait of Grace, a good likeness even in retrospect. Dr. Goodside had a series of heart attacks in the war years and was often incapacitated. His younger daughter "stayed with him there in his room. . . . I remember him barely moving." Though her stories about fathers suffering coronary disabilities feature much older men than Isaac Goodside was during World War II, this period surely fueled her description in "Enormous Changes at the Last Minute" of a man whose heart, "that bloody motor,"[5] is no longer the reliable machine it used to be. "His arteries had a hopeless future, and conversation about all that obsolescent tubing often displaced very interesting subjects" (ECLM, 121).

Grace herself contributed to her family's wartime history of painful illness by contracting pneumonia and being sick for several months before Jess Paley came back from the war. By the time he came home, she was fairly well recovered. He, however, "was really in bad shape—he was psychologically ill." Though he was certainly happy when he first came home—happy to *be* home—like other soldiers, he soon exhibited evidence of the stress he had undergone. Grace argues that the notion that only the veterans of the Vietnam War experienced shock, had terrible problems of readjustment, and suffered serious long-term depression is "really a lie." She insists that the whole generation of men who fought in World War II has very serious problems and is in fact "marked by" their experiences in that war. "It's even worse, really, because that was the 'good war.' That was the war where you should have been *glad* that you were killing people—there was no ambiguity and political dissidence."

Almost none of those men—including Grace's brother and friends and both her husbands—spoke of their experience in the ways many Vietnam veterans have, because there was no doubt in the national mind that what they had done was right and good. Her knowledge of soldiers' responses to such an analysis—and her own feeling about the military exploitation of young men—provides the roots of her commentary in "Listening," a story written after years of involvement in antiwar and antidraft work. "Poor young fellow, God knows what his experience has been; his heart, if it knew, would certainly honor the Geneva Agreements, but it would probably hurt his feelings to hear one more word about how the U.S.A. is wrong again and how he is an innocent instrument of evil. He would take it personally, although we who are mothers and have been sweethearts—all of us know that 'soldier' is what a million boys have been forced to be in every single one of a hundred generations" (LSD, 200).

When Jess returned, he "didn't know what to do with himself. He couldn't go back to physics; it had been too long a period that he'd been away." He felt that he had lost years of professional development; he had been out of school for almost three years. Jess Paley tried many jobs, but he was, like so many veterans, weary and depressed.

Grace was doing secretarial work and, with some help from her family, apparently supporting them both. She enjoyed those jobs because they were, essentially, political. She was hired by organizations that she could believe in and support. She worked as a fundraiser for Spanish refugees and for the Southern Conference for Human Welfare. Since these were all office jobs, which she calls secondary and tertiary work, she made very little money, but she "felt lucky to be there," because then she could "be with them in their work." She could be part of the organizing effort and make a living—albeit a meager one—doing it. Jess Paley, thinking about Grace's tenant organizing early in their marriage, says she's religious about her activism; remembering those early years, he calls her an activist first and a writer second.

Jess's professional rootlessness, which appears to have originated in his war years, was a cause of anxiety to his wife's family despite his growing proficiency in camera work. Victor explains that Jess was perceived as unreliable. "He didn't take a steady job when he could do the same thing by picking and choosing. He was a capable photographer,[6] but he chose not to have a steady job; he chose to be a freelance." In some ways this might have been his temperament all along, as Grace seems to suggest. He "always did what he really wanted to do. And he wouldn't do anything that he didn't want to do. If he didn't want to do something, he wouldn't do it, and that's all."

There was at least one important time when this intransigence gave way. Grace had always wanted to be a mother—she had considered having children even before the war—but Jess did not want children. She considers her attitude "part of my general optimism" and views the bearing and raising of children as not only a natural outcome of love between women and men but also a commitment to human life. She literally could not believe that Jess didn't want to be a father, that he wouldn't choose to raise children. The idea that her husband—or anyone—might consciously and deliberately reject that task and experience was simply unimaginable to Grace Paley: "I couldn't believe it, even from the first time he said it. I thought, ah, no, that can't be right. He'll change his mind. He really does" want children.

A masculine distaste for pregnancy and the presence of small children is suggested in several of her earliest stories, written between 1952 and 1959, and is featured in at least two. These characters may well be grounded in the frustration of Jess Paley, who, like many men, grudgingly accepted his children in their early years and then struggled to relate intimately to them when they grew up. Ginny's husband, in "An Interest in Life," holds that grudge and abandons her and his four children: "Oh, you make me sick, you're so goddamn big and fat, you look like a goddamn brownstone, the way you're squared off in front.... Your big ass takes up the whole goddamn bed. . . . There's no room for me. . . . All you ever think about is making babies. This place stinks like the men's room in the BMT. It's a fucking pissoir" (LDM, 95).

Corporal Brownstar, in "A Woman, Young and Old," is really just a boy himself and is startled when Josephine offers to have children for him. Lacking the experience of Ginny's husband, he is interested exclusively in her thirteen-year-old body: "No! Oh no. Don't let anyone ever talk you into that. Not till you're eighteen. You ought to stay tidy as a doll and not strain your skin at least until you're eighteen" (LDM, 32). In that same story, Josephine's and Joanna's father—who, like Ginny's husband, has no name and is described as a darkly Gallic or Gypsy type—rejects his children in a romantically understated style and later leaves them with equally charming, but obviously fake, reluctance: " ' . . . a wife,' he said, 'is a beloved mistress until the children come and then. . . . ' He would just leave it hanging in French, but whenever I'd hear *les enfants*, I'd throw toys at him, guessing his intended slight. . . . one day he did not come home for supper. . . . A post card two weeks later [read] 'I have been lonely for France for five years. Now for the rest of my life I must be lonely for you' " (LDM, 26).

Ricardo, Faith's first husband, the most prominent of the reluctant—and literally distant—fathers in Grace's stories, when drunk and holding forth belligerently on this very subject, "often shouted out loud . . . that she'd had those kids to make him a bloody nine-to-fiver" (ECLM, 35). Like him, Jess Paley left home sporadically, on assignments that sometimes carried him thousands of miles away. When Ricardo first appears, nameless, in *The Little Disturbances of Man*, he is in Chicago in one story and has just returned to New York from "the British plains in Africa" in another (LDM, 127). His contact with his two small sons is infrequent, to say the least.

With a few exceptions, that first story collection—written when the Paley children were young—presents regrettable examples of fatherhood, including Peter, who scarcely knows his daughter Judy and turns her over to a friend within minutes of their accidental reunion; Mr. Graham, whose knowledge and understanding of his daughter Cindy are nonexistent and whose interest in her is classically patriarchal in its prurience and authoritarianism; and Mr. Teitelbaum, whose relationship with his son Eddie constitutes a tragedy that provokes enough pity and terror to outclass Theseus and Hippolytus.

Grace feels that her own husband changed his mind when some of their friends had children and that he "really liked them." When his daughter was born, he "didn't object" and in fact seemed "rather interested." He didn't seem upset, she recalls, attributing this at least partially to the charm of the children themselves, who were—their mother says—"two of the most beautiful children you ever saw in your life, copper-headed, brown-eyed kids."

Nonetheless, Jess Paley was critical of his children—even when they were much too young to benefit by his analysis and commentary. Grace's assessment of him is that he was always very critical and indeed had what she called "a very critical nature," which is "a part of him to this day." "He didn't like his own family very much; he wouldn't go to see them or take the children to see them." She explains that Jess did, however, take Danny out and play ball with him. He also introduced music to Danny, which must have meant a great deal to both him and his son. When Danny said he wanted to play the flute, "Jess went out and got him a flute, and then he got music so they could play together."

Grace's stories reveal her recognition that fathers in this society generally develop minimal attachment to their young children. In "The Used-Boy Raisers," Livid, Faith's first husband, requests a reading demonstration from his elder son—whom he hasn't seen for a long time—and then admonishes his ex-wife, "Faith . . . that boy can't read a tinker's damn. Seven years old." "Eight years old," she tells the concerned father (LDM, 130). Similarly, in the later story "Faith in a Tree," Phillipp Mazzano hears Faith's nine-year-old Richard criticize his mother, and he comments, "I think I have a boy who's nine" (ECLM, 91). In fact he has three boys, as one of the mothers present reminds him—one nine, one eleven, and one fourteen. Phillipp's attentiveness to Richard, and the charm with which he evokes tenderness from both women and children in the park, lose their appeal when viewed by contemporary readers in relation to his careless fatherhood.

In the more recent story "Listening," we find a retrospective view of the situation, wherein Bob Nichols (Grace's second husband) may have joined Jess Paley as a source: "Then Jack asked, Richard, tell me, do you forgive your father for having run out on you kids years ago?" Recognizing Richard's defensive, deflective response, "Jack said, Ah ... He blinked his eyes a couple of times, which a person who can't cry too well often does." Jack tells Richard about his own father, an immigrant rag peddler, and then asks another extraordinary question: "What do you think. ... Rich, do you think my daughter, I mean Kimmy, will she ever call me up and say, It's O.K., Dad?" Richard's "Well," delivered with a nod of the head and a shrug of the shoulders, is not a heartening reply (LSD, 208). Correspondingly, in the same story collection we find "Anxiety," in which the present generation of young fathers demonstrates how much further men—even those deliberately struggling toward consciousness—have yet to go in their efforts to develop the capacity for maternal nurturing (LSD, 99–106).

Grace's own attitudes toward the care and feeding of families, despite her early tomboyhood and adolescent wildness, were typical of her gender and generation and further fueled by an extraordinary capacity for compassion and an impulse toward nurturance. Moreover, in the ordinary way, she was encouraged by her mother. Manya had actually told Grace that having her youngest child was "a very easy birth," and Grace "really took that to heart when ... having children." She assumed that "all that would be hereditary," and "it was—if it [what her mother told her] was true." Grace Paley loved being pregnant with both her children and attributes her pleasure and comfort to "genes—I think that's just what we do [in my family]. I wasn't sick or anything. My mother had me early, I had Nora at eight months (in September of 1949), and Danny was born *two* months early (in May of 1951). *That* made it very easy," she laughs.

Given the encouragement of her mother's success story, she always assumed that she would have healthy pregnancies and healthy children; "there would never be anything wrong with them." She insists that she had no anxiety about either pregnancy or either child's development. When Danny was born prematurely, weighing three and a half pounds, she says he "looked great." The hospital staff kept him "in a hot box for a couple of months," and she'd go to look at him there. She wasn't allowed to handle him; "at that time, that's how they did it." Grace remembers the nurses as being "very loving; they'd pick him up and show him to me, saying, 'Look, look.' He didn't have any meat—no flesh—so with his red hair, he was red all over. At two months, he weighed only five pounds, but at a year, he was right—he leaped ahead."

Her enthusiastic optimism—which may operate even more forcefully in a retroactive gear—is clearly the source of the tone of that telling, which ignores her longing to hold her newborn child, her fears about his vulnerability, and her desire, during that "couple of months," to bring her baby home. This is a woman for whom motherhood is an extension of a nurturant sensibility that dictates fierce pacifism and stubborn, intense personal attachments. Like the woman—surely Faith—Jack accuses in "The Immigrant Story," Grace Paley has "a rotten rosy temperament"; she "always see[s] things in a rosy light" (ECLM, 173). To that accusation, Faith replies that she sees "the world as clearly as you do," saying, "Rosiness is not a worse windowpane than gloomy gray when viewing the world" (ECLM, 174).

The rosiness of chronic optimism does not prevent Grace from taking deliberate action. Her rosy view is, as Faith insists, a clear one, and she is as decisive as she is clear-sighted. She had no other pregnancies before the children, but a year and a half after Danny was born she became pregnant again and had an abortion. She had conceived Danny only twelve or thirteen months after Nora was born, and since he was born at twenty-eight weeks, the two are only twenty months apart. "I was not in good shape. I had two little kids and things were hard for us then. I mean, hard. I experienced a lot of nausea. I was not sick or anything but I was not your bundle of energy. So it was clear that it was not the time to have another child. And yet I would have wanted it." Much of what she says about this abortion is contradictory—as is commonly the case in women's lives, even when decisions are solidly made. Jess didn't want more children; she loved spending time with the two babies she already had; their income was uncertain at best; she was a writer who already had no time to write; "And yet I would have wanted it."

"It was ugly—you had to find somebody. Oh, I remember." Grace spent those days in the park—Washington Square Park in Greenwich Village—walking, sitting, and playing with "my two little babies. This was before they were both old enough for daycare." Like the women in so many of her stories, she was friendly with the other mothers who came to the park with their children. Like the characters in "Faith in a Tree"—Faith, Kitty, Mrs. Hyme Caraway,

Mrs. Junius Finn, Mrs. Steamy Lewis, Lynn Ballard, and Anna Kraat—those women were sources and resources for each other's lives (ECLM, 77–100). "There wasn't anything that we didn't talk about together. I had my two and they were both in one carriage and I said, 'You know, I just can't have this baby.' And the woman I was talking to said, 'Yes.' She told me about this guy. And I went there with Jess; we went there together and we did it. And afterwards we went to the place that used to be where Blimpy's is now. That's what I remember."

At some point in the early sixties though, she remembered more, and she wrote her memory into the story "Living."

> I was bleeding. The doctor said, "You can't bleed forever. Either you run out of blood or you stop. No one bleeds forever." It seemed *I* was going to bleed forever.... I was frightened.... I could hardly take my mind off this blood. Its hurry to leave me was draining the red out from under my eyelids and the sunburn off my cheeks. It was all rising from my cold toes to find the quickest way out.... I felt a great gob making its dizzy exit. "Can't talk," I said. "I think I'm fainting." Around the holly season, I began to dry up. My sister took the kids for a while so I could stay home quietly making hemoglobin, red corpuscles, etc., with no interruptions. I was in such first-class shape by New Year's, I nearly got knocked up again. (ECLM, 60–61)

On the original manuscript of this story, which was typed on a manual typewriter on small white sheets of notepaper, many changes are made in both pencil and ink. The narrator's situation is at one time the aftermath of an abortion, another time a miscarriage. The final published version attributes no specific cause to what is obviously uterine drainage or hemorrhage; Grace's decision was to have her readers determine the cause of Faith's bleeding.

These years in the lives of the young Paley family were concurrent with the imprisonment of the Rosenbergs and their execution in June of 1953. Though older than Grace and Jess, Ethel Greenglass and Julius Rosenberg came from much the same background. They were born and grew up in New York City; he had graduated from City College of New York in 1939 and was in the Signal Corps until 1945. The Paleys and their closest friends, however, did not fear for their homes, their jobs, or their reputations during the McCarthy period. "We didn't even have that kind of jobs. Nobody in our crowd was like that. We were quite out of that world." The Paleys weren't in that circle—the City College crowd—but they weren't far from it either. Nor were they particularly surprised at the actions of the U.S. government. "It was no shock to my nervous system," Grace declares. "I had always paid a lot of attention to the political situation. I was not surprised or disabused" of a fantasy about democracy.

The assumption of reactionary behavior or corruption on the part of government officials is symptomatic of a common mindset in Grace Paley's characters. They may be optimists, but they are also realists, even cynics: from Rosie Lieber in the first story (who decides to live for love but is never blinded by it) to the three extraordinary major characters in the last story (the young narrator looking for a job, the multi-named "vocational counselor" who lives in a car, and the bogus entrepreneur Jonathan Stubblefield), her first collection, *The Little Disturbances of Man*, written and published during the Eisenhower administration and the Cold War years, is well supplied with characters who think and speak as their author does. Even the most hopeful, romantic, enterprising, or lucky of the people in those pages—like Shirley Abramowitz, Peter, or Dotty Wasserman—recognize and acknowledge the individual behavior and social mechanisms they suffer or struggle with; and those who anticipate and predict their losses and failures—like Anna, Frederick P. Sims, or Charles C. Charley—absorb those losses and failures with calm recognition.

Grace Paley speaks of her own lapses in much the same mood:

> I'll tell you a funny thing. You know, we did almost nothing around the Korean War. I have almost no memory of anything about the Korean War, and I'll tell you what I think [about that]. We were so unconscious, so unaware of that war. The whole country was unconscious. It was really very smart of [the government]; it came right after that huge effort, right on the heels of the other war. My generation just didn't want to pay attention. We were all exhausted. No one wanted to think about it. All we wanted was for things to settle down. It was very easy for them to move right into Korea. Even while it was happening, for Americans, it was a forgotten little war.

Grace explains that World War II had been a long presence in the life of her family and community. "We would have bad dreams at night, we would talk bad things about it during the day: the depression, the coming of the war, the war, the consequences of the war, the Cold War. All I wanted was that we would settle down into a regular life when Jess got home from the army. I don't know if that's what he wanted, but that's what I wanted. I just couldn't wait to settle down. It's true that some of our friends were moving out to the suburbs, but both of us certainly made the decision not to do *that.*" There had been over twenty years of an oppressive atmosphere —militarily, economically, politically. The Korean War was virtually hidden in the aftermath of those years, sneaked in the back door through the people's emotional exhaustion from that long, long time of grief. "So for this other war, the Korean War, there was just no place in my heart, there was no time in my life, and I simply dove into my kids."

In this way, Grace Paley was typical of American women in the fifties, encouraged to make babies and cookies and tend to them both in the kitchen. "Luckily for me my husband didn't want [four or five] kids, and I had only two." But she was having and raising small children while women were being thrust back, out of the work force, and redefined in terms of the role of wife/mother. She had never been especially ambitious for a professional career of any kind, despite her family's encouragement: "I never wanted a profession. It was of no interest. I was very glad to have crummy jobs so I didn't have to think about them. I liked being with the kids, and I liked hanging out with the other women the most. It had nothing to do with what happened after the war."

Notwithstanding such a definitive statement, Grace Paley *was* affected by the psychological transformation of women in the years immediately following the war. Her impulse to write was "frozen up for a while" in that period. "Left to my own devices, certainly I would have had more kids. I liked writing, and yet I didn't think of that as a career. I didn't say to myself [as she had in her adolescence]: 'I'm a writer.'" Grace believes that Betty Friedan's *The Feminine Mystique* presents an accurate analysis of the middle-class woman of the fifties and that "the far ends of the spectrum—like upper-middle-class" North American women—were "more deeply affected by the press of femininity" than others. She feels that the transformation from (the somewhat inaccurate cartoon of) Rosie the Riveter to (the relatively more appropriate image of) Betty Crocker in an amazingly short time reflected the lives of women who had graduated from college, women who could have had lives that included careers and professions; she says that those women "really lost a good deal. They were deprived of a lot. They married doctors and lawyers and moved to the suburbs and had children and were supposed to be happy in their kitchens. And they certainly had four children."

Before the second wave of the women's movement in the United States, Grace had "already read a very important book called *Adam's Rib* by Ruth Herschberger [first published in 1948]. She said everything. She already said everything that came up again later—all of the issues, they were all in there." Though this is an exaggeration, Herschberger did cover a lot of ground, including the linguistic use of the generic male, rape as sexual dominance, the clitoris and its uses, Freud's theories of female sexuality, witchcraft, menstruation, marriage, heterosexual romance and erotic experience, the pedestalization of femininity, the socialization of gender roles, and "equality." Though some major issues are missing, such as lesbian life, daycare, paid work, violence and abuse, and class, race, and ethnic differences, *Adam's Rib* provided an introduction to the discontent that was to come into the lives of white middle-class, heterosexual North American women in the sixties.[7]

Femininity and its attributes were undermined by the kind of careful analysis Herschberger provided. Grace Paley recognized herself as one who really never had conformed to the prescribed image: "Well, first of all, I never wore high heels. You gotta remember, I came from a socialist household. I never wore high heels. We didn't live in that style. And I never wore makeup. I'm wearing more now than I ever did then." Though it's true that Grace Paley has been seen wearing a little lipstick and the occasional dab of rouge while making a speech or giving a reading, she wore no makeup at all when she said that.

That tiny contradiction recalls the far more serious ambivalence revealed in other instances, like her abortion decision. Asked about her personal motives and circumstances, she will often insist that she is not responding to cultural pressures on women as a group, but that denial is contradicted by her candid descriptions of herself and her family. Moreover, this denial is at odds with her longtime struggle against an almost classically leftist concept of *individualism;* it seems to be based in traditionally feminine self-negation and passivity. She calls herself "lazy" as a writer or insists that her production of a relatively small number of stories—despite the demands and chastisement of critics—is based in "a character defect." But her denial carries little weight against the evidence of her life. Grace Paley is not professionally ambitious, and her explanation of that lack of ambition comes closer to the truth—not only of her life, but of the lives of women—than her contradictory denials.

Sounding strangely like Frank Sinatra, she explains:

> I just went my own way, mostly by not doing. Not by confronting or fighting. [Remember,] I didn't even quit school; I just stopped going. I just didn't go to it. They would say all of these things to me and I would just say, "Um." I would shrug my shoulders and that would be that. My mother was in despair and my father was in total despair, because they had been ambitious for me, even if I was not ambitious in my own behalf. [My family was dumbfounded] by my lackadaisical, laid-back, premature-sixties attitude. But I did want to get married, and I did want to have children. There's this split between wanting to live my own life, wanting to be totally liberated, to be a person who lived any way she wanted and do whatever she wanted to do—and wanting to have a husband and children.

Unique as any other thinking self, Grace Paley is nonetheless at one with her generation of women in these contradictions—which she would be the first to insist: "We're all creatures of our time—to the decade, maybe even to the year."

In the Eisenhower decade, though she did not name herself a writer, she wrote. She redirected her focus and, though she never stopped writing poems, began to concentrate on a different genre, the short story. So it isn't quite true that she "simply dove into [her] kids"; she wrote and published a book of stories too. Her political consciousness, bred in the house on Hoe Street in the Bronx in the twenties and thirties and fostered by her association with like-minded people and organizations in the forties, was also transformed.

The culture of the fifties that affected Grace Paley was peculiarly woman-oriented and notably motherhood-based, though often stultifying in its effects on women. The PTA and the park, her children's needs and their environment, became the sources of her art and her politics. The mothers with whom Grace formed relationships in those days inspired her to embrace the movement maxim: think global/work local. They were her local coconspirators; breathing together, they formed a bond she gratefully celebrates in her third story collection, especially the story "Friends," in which she ironically defines the connections among women as being "at least as useful as the vow we'd all sworn with husbands to whom we're no longer married" (LSD, 89).

4

A Subject of Childhood

From the late forties to the present (except for one five-year absence and a short period of peregrination in the sixties) Grace Paley has lived on one block of Eleventh Street in lower Manhattan, in the Village. Her career as a fiction writer began there, as did her motherhood. Her children grew up and went to school there, between Sixth and Seventh avenues.

At the time Nora was born in 1949, Grace and Jess Paley lived in a brownstone on West Eleventh, the first of three apartments the family would occupy on that same block. They had one and a half rooms: one room plus an alcove for the baby. That building—owned then by Jeanne Tenenbaum—is across the street from Grace's present apartment; it has three stories, and there is a small ledge, with wrought iron railings riveted across the front of the first-floor apartment. "Nora learned to walk on that balcony," Grace recalls.

When Nora was not yet two, Danny was born, and while he was still an infant, they moved across the street to a building named Rhinelander Gardens, also owned by Jeanne, where they had a full-sized apartment. In that building, Grace explains, "we were the supers"; Nora remembers it as a sort of boardinghouse, with Grace dispensing towels and linens to the people who lived there. Danny can still picture that apartment "very clearly; it was an old building, decorated with wrought iron; it even had yards in the back. Not opulent or anything, just very 'old New York.'" Nora says the apartments "were beautiful, really beautiful, set way back with gardens in front." In that apartment Nora remembers that the two children "slept in what I realize now was a porch. It had no glass windows, just screens. So it was always very cold out there, which we thought was normal. And there was a cement floor with a drain and a plug in it; when it rained we had to pull the plug to let the water out."

The Paleys lived there until the building was torn down to build PS 41 (which the children then attended until they went to high school). From there they moved farther west, to Fifteenth Street and Ninth Avenue, where they lived for five years. That isn't far, but "it was a very scary neighborhood" for raising children; Grace was worried because of the Port Authority, with its loading dock and freight trucks. She was relieved to find that there were many children already there—like the tenement Ginny and Mrs. Raftery live in in "An Interest in Life": "There must [have] be[en] at least seventy-one children in th[at] house, pale pink to medium brown" (LDM, 91), and they all went to school with Nora and Danny. "It was a much longer walk, but they would all go together. They would set out together and they would come back together."

Nora's view is different. She was sorry to leave the Rhinelander Gardens, but, she says, I

> had some of my happiest times on Fifteenth Street. It was a very big street, and it was across from the Port Authority building where all the trucks came in to load and unload. The street was always filled with trucks. And we, the kids, used to break into the trailer trucks, and there'd be great stuff in there, like chalk and tar and rope. We also did a lot of roller skating. On the weekends and at night everything was all closed up, so we could skate and ride bicycles in the street, because there was no traffic. Sometimes we could break into the building too.

Though Grace certainly knew her kids were skating and riding in the emptied street, like most mothers she probably didn't know about the rest of those exciting activities. But she has always understood that she, like her mother before her, would be ignorant of the private lives and distant actions of her children: "Their mothers never know where they are," says a wistful or disapproving woman on the subway in "Samuel" (ECLM, 104). That story is a textual rendition of a mother's worst nightmare: when kids go out into the world of trucks, subway trains, and grown-ups who aren't their parents and don't especially love them, even the most careful mother cannot protect them.

Danny Paley says that on Fifteenth Street they lived in "an old run-down tenement" and had very little money. He remembers hearing his parents talk about how they didn't have enough money to pay their rent. Jess was offered—and took—assignments doing commercials, and he made a lot of money on occasion, but that income wasn't steady, and Grace made almost no money at all when the children were both very young. Danny knew that his father

> had always refused to work for anybody. He would only freelance, take a job here, a movie there—rather than have one employer. And so when there weren't jobs there wasn't money. I remember in the early years, when we lived on Fifteenth Street—I'm talking now about the years before 1960, up until the time my mother's first book came out—we were really poor. But you know, if I compare the kids I teach—I'm a teacher of a sixth grade class and I have about thirty kids—about one-third of them live in the homeless shelters, or they live in these terrible hotels; that's what I think of now as poverty.

In those terms, "we weren't really poor, because we had food and we had an apartment. In those days in New York you could be poor and still have an apartment." There were "no nights when we couldn't eat. Maybe we couldn't have anything great, but. . . . "

Then "all of a sudden," Danny recalls, things started to change, around 1960. Jess started getting more work, and Grace's first book came out. The Paleys moved as soon as they could, to the apartment Grace still lives in on their old block of Eleventh Street. Much discussion preceded the decision, because of worries about whether they would be able to make the rent, which was $125 a month. "But it was such a nice apartment, it was so much bigger, they took it anyway," Danny says.

The family came back to Eleventh Street at the end of 1960 or early 1961 and took an apartment in the building named Unadilla, right next door to the new grammar school. Nora says that she was *really* sorry to leave Fifteenth Street, but "my parents weren't so happy about the things we liked there, and I don't think my father liked it there at all. It seemed big to me, but it must have been pretty small; the new apartment on Eleventh Street was much bigger." She and Danny each had their own room there.

No one else lived with the four Paleys; there was no extended family on the scene in this generation. Danny says, "I don't think anybody could stand it anymore." Their grandfather never came to their house, though they often went to see him. He lived "up at the last stop on the subway," Nora remembers. When she was growing up, she thought that all old people spoke Russian; identifying the language and accent of her mother's elders with oldness itself, she thought that when she got old, she would have an accent too.

Danny also remembers going up to the Bronx to visit his grandfather, especially with his aunt Jeanne, who would drive them up there in her car. Jeanne is not a mother and says that over the years Nora and Danny "have been as close to me as though they were my own." No longer living together, or even in the same neighborhood, the Goodside family maintained relatively intimate relations. (The Ridnyiks had never been as close to Grace and her children as the Goodsides were; apparently Manya did not cultivate her side of the family.) Grace's father was the most prominent elder in the Paley children's lives. He would tell them stories, Danny remembers, "and we always had a good time with him. He was very affectionate. He had been kind of a wild radical in his youth in prerevolutionary Russia. And so of course he would tell millions of stories about those days, about being sent to Siberia and then coming to this country. My sister and I were both very close to him."

Grace Paley was married to a man who absolutely refused to live as her father had, a man who seems to have been the opposite of that immigrant photographer/doctor who "worked harder than anyone" to support not only his wife and children and mother and sister, but many others as well. Wives often speculate about whether they have chosen husbands who are duplicates or opposites of their fathers—consciously or not. Grace Goodside, like many women, had managed to effect a compromise: she found a man who had her father's authority, personal power, wit, aesthetic sense, and intellect, but who would not relate to his family—or anyone else—in terms of those standard social or familial contracts and agreements that had bound her father to forty years as "the burdened man."

Danny remembers going to summer camp at the age of six; IRS refund checks paid for the weeks he and his sister spent in the country. Grace, like Manya Goodside, wanted them to lie down in the tall grass and see wide blue skies when they looked up, but she knew that going to camp wasn't a bucolic fantasy for them. "I think they hated it," she says, and writes that thought into one of Faith's funny complaints in "Faith in a Tree": "I could be living in the country, which I love, but I know how hard that is on children—I stay here in this creepy slum. I dwell in soot and slime just so you can meet kids like Arnold Lee and live on this wonderful block with all the Irish and Puerto Ricans . . . " (ECLM, 84). Danny says that when he and Nora were at camp his father "would never write but my mother would write regularly. She would tell me the news of what was going on in New York, and send me little newspaper clippings. This was before I could even read. My counselor would read me the letters and I would try not to cry hearing them."

One of Danny's earliest memories is of the separation struggle between mother and child. Of course, mothers want their children to be with other youngsters and learn to make their own lives, but they also want their children simply to go away—just to be, sometimes, somewhere their mothers aren't. "I remember her taking me to nursery school on the first day. I was very upset; I didn't want to be separated from her, so I kept crying. When she'd try to leave me in the room, I'd run back out again, and she'd hug me again, and then I'd go back in. This happened a few times," Danny recalls, "before finally I stayed." The mother's point of view in a complementary scene is delineated exquisitely—excruciatingly—in "A Subject of Childhood":

> "Now listen to me. I want you to get out of here. Go on down and play. I need ten minutes all alone. Anthony, I might kill you if you stay up here." . . .
> "O.K., Faith. Kill me." . . .
> "Please," I said gently, "go out with your brother. I have to think, Tonto."
> "I don't wanna. I don't have to go anyplace I don't wanna," he said. "I want to stay right here with you."
> "Oh, please, Tonto, I have to clean the house." . . .

"I don't care," he said. "I want to stay here with you. I want to stay right next to you."

"O.K., Tonto. O.K. I'll tell you what, go to your room for a couple of minutes, honey, go ahead."

"No," he said, climbing onto my lap. "I want to be a baby and stay right next to you every minute."

"Oh, Tonto," I said, "please, Tonto." I tried to pry him loose, but he put his arm around my neck and curled up right there in my lap, thumb in mouth, to be my baby.

"Oh, Tonto," I said, despairing of one solitary minute. . . .

"No," he said, "I don't care if Richard goes away, or Clifford. They can go do whatever they wanna do. I don't even care. I'm never gonna go away. I'm gonna stay right next to you forever, Faith. . . . "

"I love you, Mama," he said.

"Love," I said. "Oh love, Anthony, I know." (LDM, 144–45)

Danny remembers his mother "always being there at home, and just being very warm and affectionate; I don't remember her blowing her stack too much, or getting too angry about anything we did." Grace Paley has obviously experienced the desperation she describes so poignantly—"always being there"—and had the great good fortune to understand the contradictions of early motherhood while she lived it.

Grace was not a mother who made many rules or deliberately tried to implement her expectations in her children's lives. For instance, even though she wanted them to embrace Jewish identity, she maintained a laissez faire policy on that issue. She says that a Jew is "a person whose family is Jewish. I raised my kids to know they're Jewish, to like the idea, not be displeased with it, not try to hide it. To not be like in my generation, [where] there are many people who are ashamed of it." She probably would have raised them even a little more Jewish, but her husband opposed overt Jewishness in their home. They didn't attend services, and there were no longer any family members—as there had been in Grace's childhood—who might have taken the children into religious situations and ceremonies, but "I raised them to know they were Jewish children."

As Danny recalls his childhood, Jewishness was rarely discussed in the family. His sense of the family history is that both "my parents come from antireligious backgrounds. In fact, we had a Christmas tree when we were kids." His mother's tolerance and affection for that symbol of Christian December is a prominent feature in one of her earliest stories, "The Loudest Voice": "On the street corner a tree had been decorated for us by a kind city administration. In order to miss its chilly shadow our neighbors walked three blocks east to buy a loaf of bread. The butcher pulled down black window shades to keep the colored lights from shining on his chickens. Oh, not me. On the way to school, with both hands I tossed it a kiss of tolerance" (LDM, 60). Danny says that as a boy he knew very little about Judaism. "My mother took us to synagogue maybe two times total. My father hated synagogues and rabbis and churches and all organized religion, and my mother was brought up" that way too. Danny, like his grandfather, was not made a bar mitzvah, "which is almost unheard of" in his generation. "Although my mother did give me the option to do it. It wasn't that she didn't want me to. She asked me when I was about eleven or twelve, would I like to, and I said no."

Nora was also aware of her father's antipathy to Judaism and other religions, but she says that Grace often read the children Bible stories when they were small. "I had a sense of Jewishness, you know—my family *was* Jewish." Given their names—Nora, Danny, Grace, and Jess—the children's auburn hair, and the fact that not one of the four has the stereotypical features attributed to Jews in the West, their Jewishness has never preceded them in a situation, a relationship, or even a conversation. Grace has been assumed to be "New York Irish" by neighborhood people who knew her, and Nora speaks of frequently encountering and overhearing outspoken anti-Semitism because gentiles assume she is Christian and speak freely in front of her. Like her brother, who is interested in Jewish history, she identifies as a Jew more strongly now than in her youth.

The socialization of the genders and cultural distinction between them received even less consideration than did ethnic identity in the Paley family. Grace had no preference before Nora was born, but once she had a girl, she wanted a boy during her second pregnancy. She thought little about sex-role stereotyping when the children were growing up. "I thought about how much I wanted them to be decent human beings. I thought about that a lot." Her concern is voiced by Jack, who, in "The Story Hearer," doesn't want Faith to want another baby: "The kid might be very smart, get a scholarship to M.I.T. and get caught up in problem solving and godalmighty it could invent something worse than anything us old dodos ever imagined" (LSD, 143–44).

She was more worried about Danny than about Nora though. Despite the fact that she didn't think about maleness per se, "didn't think the word *male*," she did think about the draft, about the *idea* of the military, about the way the military is perceived and imagined in this society, and about how it works, in terms of law and political exigency, in the lives of boys and men. She recognized there were "all these people [who] want these kids to go and fight and die—and I didn't want that for my kid"—or for anybody's kid really, a sentiment that was the basis for her later draft resistance work. She hated that people would say to Danny—or to Nora for that matter—"You stand up for yourself! You have to fight back." Even in her youth she had rejected violence as a response to offense. "I always felt that Danny should not be called upon to beat some other kid up. He didn't have to do that." In the mid-sixties, as escalation of the Vietnam War steepened, Grace defined the absurdity of that demand by putting it in the mouth of a police officer in "Faith in a Tree." He addresses Faith's Tonto—who is still more a baby than a boy—in just the kind of shame-making terms that push young boys into violent responses: "Listen Tonto, there's a war on. You'll be a soldier too someday. I know you're no sissy like some kids around here. You'll fight for your country" (ECLM, 98).

During the mid-sixties, she wrote the male code of everyday violence into "Samuel," a story in which the natural exuberance and adventurous spirits of children have been guided into masculinity training. Four boys who have gone to see "the missile exhibit on Fourteenth Street," a show designed to create and foster interest in the military, are shooting off make-believe machine guns as they balance on the small platforms between speeding subway cars (ECLM, 104–5). "Samuel laughed the hardest and pounded Alfred's back until Alfred coughed and the tears came. Alfred held tight to the chain hook. Samuel pounded him even harder when he saw the tears. He said, 'Why you bawling? You a baby, huh?' and laughed" (105). The boys have been watched by both men and women inside the cars, and the author has made a distinction between those men who identify with the boys and those who disapprove of their behavior. One of the latter pulls the emergency cord in an effort to make the boys come in off the dangerous platform, and the train stops "at once." "Samuel had let go of his hold on the chain so he could pound Tom as well as Alfred. . . . he pitched . . . forward and fell head first to be crushed and killed between the cars" (ECLM, 105–6).

Samuel's death is the result of more than chance; it develops out of a complex of male motives and actions, all of them built into the social construct of masculinity. The men riding the train are described in terms of responses to the requirements of their own masculinity training. Some of them, the narrator explains, "were once brave boys like these." Others had been "boys who preferred to watch" the daring ones, like the man who won't confront the boys but pulls the emergency cord in the story (103). Both kinds of men had long ago learned what Samuel, Calvin, Tom, and Alfred are learning—that they will be measured by, and must measure themselves against, a standard of adventurous daring, a model of individual heroics.

Grace recalls how Danny "loved to wrestle. He had lots of buddies," and in the schoolyard they would be encouraged to fight, but when they were at home or in the park—private time—the little boys would wrestle for hours, for the sake of intimate contact and the exhilaration of using their bodies. Understanding the children's need to be close despite the codes of behavior that deny physical intimacy to boys even when they are toddlers, Grace says that "they were hugging really, just hugging a lot. Knocking each other down, picking each other up. But it had nothing to do with violence at that time." She argues that they didn't really want to hurt each other and asserts that they *didn't* hurt each other. "Of course there were always a couple of kids who did want to hurt, and Danny hated them. There was one kid who had a real big stomach, who used to fight with his stomach, go up and bounce into people with it."

That boy, irrevocably doomed as "the fat kid," was probably malicious out of his own pain. The family portrayed in "Gloomy Tune," a composition of the early sixties, contains children whose low economic status and painfully meager parental attention define another kind of doom, virtually irreversible in the terms of the text. In this story, mindless, pointless violence—verbal and physical, effortlessly learned—renders genuine response an impossibility between Yoyo and Chuchi. The boys are suddenly and accidentally thrust into a situation that calls out the set of masculine responses they have memorized.

> Chuchi Gomez slipped in an olive-oil puddle left by a lady whose bottle broke. . . .
>
> Chuchi said, turning to Yoyo in back of him, Why you push me, bastard?
>
> Who pushed you, you dope? said Yoyo.
>
> You dumb bastard, you push me. I feel over here on my shoulder, you push me.
>
> Aah go on, I didn push you, said Yoyo.
>
> I seen you push me. I feeled you push me. Who you think you go around pushin. Bastard.
>
> Who you callin bastard, you big mouth. You call me a bastard?
>
> Yeh, said Chuchi, the way I figure, you a motherfuckn bastard.
>
> You call me a motherfuckn bastard?
>
> Yeh, you. I call you that. You see this here oil. That's what I call you.
>
> Then Yoyo was so mad because he and Chuchi had plans to go to the dock for eels Sunday. Now he couldn't have any more plans with Chuchi. (ECLM, 55–56)

They continue their exchange until words give way to blows and Yoyo smacks Chuchi on the shoulder with a board with two nails in it. The author shows the boys' friendship, apparently developed out of genuine interest, destroyed by the demands of their masculinity training.

Following the theoretical separation of traditional parental roles along gender lines in this culture, most mothers, like Grace Paley and her characters, are the ones who take care of business in the home—and in the lives of their children. Like her children, Grace's friends and colleagues describe her as loving, attentive, and utterly involved in the lives of her children when they were small. Her longtime friend Sybil Claiborne explains that she was "very loyal, very, very loyal." She supported her children's choices and points of view; if there was a fight between one of Grace Paley's kids and another kid, Sybil remembers, Grace wouldn't necessarily say the other kid was wrong, but whatever Nora or Danny said, she would support. Even in a disagreement with a teacher, she would take the side of the child.

Grace Paley's politics of motherhood were different from those of the immigrant generation of her parents—and many members of her own generation as well—who thought not only that teachers and schools represented the American way, but that this way was by definition good and right. Many parents of that era wanted their children to fit a specific pattern of citizenship and daily behavior, just as the Goodsides had expected—and came to despair of—a certain kind of demeanor and accomplishment from their youngest child.

When Jess was at home, the aesthetic and intellectual interests of the two parents broke down into standard mom and dad patterns. Danny remembers that they "always helped us with homework and projects. My mother would help with the writing part, and my father with the math and science." Nora, however, thought of her mother's and father's work in terms of the professional dynamic they seemed to represent: "He did this visual thing, and was always thinking about light. She was a writer, and was always thinking about language."

Their father's presence in the children's lives was marked by frequent long absences as well as notable actions, rather than an ongoing mood, tone, or feeling. For instance, Jess designed and installed headphone sets for Nora and Danny to wear while they watched television—the sound of which their father hated. His presence was thus as memorable as his absence. Danny recalls:

> When I was a young child my parents were very close. The four of us would take trips to the country. Let's say my father would be shooting a film, and he'd have a list; he'd need shots of an elm tree with a field behind it. Or a certain kind of flower by a brook. It would be very specific. My mother and he would be in the front seat, and she would help him find all these things. And we'd drive around until he'd say, "OK, this is it exactly," and then he'd take pictures of that. I have mostly good memories from my early childhood; I don't remember them fighting too much. But I do remember my father being away a lot.

When Jess was working, more often than not he was out of the country. He worked several times for Twentieth Century, usually on documentaries. His children remember him traveling to Mexico and Israel and to Laos and Thailand before the proliferation of wars in Southeast Asia. Nora says that "he had a lot of real interesting jobs. He went away to amazing places—we have these beautiful pictures, slides, of places that are completely gone now." There were long periods of time, however, when he didn't work, times that were, she says, "grim." Her mother wrote that grimness into wry humor, projecting the economics of her own marriage into Faith and Ricardo's divorce. Faith makes "reasoned statements" about the situation in "Faith in the Afternoon": "odd jobs were a splendid way of making out if you had together agreed on a substandard way of life. For, she explained to the ladies in whom she had confided her entire life, how can a man know his children if he is always out working?" (ECLM, 35–36). Not divorced but frequently without her husband, Grace was surrounded by other women living with their children in the neighborhood. "All these women that I knew," she says, "I was very impressed with them; I was very interested in all these women living these lives. And I really wasn't so different from them, because Jess would go away for long periods at a time, and I would be alone with the kids."

We need to know that *alone* is not really the operative word here. Family life at the Paleys' place was what has been—for much of the twentieth century—considered quintessentially "bohemian." That is, as her sister Jeanne explains, "she had a very disorganized household. Very disorganized. Nothing was in its place. Everything [Jeanne chuckles]—even the children—was out of order. There were always a million people in her house." This domestic scene might be called "woman artist with children." Never a still life, always employing chaos as a thematic element, such a picture is the antithesis of images like that of Virginia Woolf, writing at her tall desk, gazing out over the garden and water meadows.[1]

The backyard at Rhinelander Gardens was filled with children, swarming over the jungle gyms Jeanne bought. There, and then later on Fifteenth Street, the neighborhood kids were always in Grace's house, and so were their mothers. "Her household was always filled," Jeanne recalls, "and her door was never closed."

People came in and out, "using the refrigerator as though it were their own." When Nora and Danny were both old enough for full days of school, other students would come home with them in the afternoons, drop their books at the Paleys' house, and run out to play. Not until their own mothers came home from work, or maybe even dropped by, would they get their books and go home.

Danny says that even when they had very little money, Grace was always giving it away, helping out everybody she could. "People would be coming over to borrow money constantly—not that she would ever get it back—but it never seemed to be important to her, whether she got it back. And when I was a kid, if somebody needed a place to stay, even if it was for weeks or months, they could stay with us."

That style, dependent on a constant vital exchange amidst a virtual tribe of mothers and children—built to some extent on her own childhood of immigrant "guests" who stayed weeks and months—is associated with a particular class or subculture. Nora recalls that the first time she thought Grace was different from other people's mothers was one year at summer camp, when all the families came for a visit. Nora looked at her parents and suddenly saw that they were completely different from the others. They were in a different class, by virtue of not only their low income, but also their politics and culture—in the anthropological sense; their style of clothing, their demeanor, and their conversation were all dictated by such differences.

Grace and Jess may have even walked and talked differently from the majority of the campers' parents; people who make art, and whose income comes from "money jobs" that support that art, are a hybrid class. They may have been born or raised in the middle class, but they have neither the money nor the inclination to live among the bourgeoisie. This couple visiting their children at summer camp consisted of a freelance cameraman and a writer of short stories who had chosen to raise those children in a "bohemian," "beat," or "hippy" neighborhood, a community long-recognized as the home of artists, leftists, and poor people. Grace uses that image of her "dangerous" neighborhood ironically in "An Irrevocable Diameter," when Mr. Graham interrogates Charles about his date with Cindy:

"You sonofabitch, where the hell were you?"

"Nothing to worry about, Mr. Graham. We just took a boat ride." ...

"Where to?" he said. "Greenwich Village?" (LDM, 110)

When Nora was a child, she had no idea about the family's class or income. She first thought about it when "a friend of mine's family had a car and we didn't. And they had a summer house. Then I knew that *they* were rich." This same friend couldn't go to Greenwich House daycare because her family had too much money. "They weren't poor enough; they were over the line." It is interesting to compare this situation with Grace's own childhood, in which *she* was the little girl with the summer house. Thirty-some years later, they were "so broke . . . [one] time, we were at the lowest level of income at Greenwich House," which rose from three to ten dollars a week through the fifties.

But she was still, Grace explains, "a middle-class person." Like Danny speaking of his students, she says, "I knew we were broke and I felt very bad that we didn't have any money, but if you had said 'poor' to me, I would have said, 'What?' I would have said that we just happened to be broke this week. I would think to myself, 'After all, we're not poor people.' And then I would think, 'Jesus Christ, if we don't get out of this hole soon I don't know what's gonna happen.' But we weren't poor people."

At the time Grace and Jess Paley's children were growing up, Greenwich Village was filled with young people who made lots of children and hardly any money. The men wore beards, the women wore their hair and earrings long, and both women and men wore black a lot. Nora says there wasn't much distinction between "artists" and working-class people. "Everybody was working. My mother never hung around with artists. She wasn't part of a community of artists," and in fact her daughter recalls knowing no other artists in those early years. Her friends' mothers were the people Grace spent her time with then, so the children saw no distinctions among them. Being "an artist" just seemed to be one of the ways people lived. Not until she went to college did Nora recognize that in the society at large, making art is considered different and unusual.

But Nora always knew her mother was a writer, "before she had published a book or anything. I think she was always writing. I remember her typing; my brother wrote a poem about a lady typing, because that was the way we always saw her. Writing was what my mother did, like my friend Nancy's mother worked in the Bible society; it couldn't have been more normal." Nora and her brother grew up feeling that writing was a part of thinking—a private, personal act. Nora read her mother's stories "from the beginning. It just seems like it goes way back. My own interest was really more with the poems, because I was writing poems very early myself. And she would encourage that, so we read and wrote a lot of poems together."

Danny knew his mother was a writer by the time he was six: "I knew she was always writing. I read her first book when I was eight or nine years old." He says that her habitual periods of consideration and reconsideration, her painstaking editing process, were evident in his childhood; it "took her a long time to finish anything." He recalls Grace "typing away; I always saw her typing." He mentions the poem Nora refers to, a childhood memory like the "lady writing" in Virginia Woolf's *The Waves:* "It's about a woman who kept typing—and the minute she gets done typing, she types the thing again."

Like his sister, he recalls his mother's support and approval of her children's writing. "My sister's always written more than I have. I remember her writing poetry at a very young age. Grace always encouraged us to write; and she always told us [that what we wrote] was good—I don't know whether she meant it but she always told us it was good." Danny often submitted his work to a monthly magazine of children's writings and was frequently published. Once a story of his was not taken; "I don't remember what the editor said but he was very diplomatic. And my mother said to me, 'That's how it is. You've just had your first rejection.' " Faith has a similar attitude toward her children's writing and is equally committed to enthusiastic support in "Faith in a Tree."

> *"The ladies of the P.T.A.*
> *wear baggies in their blouses*
> *they talk on telephones all day*
> *and never clean their houses."*

He really wrote that, my Richard. I thought it was awfully good, rhyme and meter and all, and I brought it to his teacher.

I took the afternoon off to bring it to her. "Are you joking, Mrs. Asbury?" she asked. (ECLM, 90–91)

As a child, Nora recognized that Grace's writing was her work, as well as a source of intellectual and aesthetic pleasure. "I always knew she was doing work." One's work, then, was part of one's life; it was not separate from the rest of daily existence. "I didn't think it was easy, but it was woven into the fabric of our life—mother and kids, and what we all were doing." The issue of productivity—number of texts produced—arises here, for Grace Paley has always refused to isolate herself for the sake of her writing. She has never been ambitious in the traditional sense: she has no career goal toward which she moves as a writer—only the goal of the immediate project, its truthfulness, and its quality of expression. Keeping the writing integral to the rest of her life, she has rejected the romantic image of the (archetypically male) artist as lonely seeker and inter-preter of truth and beauty. Her other commitments—not only to her children, but to other people, her community, and her growing political involvements—have always taken as much of her time and energy as her art.

It is also true that in these early years, as a mother with no "disposable" income, she did not have much choice, though she never railed against that circumstance. She refuses to consider motherhood a sacrifice or a form of self-denial, insisting that even when Nora and Danny were growing up she chose to live as she did. This is not to say that she did not recognize the conflict between her longing to write and her love for her children. The woman who wrote that long exchange between Faith and Tonto in "A Subject of Childhood," defining a quintessential maternal struggle in our time and place, was clearly conscious of the issues.

But she has continued over the years to maintain an unusually high level of integration in her life as a writer, teacher, mother, activist, wife, and friend. As her income rose and her fame spread, eschewing the male model of productivity and ambition, Grace Paley still did not assign greater importance to her writing than to her other activities. When her third story collection was published in 1985 and she read from it for weeks at bookstores across the country, the question asked most often by her audience was, "Why so long between books?" or "Why do you make us wait so long for these stories?" Her answer is always the same: "I have other things to do. Writing isn't all I do."

Nora, like some others close to Grace, occasionally regrets that her mother has not taken more time for writing:

> There wasn't very much separation [between writing and the rest of her life; that was good for us but] probably for her sake there should have been. She should have had a door to close and be behind it—but none of that happened; it wasn't like that. I don't know when she got the time, how she did it. She must have done it sometime—maybe it was while we were in daycare. I know some of that time she was working [for pay] but maybe she was also doing her own stuff. It's not like my father took us to the park so she could work—none of *that* was going on yet.

Neither Nora nor Danny understood, when they were children, that mothers weren't supposed to be writers or that there were negative sanctions and endless restrictions on women who tried to write.[2] Grace Paley's writing was part of her life in the same way that her life appears in, and is part of, her writing. Despite Nora's retroactive wish for her mother to have had more worktime and privacy, Grace Paley's life reveals none of that apparent but decidedly artificial separation between life and art or life and work.

Her work has always been based in her family experience, as a Goodside and as a Paley. All of her stories deal with or connect to women and children, to family life in the urban world of apartments, parks, streets, and schools—even when they also focus on a broad range of other subjects, including the Yiddish theater, sexual struggle and tenderness, racism, employment, the uses of depression, poetry, revolution, death, old age, writing and language, war, kidnapping, marriage and divorce, drug addiction, the state of Israel, Russia, immigration at the turn of the nineteenth century, China, poverty, reading, medical technology, socialism, racially mixed families, pinball games, surgery, heterosexism, music, libraries, senility, police officers, drinking, and horticulture.

Like many writers, Grace was able to write her stories when she realized that the things of her life could be put to use in art and that her own language could make "literature." She began to write stories in 1952. "I'd been writing poetry all that time and sending it out. I would have loved to be published. I read little magazines all that time." She had none of the fear or hesitation that new writers sometimes express about seeing their work in the hands of an uncaring or unworthy public: "I have no oppositional feeling, no precious feeling, about sending stuff out."

Jess Paley says that he believed the short story form was the coming thing, that people don't have time for novels, and they like to sit and read a story. With that belief, he joins the vanguard of American literary criticism. The short story genre, long denied serious consideration by scholars, academic critics, and some fiction writers themselves, was even scorned by most book publishers, who posited a theory of textual evolution and insisted the novel was a higher form of life. Throughout the past four decades, however, the story form has gained in status and sales, and it is no longer considered an exercise, a brief drill to be performed by fiction writers before they undertake the real work of writing a novel. Grace Paley's choice has been serendipitous.

Jess urged Grace to write stories for publication—he says he always knew she was a writer—just as she had encouraged him in his film work. "Jess said to me, 'You have a sense of humor, you can really tell a story. Why don't you write stories?' And I knew that was true. I had known it for a long time." Some friends of theirs were writing stories, and she had heard or read some and thought, "I could do that. I *could* do that." Jess pointed out to her that she had always been a story hearer; she had always been interested in the way people talk and what they talk about. Her interest in dialogue—which has developed into her extraordinary ability to render the ostensibly spoken word as printed text—was an impor-tant element in bringing her to the short story. She realized that, as she told her story-writing class at Sarah Lawrence College in the spring of 1988, "dialogue is action; it's gotta do some work" in the text. She recognizes that her analysis—political in its insis-tence on the social value of conversation—"was really a kind of breakthrough."

"I just decided to write stories. I just decided that I could."[3] After this declaration, she speaks haltingly—not a Grace Paley habit. "You know, when I began to write stories, I was really getting——I began——I was——I was really getting very—— that was when I began to get very concerned about women.

Consciously thinking about women. I'm not saying I was consciously political. I wasn't thinking feminism. I was just thinking about their lives, the lives of women. I was really thinking about it a lot." Her hesitation here comes from trying to locate the real feeling of that time, in memory—and trying to keep that feeling clear of her present political sensibilities. She is trying to avoid the imperialism of memory, which retroactively incorporates current thinking with past thought and action.

"Now you know, it wasn't as if I had never written paragraphs in prose. But I'd never *finished*. . . . I mean, I had small kids, right? And I had a man who was trying to get into a business, you know. And not a lot of money. And I wasn't really thinking about [writing] all the time. I was hanging around in the park a lot [with other mothers and small children]." How did she eventually find the time? "Literally, with the first couple stories, I was sick. I can't remember what I had; I had a miscarriage—or the abortion—and I was quite ill afterwards. No, I think it was something else; I had some sickness. It's funny you don't remember these things."

Grace knows she began to write stories late in 1952. Her abortion was near the end of that year and, in a sharply ironic turn, probably was the circumstance that afforded her the time to write fiction. We often use metaphors of motherhood and birth when we speak of writing, or any kind of creative work. Women realize that we must make choices about time for children, time for work— balancing and juggling, arranging lives to include what can be done, to produce what can be given. Writers—often men or childless women—may even speak of manuscripts as their children. If that abortion was indeed the source of her first story-writing time—time without noise, interruption, and the consuming needs of children, time for creations of the spirit and mind instead of the body—it becomes a singular representation of the forbearance and irony entailed in the "choices" of women artists.

Grace remembers only being told to " 'take it easy, don't work for a while, send the kids to daycare and keep them there as long as you can.' So I would drop them off at school and someone else would pick them up and take them to the daycare center. Then I had all this time and I began writing these stories. Suddenly I was getting time, time for myself." That time, of course, was given to her—she did not seize it; it was a gift, maybe even an order, which is why she could take it. Somebody with authority—a doctor, like her father—told her that she had to do it.

She would not have—and has rarely since—taken so much private time and space for her writing. She understands too that the doctor's admonitions would have been meaningless if there had been no daycare she could trust and rely on. "Whenever I go out to talk I tell everybody how important the daycare was; I couldn't really have done anything without good daycare." The daycare center available in Grace Paley's neighborhood qualifies as a bona fide miracle. Greenwich House was a forgotten leftover from the insufficient federally supported programs and institutions created for working mothers during World War II. Grace believes that "they hadn't killed it yet" because it was in an old, poor neighborhood; probably no one with any power noticed or remembered its existence.

In that period too she read a great deal. She read "all the people that were read in my day"—Joyce, Flaubert, Chekhov. She read "all the moderns" and was conscious of their style, was "very aware of their way of writing." She remembers reading James Joyce and Virginia Woolf. "I guess I was more affected by *Mrs. Dalloway* than anything else—without being aware of it at the time. It seems to me, looking back, thinking about when I was going to school, I was always very interested in how she did it." She also liked *To the Lighthouse*, and, she says:

> I was crazy about Gertrude Stein, about *Three Lives*. Remember, I had tried to write a couple of stories earlier; I had learned from reading *Dubliners*. I thought about technique a lot—and you know, I always read a lot of poetry, I mean, really a lot. I'm surprised by how much. Every now and then I'll open an anthology from the forties and I'll find that I know a lot of poems by heart. People always ask what influenced me, and I see lines in these books that *really* must have influenced me because I still have them in my head."

Interestingly, given her later choice to write stories, she didn't read much short fiction, favoring novels when she read prose. And she didn't read "those guys"—the standard list of American fiction writers. "Hemingway, for instance, didn't really interest me. I wasn't mad at him like a lot of people got to be later. I just wasn't interested. I was interested in that idea of using my own voice to make someone else's voice. Or actually using someone else's voice to get to my own."

Then, one evening, someone read a story at her house, a story that "was on Jewish themes," and she "all of a sudden felt that somehow *I* was given permission to write, by that story." She realized then that stories could come out of her own life, could be about what she knew, what she cared about and wanted to tell. "And then of course the first story I wrote was 'Goodbye and Good Luck.' I wrote that story for my aunt—for all my aunts—and for Jess's aunt. It was all about being Jewish and about the lives of women." It was also "all about" the Yiddish theater and the culture that grew up around it on Manhattan's Second Avenue and environs. The romantic leads are Volodya Vlashkin, "the Valentino of Second Avenue" and author of *The Jewish Actor Abroad,* and Rosie Lieber, who worked first in novelty wear, then in a theater ticket booth and on stage as an extra, made artificial flowers at the kitchen table in the mornings because she "had to give Mama a little something" (LDM, 13), and wound up again in novelty wear, when she was "a lady what they call fat and fifty" (LDM, 19).

Her earliest stories also included "The Contest," with its unforgettable "Jews in the News" puzzle series, and "The Loudest Voice," in which a whole neighborhood of first and second generation immigrant Jews debates the required celebration of Christmas in their children's school pageant. In the next six years, during which Grace wrote eight more stories, she produced "In Time Which Made a Monkey of Us All," which takes place in the Bronx neighborhood of her youth and is strongly Jewish in characters, references, and mood, and "The Used-Boy Raisers," in which Faith makes a short passionate speech about the proper position and role of Jews in human history and about the 1948 creation of the state of Israel.

Clearly that moment of revelation, in this case hearing a story "on Jewish themes," is essential to the writer who is not among those listed—or perhaps we should say loaded—in the traditional literary canon of the West. Young Mrs. Paley was not Irish like James Joyce, nor was she British, like W. H. Auden. Female like Virginia Woolf and Jewish like Gertrude Stein, she was nonetheless "other" than they in their childlessness and class privilege and, perhaps most important, in the language of that privileged class. The story she heard that day in her own home came from someone like her; it might have spoken in the language of immigrant voices, of the Bronx or its equivalent. Only when she knew that stories *could be told* in voices like hers, could she take W. H. Auden's good advice. Easy for him to say, "Write in your own voice." *His* own voice was the voice of ENGLISH LITERATURE; born with a silver voice in his mouth, a descendant of Shakespeare and Dickens could say anything. The story of Grace Paley's beginning to write stories illustrates her now-frequently repeated teaching: a writer begins by finding her own voice and is thus enabled to reach toward the other, to speak in tongues—bringing her to knowledge of both self and other.

She says, "I'm really embarrassed. I can't remember [for sure] which I wrote first, 'Goodbye and Good Luck' or 'The Contest.' But those were my first two stories." After many rejections—"both those stories were sent back by every other magazine"—the two were published in *Accent: A Quarterly of New Literature*, based at the University of Illinois at Urbana-Champaign. *Accent*, founded in 1940, was publishing established writers (like Wallace Stevens, Katherine Anne Porter, Eudora Welty, Richard Wright, and John Dos Passos) as well as the work of new writers. Like Grace Paley, Flannery O'Connor, J. F. Powers, and William Gass were first published in *Accent*. These editorial choices were the result of a "conscious effort to locate and . . . undeniable success in finding and publishing the talented, unpublished writer" (Hendricks, 4). *Accent*'s longtime editor Kerker Quinn expressed a preference for "a more suggestive, concise technique" (Hendricks, 25) and was noted for his "truly eclectic" choice of fiction, the majority of which was "highly experimental in either form or subject matter" (Hendricks, 139). Such a purpose and sensibility must have been necessary for the initial acceptance—in those New Critical times—of Grace Paley's first-person narratives about women, stories that are noncanonical in both style and subject.

Having written those first two or three stories during her convalescence, she did not try to publish them right away. Sybil Claiborne, whose son was one year ahead of Nora in the park and Greenwich House and whose kitchen provided the opening scene in the first Faith story ("The Used-Boy Raisers"), says that "Grace wouldn't let them out of her clutches," but Jess showed the stories to some people, and Sybil was among them. All of those first readers were more than appreciative, she reports; they loved the stories.

The publication of Grace's first story collection is itself a good story, a tale of good fortune with a happy ending. Like most of the stories Grace Paley writes, it is grounded in a network of women's and children's lives. Nora and Danny had some friends whose father worked at Doubleday. This fact became a stroke of luck when he once arrived at the wrong time—too early or too late or on the wrong day—to pick up his kids for his weekly visit, and his ex-wife said, "Well, why don't you read Grace's stories while you wait for them to get ready?" Whether this, or one of the other versions people tell, is what actually happened, the point is that Grace's children's friends and their mother gave the stories to a reader who not only liked them very much indeed, but also was in a position to act on his appreciation.

After reading "The Contest," "Goodbye and Good Luck," and "A Woman, Young and Old," Ken McCormick spoke to Grace. "Write seven more and we'll publish them as a book," he said. He offered her a contract, which she negotiated through Tom Bowman, a friend from a college short story class, who acted as her agent for that first book. Though McCormick had asked for seven, Grace wrote eight more stories (the extra one is in the set that introduces Faith Darwin, called "Two Short Sad Stories from a Long and Happy Life") "much faster" than she wrote the first three. As she wrote during those years—*The Little Disturbances of Man* was published in 1959—she regularly sent her work out to magazines; with the usual amount of disappointment, she experienced the new writer's typical fate of frequent, if not constant, rejection.

Doubleday, however, accepted her stories and forbore editing them as well. Equally important, the author had control of their sequence, which she has maintained with each of her subsequent collections (including *Leaning Forward,* a book of poems). *Little Disturbances* presents its eleven stories in an order relatively close to the order in which they were written, but this is not so much the case with her other books. The second and third collections create and maintain an ongoing community of characters within a complex of evolving themes: a story cycle. By 1974, when she published *Enormous Changes at the Last Minute,* Grace was even more obvious—whether consciously or not—in her repeated use of maturing characters and the creation of thematic patterns by means of story sequence. Neither so fully integrated nor so deliberately constructed as *Winesburg, Ohio,* Grace Paley's stories, written over a thirty-five year period, are perhaps more like the cycle of Faulkner's Yoknapatawpha tales; they describe and populate—with few exceptions—a neighborhood of characters who share and exchange knowledge of their mutual history.

The order in which these stories are arranged creates a chronology for the lives of the major characters, emphasizing certain themes repeatedly. Moreover, some stories clearly are deliberate continuations of earlier ones or refer directly to episodes and conversations that have taken place in earlier stories. For instance, Faith and Jack's conversation about having a baby late in life in "The Story Hearer" (first published in 1982 in *Mother Jones*) is continued in "Listening," which Grace recalls as one of the last stories written for her third collection (1985)—at least three years, and maybe as many as five years, later.

This coherent ongoing fictional world might have been lost, were it not for the network of mothers and children—like those in her stories—that Grace, Nora, and Danny belonged to. She says now that "if [Doubleday] hadn't taken [those first stories] for the collection . . . and [then] said to me, 'Write more,' for all I know, I would have just written the first three stories. That's a possibility. That's why I've always understood how people need encouragement to write."

The young woman who realized at the age of twenty that her family considered her "a dud" now, in 1959, had to reassess that realization—and so did her family. Victor Goodside, who had seen his little sister's early poetry and had been "startled by the quality of it—she was quite young"—says that when "the first book came out there was this real feeling in the family that Grace had come through." Victor, realistic in his judgment, was also aware that Grace's stories were not spontaneous outpourings of the creative spirit. "I do have the sense that it was a struggle [for her to write]. And I guess you might say I was a little unhappy about it. I thought that her life was unnecessarily a struggle." He thought that "if Jess would only get a steady job"—he chuckles as he says this—"and take care of things," Grace would be able to write more stories. But he "accepted it as the way some people live in the Village, the bohemian life" of artists.

Jeanne Tenenbaum has also been aware of Grace's struggle to write, especially in terms of the competition among all the activities in her sister's life. She wishes that Grace had chosen a life that allowed her "to sit down, alone, every day, to write"—and she hopes that now, having attained literary eminence, Grace will do that. When Jeanne read the first published stories, she too recalled that early promise and the family's hopes for Grace. "I couldn't believe what I read. I was so taken aback, astonished, so amazed at the beauty of her work."

She says that their father had some criticisms, however. "He would say to her, 'Why do you write this way? What makes you write this way?'" Isaac Goodside himself had written a book, an autobiography, for which he wanted his children to find a publisher. The father-as-poet appears in Faith's life when Gersh Darwin recites his work to his daughter, translating from Yiddish as he speaks.

Childhood passes
Youth passes
Also the prime of life passes.
Old age passes.
Why do you believe, my daughters,
That old age is different?

"What do you say, Faithy? You know a whole bunch of artists and writers."

"What do I say? Papa." She stopped stock-still. "You're marvelous. That's like a Japanese Psalm of David."

"You think it's good?"

"I love it, Pa. It's marvelous." (ECLM, 46)

This excerpt from "Faith in the Afternoon," in which Faith's father is modest and his daughter admiring and encouraging, is markedly different from their exchanges in the later story "Dreamer in a Dead Language," when he is arrogant and ambitious and she is dismayed at his interest in publicity and marketing (LSD, 11–38).

Isaac Goodside "thought he was a great writer," Jeanne says. "My father thought he was a great everything. And he wanted to give Gracie suggestions as to how to write." Those "suggestions" became the heart of Grace Paley's most analyzed story, "A Conversation with My Father," in which the father-as-critic argues with his daughter about her writing.[4] He says to her, "I would like to see you write a simple story just once more ... the kind de Maupassant wrote, or Chekhov. ... Just recognizable people and then write down what happened to them next." The daughter, who says she wants "to please him," writes and offers her story to the father, who says, "You misunderstood me on purpose. ... You left everything out" (ECLM, 161–62). The fictional father's objections are stylistic, but they are moral, ethical, and philosophical too. He wants her characters to be described physically and to be given personal histories, but they must also subscribe, within the plot, to the social mores he approves.

> " ... Pa, what have I left out now? ...
>
> "Her looks, for instance."
>
> "Oh. Quite handsome, I think. Yes."
>
> "Her hair?"
>
> "Dark, with heavy braids, as though she were a girl or a foreigner."
>
> "What were her parents like, her stock? ... What about the boy's father? Why didn't you mention him? Who was he? Or was the boy born out of wedlock?"
>
> "Yes," I said. "He was born out of wedlock."
>
> "For Godsakes, doesn't anyone in your stories get married? Doesn't anyone have the time to run down to City Hall before they jump into bed?" ...
>
> "Married or not, it's of small consequence."
>
> "It is of great consequence, he said." (ECLM, 162–63)

Additionally, the fictional father wants his writer-daughter to accept his definition of tragedy—not only in her fiction, but in her life as well.

> "The end. The end. You were right to put that down. The end."
>
> I didn't want to argue, but I had to say, "Well it is not necessarily the end, Pa."
>
> "Yes," he said, "what a tragedy. The end of a person. ... You don't want to recognize it. Tragedy! Plain tragedy! Historical tragedy! No hope. The end."
>
> "Oh, Pa," I said. "She could change."
>
> "In your own life, too, you have to look it in the face." (ECLM, 166–67)

This fictional quarrel, which reflects current arguments about critical sensibilities in postmodern American fiction,[5] is fundamental to the ongoing philosophical disagreement between Grace Paley and her father. Even when the composition of the story-within-the-story (in which a mother and son are juxtaposed with the father-daughter pair in the external framework) was not the issue, Isaac Goodside and his daughter Grace fought together for nearly forty years. Jeanne says that when Grace would visit their father, his eyes would light up. Isaac "was crazy about her whenever she came. They'd fight, but he was crazy about her all the time. And she'd spend the time arguing with him, both of them arguing at the top of their lungs. But he couldn't wait until she came again."

The family's response to her published work, with or without argument, was like Grace's own: recognition that yes, she was a writer. Once her first collection was complete, she felt that she really *had* to continue writing. "But then I also had to get a job." The children were nearly nine and eleven years old, and the Doubleday money couldn't take them very far, "so I went to Columbia University. And the pay was so minimal that they were embarrassed." She was typing for the university and says they were "so embarrassed" that they actually would tell her, "Well, take your time, work an hour and rest an hour." In that "rest" hour she could do her own writing. "Well, maybe they didn't say that. But that's what I did," at least for the short time she worked there.

Sometimes she would bring stories written in longhand to transcribe at the typewriter; sometimes she would compose as she typed. She was not one of those writers who wakes up at 3:00 A.M. to write while the world—and her children—sleep. She laughs at the suggestion, saying, "That's not me—that's Bob Nichols—not me. When Bob lived in New York and had jobs [in the city] he would get up at 5:30 and write before he had to go to his job." In full sunlight, then, and on a very slim paycheck from Columbia University, Grace Paley continued to write.

5

The Loudest Voice

Positive response to the publication of *The Little Disturbances of Man* crystallized Grace Paley's early reputation as a writer. One year before that collection appeared, the editors of *Accent* noted when they published "The Contest" that "Goodbye and Good Luck," the collection's compelling opener, had "attracted wide attention" when they printed it in 1956. This first book received national reviews. Praising the book, Virginia Kirkus was undisturbed by Grace's unusual style, finding that the stories revealed "a penetrating wry wit and a poignancy which avoids the sentimental"; she decreed "this first book . . . a demonstration of a considerable talent." The *New Yorker* bestowed a mixed blessing: "Mrs. Paley's writing is fresh and vigorous, and her view of life is her own, but she juggles her phrases at such a dizzy speed, executes so many sleights of hand . . . that it is not easy to see whether she is telling a story or merely performing tricks with words."

Grace Paley had no wish to become the newest radius in New York's literary circles. She wanted, she insists, to "stay with" her friends: "I was so interested in my friends. I didn't want to leave them." For many more years, Grace believed that to identify as a writer, she would have to leave her chosen social and political world, "my sphere—which, interestingly or perhaps ironically, was creating my literature. I was very afraid . . . and my fear was the fear of loss, loss of my own place and my own people." Had she understood then what her characters learned nearly twenty years later, she might not have been so afraid. In "The Expensive Moment," the narrator explains how American artists responded to the revolutionary Chinese view of the artist as one who works to develop the culture of her people: "All sorts of American cultural workers were invited [to greet the Chinese visitors]. Some laughed to hear themselves described in this way. They were accustomed to being called 'dreamer poet realist postmodernist.' They might have liked being called 'cultural dreamer,' but no one had thought of that yet" (LSD, 189).

Grace Paley has explained to dozens of interviewers and audiences over the past three decades that she was always active in "local things" and really didn't want to become "a literary person." She was wary of the mystique of professional writers, both the academically and the aesthetically inclined. She wanted to stay "on the block"—that is, not only did she wish to remain outside the culture of the literati, but she perceived the literary world almost wholly in terms of its most negative, and exclusive, reputation. She assumed, for instance, that association with other writers would necessitate leaving her friends and abandoning her political commitments. Bob Nichols even now refers to her as "a neighborhood type, not a coalition or abstract-level type."[1]

The neighborhood not only is the most common locale in her stories, defining the milieu of her recurring character groups, but also represents a feeling in Grace Paley, the sense of community and connection, the sense of being at home. In 1986, long after she had become comfortable with the appellation "writer," she was the first winner of the Edith Wharton Citation of Merit and was named State Author of New York. In her brief acceptance speech, she expressed gratitude for the honor, and admiration and respect for the committee of writers who chose her, by saying that "the only nicer thing maybe for me would be if I got an award from my block."

Her desire to stay small and work locally was a tactical decision and the choice of a good radical, as well as the result of the fears she describes. Being a woman was basic to her decisions as well. In her choices, Grace Paley was also refusing to take up space, rejecting the possibilities of her own energy and talent. Her gender—like her motherhood—is not inconsequential here. She didn't become a public speaker until the early sixties; "I wasn't in that kind of situation, and I tried very hard not to be." Her trying to keep small, to stay in the family and on the block, not only was motivated by a fear of losing her homeground, but also is a classic woman's maneuver; we learn how to keep our place. Ironically, in her efforts to keep from getting too big, becoming too important, wielding too much power, she learned to prosper in the small plot she chose to cultivate.

Grace Paley's small plot was just like those of other young mothers in the fifties. When Nora entered elementary school, Grace went to her first PTA meeting. At that meeting, her sister Jeanne recalls, something was said or done that evoked a strong response from the new member, Mrs. Paley. "She had never gotten up to speak, she had never spoken, but she got up and said what she wanted to say—and she told me that she liked [doing] it. From then on it was easier for her. That was the beginning of her ability to get up and talk and say her piece.[2] She grew active in the PTA and one thing led to another."

When Grace became politically active in the neighborhood, Nora perceived her actions as a function of motherhood, because "she began with going to the school and sticking up for her kids. And it just seemed like this is what mothers do." Moving outward, from the family onto the block, into the park and the wider neighborhood, was a natural extension of the maternal sphere. "From my point of view, since I was very little when she began, it was just an outgrowth of her motherhood. All the [important] action was always taken by the mothers," Nora says. In "Politics," Grace describes some of that important action, displaying the accuracy of Nora's analysis with hilarity, as well as the irony intrinsic in all municipal business:

> A group of mothers from our neighborhood went down-town to the Board of Estimate Hearing and sang a song. . . . [the soloist's lyrics and the "recitative," which all the attendant mothers deliver in chorus, request the construction of "a high fence" for "the children's playground" to keep out "the bums and tramps," the "old men wagging their cricked pricks," the "junkies," "Commies" and other assorted "creeps."] No one on the Board of Estimate, including the mayor, was unimpressed. After the reiteration of the fifth singer, all the officials said so, murmuring ah and oh in a kind of startled arpeggio round lasting maybe

three minutes. The comptroller . . . said, "Yes yes yes, in this case yes, a high 16.8 fence can be put up at once, can be expedited, why not. . . . " Then and there, he picked up the phone and called Parks, Traffic and Child Welfare. . . . By noon the next day, the fence was up. (ECLM, 139–41)[3]

Danny explains the connection between Grace's politics and her motherhood: "As a mother she wanted to help make the world safe, help make a world that would still exist when her children grew up." Grace's style of mothering is an expression of her general politics, which grow out of a radical compassion—that same concern she exhibited as a child during the Great Depression. Though she might feel angry, frightened, or indignant when she organizes or takes to the streets, these emotions are not the root of her activism. Sybil Claiborne speaks of her "as a nurturer rather than a mother, because that [meaning] spills over into so much of the world—her concern about the environment—everything goes beyond her being the mother of two children. You have to be careful with a word like 'motherhood,' because it can be so restrictive and so selfish. Being a mother was what rooted her in her community, and pushed her into a certain kind of activity at a certain time in her life. Grace says, 'Your politics is where your life is.' "

While Grace's writing and her political work were constrained by the narrow range afforded women, at the same time they were powerfully fueled by doing "woman's work" in "woman's place," a contradiction integral to the lives of women in this society. Her present feminist consciousness was engendered within those restrictions, and it has produced her current analysis of the integrated nature of such seemingly disparate issues as women's reproductive rights, global militarism, the proliferation of nuclear power, daycare, racism, poverty, and gender equity in the workplace.

Danny remembers when Grace became involved in antiwar and antimilitary activities in the late fifties, "though back then they called it the 'Ban-the-Bomb' movement." By the time he was six or seven years old, he had begun to worry about the future, his future. "Was I going to get to grow up? What was going to happen?" So he asked his mother, "and she more or less promised me that by the time I was grown up there wouldn't be any more war." He remembers that she didn't waffle either; no "Let's hope...." She was definite; "I was so relieved."

Despite the inaccuracy of this prediction, Grace Paley was an effective teacher as a mother. The children learned from her, and when still quite young, they were actively engaged in community struggles. Both Nora and Danny pulled away and reacted against Grace to some extent during their adolescence in the sixties. Danny recalls that though he was involved with both the peace movement and the civil rights movement and "used to go to a lot of demonstrations," as a teenager he went through a period when he "didn't want to have anything to do with the political movements she was involved in." Adolescent disaffection notwithstanding, Nora explains that, for Grace's children, political action—like writing—"was what you did; it was what was happening, what was going on, especially in the sixties."

Tonto and Richard in the Faith stories are children of a politically conscious and active mother; their pronouncements and arguments are drawn from the dinner table debate they grew up with, just as their author's earliest political inclinations were fostered in the dining room on Hoe Street in the Bronx. Grace says that her daughter Nora's politics were clear very early and that even when teachers threatened to fail her for refusing to participate in bomb drills, she said, "I don't care, I'm not going to." Nora explains that "I really just watched her, and I got involved myself with people my age, and it was all just sort of natural."

The first political action Nora ever undertook herself was in elementary school during the fifties, when her mother was eccentric, unusual—not yet a member of that vast sixties movement. "We had these shelter drills. And I remember being totally horrified by it, and I refused to do it. It was the first action I ever initiated." She knew the precautions she and her classmates were being taught were ridiculous, and she resented the hypocrisy of their being mandatory, so she protested and opposed civil defense drills in her school. Her motivation, she says, was just "the terror. I mean, I was terrified. We were terrified by what we learned about the bomb. That was something I decided to do myself, but it came out of my knowing something that the other kids maybe didn't know—I knew about it because it was talked about in my house."

Most of the political actions the Paley children observed or took part in seemed "natural" because they were, literally, right in their neighborhood. The earliest community conflict Danny remembers was the one about the city buses; they would drive down Fifth Avenue, come through the Washington Square arch, lumber into the park, and turn around. They kept coming farther and farther into the park itself, and the transportation people wanted to route them all the way through. "Of course," Danny says, "this was where the kids were playing, so my mother mobilized the community to stop them—and they won that one. It was probably the next year that [the city] wanted to ban the folksinging."

Yes, it was soon after that that the city administration attempted to ban the playing of music in Washington Square Park. At that time people sang—mostly folk music—in the park every weekend and often during the week in spring and summer. "And this was even before portable amplifiers were invented, so it wasn't a question of loudness. They just wanted to ban it." That absurd ban is mocked in one of Faith's numerous digressions as she tells the story of a day in the park from her perch in "Faith in a Tree":

> all the blue-eyed, boy-faced policemen in the park are worried. They can see that lots of our vitamin-enlarged high-school kids are planning to lug their guitar cases around all day long. They're scared that one of them may strum and sing a mountain melody or that several, a gang, will gather to raise their voices in medieval counterpoint.
>
> Question: Does the world know . . . that, except for a few hours on Sunday afternoon, the playing of fretted instruments is banned by municipal decree? Absolutely forbidden is the song of the flute and the oboe. (ECLM, 80–81)

One day, which Danny remembers "very clearly because it was so violent," all the folksingers came with their guitars to protest the city's ban. "I was there with my mother. And to my great shock, because it seemed so peaceful—they were just sitting there playing their guitars—the police came, and they started clubbing everybody in sight. No provocation. You know, it was so peaceful, just people playing music. They started clubbing everyone, and I got scared—naturally."

Grace's response was a revelation to her small son:

I saw something in my mother that I'd never seen before. This big cop grabbed me—I don't know, by the hair or the back of the neck, but he grabbed me. And my mother, who was about half of his height, pulled me away, pushed the cop and said, "Don't you ever touch my kid!" And she said it in such a way that he backed off immediately. Here was this guy who was just clubbing people! And he was so big, with his gun and his club. I looked at her in a different way that day, because I had seen something in her, a kind of toughness, that I had never seen before. And I remember being really impressed by that. I was six years old, and that day has always stayed with me. And then she gathered together with other people and they defeated that ordinance. They defeated all those stupid things the city tried to do.

People still sing in that park, and the buses don't go through the arch. "They remodeled the park around 1970, and in fact Bob [Nichols] was the architect of the new design."

Nora explains that she was "very proud of [Grace], always. But in the dangerous parts I was always very frightened." Like Danny, she tells of seeing her mother respond to danger and brutality with courage. At a demonstration in Times Square, there was a great crowd of people, and one cop was coming toward Grace and the children, moving through the crowd, swinging his billy club— "probably in an arc, but back and forth, back and forth." He was getting closer and closer to them, when Grace moved toward him and put her hand up—"very fierce." She stopped him cold, saying, "Get away from my kids."

In "Ruthy and Edie," in the fiftieth birthday party section written in the early eighties, one of the friends recalls an antidraft demonstration. Echoing Nora and Danny Paley, she talks about Ruth Larsen, who, in the third story collection, joins Faith Asbury as a strongly autobiographical character:

we were sitting right up against the horses' knees at the draft board. . . . And then the goddamn horses started to rear and the cops were knocking people on their backs and heads— remember? And, Ruthy, I was watching you. You just suddenly plowed in and out of those monsters. You should have been trampled to death. And you grabbed the captain by his gold buttons and you hollered, You bastard! Get your goddamn cavalry out of here. You shook him and shook him.

He ordered them, Ruth said. . . . I saw him. He was the responsible person. I saw the whole damn operation. I'd begun to run—the horses—but I turned because I was the one supposed to be in front and I saw him give the order. I've never honestly been so angry. (LSD, 123–24)

Ruth's experience is based in much of Grace's own, some of which is described in the essay "Cop Tales." A series of recollections about personal confrontations with police assigned to political demonstrations, the essay recounts an incident at the Whitehall Street Draft Induction Center at dawn, obviously one of the sources for the episode in "Ruthy and Edie." The demonstrators surrounded the building; Grace and her pals ("our group of regulars") were at the back: "Between us and the supply entrance stood a solid line of huge horses and their solemn police riders. . . . Off to one side, a captain watched us and the cavalry. Suddenly the horses reared, charged us as we sat, smashing us with their great bodies, scattering our supporting onlookers. People were knocked down, ran this way and that, but the horses were everywhere, rearing—until at a signal from the captain, which I saw, they stopped, settled down, and trotted away" (24).

Grace Paley's opinions and experiences are part of the landscape in her stories. Her stories are not didactic, nor do they present a particular party line; nevertheless, they are the natural outgrowth of what Grace calls her pacifist anarchism. Most of them introduce people who live the same kind of life, and are motivated by the same kind of needs and ideals, as their author and her friends and family. Often the stories display the conflicts that dog one party line or another as it makes its propagandistic way along the street.

The most autobiographical of Grace Paley's characters quarrel— even "holler" like the Goodsides—about their beliefs and ideals. This has been true since she began to write short fiction. We can trace these ongoing debates from their appearance in the first Faith stories in the fifties: "The Used-Boy Raisers" and "A Subject of Childhood," in which Pallid and Livid outrage each other with their opposing views of the Catholic church and Faith is driven to violence in her fight with Clifford about the proper raising of children

(LDM). We can follow it all the way through the story collections to the last story in the third volume, "Listening," in which Faith and Jack argue about the value of optimism in the face of reality, Faith and Richard differ about the meaning of the intelligentsia, Jack and Richard disagree about both the revolution and the proper treatment of Faith, and Faith and Cassie struggle with the suddenly open acknowledgment of Faith's heterosexism (LSD).

It is important to understand how the absolute reality—fact for fact—of Grace Paley's life need not appear in her stories to render them peculiarly her own. For instance, in the sixties, as her son observed, she "always seemed to have these FBI agents following her, and I thought that the phone was tapped because it was always clicking—I'm sure it was tapped."[4] This kind of experience designed and molded the consciousness that created "In the Garden," a story in which no autobiographical elements or characters appear. Written after a trip to Puerto Rico and informed by the ambience of that country, the text draws on her knowledge of U.S.-style political secrecy, surveillance, corruption, and arrogance of power.

The integrated quality of Grace's work—political experience informing the writing—is not a simple case of writing stories that are "about," or demonstrate, specific positions, attitudes, or ideas. She does not write stories that purposely illustrate certain circumstances and attempt to effect certain responses in her readers. For instance, the core of "In the Garden" is not necessarily to be found in its presentation of the multiple issues of crime, money, capitalism, and patriarchal power but is revealed in the mind of an aging woman who "had become interested in her own courage" (LSD, 44).

There is only one story Grace says she consciously wrote to influence her readers in a particular direction: "Anxiety" (LSD, 99–106). In that story, she definitely wanted to deliver a message, to say to the "new young fathers," "Now, listen, you guys...." Despite its overt message, however, even this story is not marred by didactic stiffness:

> The young fathers are waiting outside the school. What curly heads! Such graceful brown mustaches. They're sitting on their haunches eating pizza and exchanging information. They're waiting for the 3 p.m. bell.... The children fall out of school, tumbling through the open door. One of the fathers sees his

child.... Up u-u-p, he says, and hoists her to his shoulders.
U-u-p, says the second father, and hoists his little boy. The
little boy sits on top of his father's head for a couple of seconds
before sliding to his shoulders. Very funny, says the father.
(LSD, 99)

Grace Paley opposes the subordination of art to propaganda,
and though her political sympathies may lie with certain concepts
and authors, she absolutely resists the idea that writers should
strive to render their texts impervious to multiple interpretations.
In a symposium on contemporary fiction in 1975, some years before
academic reader-response theory was widely accepted, Grace argued
with William Gass about the role of the reader.

> *Paley:* I think what you're forgetting, what you're underesti-
> mating, are the readers.... art ... [is] two things, it's the reader
> and the writer, and that's the whole of the experience.
> *Gass:* You want the creative reader.
> *Paley:* You've got 'em. I mean, he's there.[5]
> *Gass:* I don't want them.
> *Paley:* Well, it's tough luck for you.
> [Donald Barthelme interposes a remark.]
> *Gass:* What I mean by this is that I don't want the reader
> filling in anything behind the language.
> *Paley:* Right, that's what's wrong with you. You don't leave
> him enough space to move around.... but that reader move[s]
> in, by God, where there [is] space, and he always will.
> *Gass:* Oh yes, it can't be helped.
> *Paley:* Well, I'm glad. ("Symposium on Fiction," 7–9)

On the other hand, she accepts and insists on the social responsibility of the artist, encouraging the consciousness that one's work has
an impact on both the individual and the society at large:[6]

> I consider that as a writer I have several obligations and one of
> them is to write as damn well as I can. I take that very
> seriously and responsibly and write as truthfully as I can, as
> well, and I do really feel responsible for the future of literature.
> ... The moral word is "ought to be" which people don't like to
> use too much these days. What ought to be? People ought to
> live in mutual aid and concern, listening to one another's

stories. That's what they ought to do. . . . I want to find out a way. Is there a way for people to tell stories to one another again and to bring one another into that kind of speaking and listening and attending community? ("Symposium on Fiction," 31)

Her disagreement with William Gass is notable because it helps us understand Grace Paley's position among her peers—postmodern writers of short fiction in the United States. Her stories—which are straightforward, apparently autobiographical, often called realistic despite their unusual chronology and occasional fantastic elements—affect us in the same way that photography, film, and even photographic realism in painting do: they manipulate the "reality" they seem merely to mirror; they rearrange "reality," making it more visible than it could be as its "real" self, rendering it more understandable, perhaps even more accessible, than in its actual, nonart, condition.

The essentially political quality of her fiction has distinguished her among innovative and experimental postmodern writers whose work, both in structure and content, directs and reflects the practice of the art of contemporary prose. Grace Paley corrects herself when she talks about literature: "I shouldn't say a work of art; I mean a work of truth."[7] In contrast, William Gass promoted one of the tenets of postmodern art when he told the symposium audience that "we ought to abandon truth as an ideal as artists. I think it's pernicious" ("Symposium on Fiction," 5).

Indeed, when a reader in that audience referred to Gass's *The Tunnel* and asked about the issue of "what Germany is like" in the book—referring, presumably, to what Gass thinks the actual country Germany "is like"—Gass insisted that he hadn't "the vaguest idea what Germany is like" ("Symposium on Fiction," 17). But Grace, who says, "When I write, I'm trying to understand something which I don't understand to begin with," insisted on pointing out that in *The Tunnel* Gass "picked Germany for a reason. Why didn't you say Luxembourg or Italy or something[?]" (18, 17). She is unwilling to accept the abandonment of social responsibility inherent in Gass's precepts; she rejects the writer-as-ingenue postulated by Gass:

I think you know more than you say you know about Germans, Fascism and so forth. Also I think that what happens is the reader will come in to your book, and he isn't a total dummy. That reader has been alive and has been reading the papers and books, or if they're as old as me, they've lived through that whole period and they know a good deal about it. The whole business is joined and more knowledge occurs in your work, or more truth . . . than you know, or than you planned, or than you even wished. ("Symposium on Fiction," 18–19)

Readers of Grace Paley's stories encounter characters and narrators who, like their author, are advocates. A writer for whom Russian, Yiddish, and the multiple ethnic and racial dialects of the Bronx and lower Manhattan constitute a mother tongue, she uses speech in the mouths of characters and narrators in such a way as to make it seem "real." Speech, which is the most prevalent mode in contemporary Western fiction—appearing as both dialogue and first-person narration far more frequently in the past several decades than in previous eras—is the primary mode in Grace Paley's stories.[8] Helmut Bonheim suggests that the prevalence of one mode or another "has to do with the purposes to which" writers put their stories, "or at least with" their "assumptions about [the] stories' functions" in the world (14). Grace Paley's purposes and assumptions, as revealed in her debate with William Gass, are served by the predominance of speech in her texts.

Speech may be the most apparently autobiographical narrative mode because it creates an atmosphere of immediacy and intimacy. Moreover, its immediacy and intimacy render speech persuasive; it is rhetorically—and thus politically—effective. Much of what Grace Paley asserts in her stories, as in political action, is the strength and force of individual character embodied in human presence; it is that presence that carries her program and is heard in her fictional voices. Crafted by one with an ear for the music of language, a writer trained as a story hearer, the written "spoken" word in her stories appears to be as open to spontaneous response as it is in actual conversation; the felt possibility of instant rejoinder, or even contradiction, is sustained.

The Paley trademark is a sharply honed prose that echoes the spoken word for her readers. She does not merely listen carefully and then "record" the spoken word; in the age of techno-sound we have all heard the halting, slurred, and repetitious quality of "realtalk" in unedited recorded conversation. She extracts the essence—rhythm and diction, feeling and consciousness—of speech and then *creates the illusion* that people are speaking. Grace Paley as "voice" differs from those classical American writers of short fiction who often employed the first-person narrator. Edgar Allen Poe never attempted to make us believe, for instance, that we were actually in the presence of Fortunato and Montresor; Montresor's first-person voice does not suggest the spoken word. It is a "writerly" voice, obviously and deliberately an element of written narrative.

Most of the collected stories—thirty-one out of forty-five—are told in the first person; the voice is that of "I," a character in the story who speaks to us, to other characters, and often to herself or himself in meditation or ironic consideration. Of these thirty-one, at least twenty-two (including Faith in more than a dozen cases) are narrators who may be identified with the author through specific autobiographical elements or through her increasingly well-known politics and world view. Her first-person narration, projecting a consciousness that is apparently present, relates to its readers familiarly and so, like a friend or acquaintance, seems unconsciously to disclose more of its apparent "self" than a third-person voice could do. (We might, of course, simply move back yet one more step and say that third-person narration is itself always delivered by a "first" person. Some presence is suggested; someone has written those words.)

One of Grace Paley's most effective devices in this area is the *overheard narrator.* Subject to the influence of a sliding conscious-ness (which suggests the author's presence in the text), characters comment on the remarks and answer the questions of the nar-rator, who is not—even if also a character—speaking to them and may not even be present when they speak. In "Goodbye and Good Luck," when Rosie Lieber, a first-person narrator, is introduced to Volodya Vlashkin, she tells her niece Lillie—and the reader—"I took one look, and I said to myself: Where did a Jewish boy grow up so big? 'Just outside Kiev,' he told me" (LDM, 10).

Additionally, Grace went on to create third-person narrators who are omniscient to the point of transcendence; their storytelling is unaccountably overheard by other characters, who respond to dialogue they could not actually have heard. For instance, in "Enormous Changes at the Last Minute," the third-person narrator tells us that Alexandra, while in conversation with Dennis in his taxi on the way to visit her father, "wondered: What is the life expectancy of the mind?" The text then moves to a small block of white space—a technique that generally signifies movement in time or space, as it does here—and then to the hospital room of Alexandra's father, who immediately responds to her wondering: "Eighty years, said her father, glad to be useful" (ECLM, 121).

Her creation of the overheard narrator is no doubt a result of her disdain for transitions. She explains, "I'm not afraid to make great leaps. . . . I hate the word 'transition'—I just like to make a good jump" (Bonetti). The same kinds of transitions—or nontransitions —occur in other stories, linking characters and scenes through time and space by means of the initially external third-person narrative voice, which, by sliding into the dialogue, seems almost to abdicate its omniscience.[9]

That almost-abdication is typical of the politics of the writer-reader relationship in these stories; Grace Paley's texts are open, accessible. Her aberrant punctuation—especially the nearly total elimination of quotation marks from the dialogue of her later work—and her intimate conversational style help to keep her stories from stiffening into a flat minimalism. Readers respond to the words on the page as people respond to the author herself in person. She is an effective translator, creating apparent truth and the suggestion of autobiography by her written rendering of the spoken word; the successful translation is clearly demonstrated whenever a reviewer attributes the words or thoughts of characters and narrators to their author. Nancy H. Packer, for instance, equates "the loudest voice" of young Shirley Abramowitz from the fifties with the author's own voice in her latest collection (34). Similarly, Burton Bendow, writing about "The Long-Distance Runner," refers to Faith as the "heroine, the intrepid Paley without disguise" (598).

Grace's readers believe that they know her, that they really know who she is. Even readers who know none of the facts of her life, who have read only one story, often insist that Grace Paley embodies the voice of the narrating speaker. Indeed, Nora Paley reports that when she is introduced as her mother's daughter, new acquaintances—thinking of Faith—invariably comment, "Oh, I didn't know Grace Paley had a daughter; I thought she had two sons."

Nora says that "this happens all the time. I can't believe how often it happens and how intense it is. I'm always shocked."

Grace's technique induces acceptance, and often belief, by means of a compelling rhetorical device. The author puts forward a "self" in the text, a character for us to identify with, to like and accept, and then to believe. Other writers, whose characters' philosophical alignment is enormously different—like Philip Roth's mother-blaming, woman-hating men, filled with fear and shame of their Jewishness and resentment at their maladjusted masculinity—are equally successful at capturing the sympathy of readers with this device.

In Grace Paley's own work, we find the compelling power of narrators whose easy familiarity and accessibility urge us toward an acceptance of what we might otherwise find unacceptable. In "The Little Girl," a story in which a young girl is raped and killed, the narrator's conclusion, which concludes the text itself—giving him the last word—is that Juniper, the little girl, has killed herself. "That is what happened," Charlie says in the story's final line. Finding herself "tore up, she must of thought she was gutted inside her skin" after being beaten and raped, her flesh bitten and torn, so "she made up some power somehow and raise herself up that windowsill and hook herself onto it and then what I see, she just topple herself out" (ECLM, 158).

In "A Conversation with My Father," written a few years earlier than "The Little Girl," (at least) two distinct points of view are presented and identified with specific characters, and the final word is given to one that appears to oppose the (strongly auto-biographical) narrator's. In "The Little Girl," however, the author has chosen to offer one perspective only and to give the power of conclusive placement to that vision.

Unlike that of Grace Paley's other sexually adventurous young girls, Juniper's fate is realistic. In contrast to the adventures of Cindy and Josephine, those other two sexually obstreperous adolescents, Juniper's experience as a runaway teenager, including her death,[10] is more probable than either of their exploits. The racial implications alone may be a shock to the reader: though Grace has given narrative power to a Black man, she has also made him complicitous in a heinous crime and has had him blame the victim for her own death. She has also placed his story in the midst of a collection that deals, with the exception of the very short story "Samuel," almost exclusively with white people. What is the effect of this double or triple shock?

The story juxtaposes an old stereotype—the scenario of black-on-white rape—against the persuasively effected identification of the reader (of any race and either gender) with a Black male narrator. A reader's sympathy for the thoughtful, compassionate, wise narrator Charlie (in conjunction with disgust for his roommate, the white villain ironically called Angel) leaves Juniper as emotionally isolated in the reader's world as she is in her own. Little white Juniper gets just what she deserves for running away from home and wanting to have sex with a Black man.

Grace's longtime friend Karl Bissinger, who read this story in manuscript (and advised Grace not to publish it), explains that Charlie is telling a story that was actually told to Grace. The "real" narrator—whom Karl also knew—was Bill Dixon, a friend of the author until his death a few years ago. He and Grace met when both were working in the Southern Conference for Human Welfare during World War II. Grace says it was through Bill that she learned much of what she uses in her Black characters, much of what she puts into her Black voices; she speaks through him. "That's him talking in a couple of my stories," she says.

Like Grace, Bill spent a lot of time socializing in Washington Square Park; he was from the South, a modest, easygoing man, often humorous. Here is a case where factual information produces one of the primary problems in biographical criticism. Once we know about the people whose lives influenced the writer, affecting the choices she has made, we begin to think differently about, for instance, the authorial decision to give the heaviest weight, the most narrative influence, to the man who says that Juniper killed herself, the speaker who places the final burden of the little girl's destruction on her own thin shoulders.

This story presents us with contradictory and apparently mutually exclusive choices: blaming the young white girl who ran away, flirted, and suddenly found herself trapped; blaming the initially engaging young Black man who beat her up, raped her, and may have killed her; blaming the white junky who probably did ravage and kill her; or castigating and rejecting the trustworthy older Black man who names her the cause of her own death. The last interpretation is perhaps the least likely choice for Paley readers, even though Charlie, who serves as our source and guide throughout, reveals at least a touch of unreliability. His sources of information are unclear; some of what he tells, according to the facts of his own narration, he could not possibly know. This story, with its multiple conflicts, is an extraordinary example of the use of direct speech—especially in the mouth of a first-person narrator—as the mode of choice for fictional storytellers who are arbiters of morality and ethics, judges of motive and definers of the situation who lead readers to engage in considerations that are fundamentally political.

Though distinguished from many contemporary storytellers by her work's readily discernible sociopolitical context and content, Grace Paley is among those fiction writers whom literary scholars and theorists have recently come to call *metafictionalists*.[11] Her work is self-reflexive; her stories are often about the telling of stories, and her subject is frequently the recounting of lives. But, unlike stories that are *primarily* about stories—that is, about narrative, about fiction, about writing—Grace's texts maintain a definite social, and thus political, component. She has included her assessment of this combination in "Debts," written in the late sixties: "It was possible that I did owe something to my own family and the families of my friends. That is, to tell their stories as simply as possible, in order, you might say, to save a few lives" (ECLM, 10).

Metafictionally speaking, Grace Paley writes about storytellers and story hearers; her characters sometimes use language that calls attention to itself *as* language. The story called "The Story Hearer," for instance, is a text in which language—as an issue, as a topic—is discussed by major characters, used as a metaphor, and mentioned casually in passing. Treadwell Thomas, "a famous fussy gourmet," describes his former career in "the Language Division of the Defense Department," when his assignment was "to develop a word or series of words that could describe, denote any of the Latin American countries in a condition of change—something that would by its mere utterance neutralize or mock their revolutionary situation. . . . [He] came up with 'revostate'" (LSD, 138–89). When Faith, as narrator, later recalls her small-mindedness in part of their conversation, she asks her readers, "Don't you wish you could rise powerfully above your time and name? I'm sure we all try, but here we are, always slipping and falling down into them, speaking their narrow language, though the subject, which is how to save the world—and quickly—is immense" (LSD, 140). And Faith includes a brief consideration of language when she muses about having a baby late in life: "there *was first* the little baby Isaac. . . . before he was old enough to be taken out by his father to get his throat cut, he must have just lain around smiling and making up diphthongs and listening . . . " (LSD, 144).

Similarly, her characters sometimes talk about each other *as* characters. For example, Mrs. Raftery, who is Ginny's interested neighbor in "An Interest in Life" (LDM) and who narrates her own story in "Distance" (ECLM), is also Faith's neighbor in "The Long-Distance Runner" (ECLM). In that story, Faith narrates and tells us that Dolly Raftery not only has a history of being liked, loved, and endured by her, but was in fact invented "by me" (180). Faith, the narrator and ostensible writer of the story, made up Mrs. Raftery and tells us so.

An instance that extends through nearly the whole story cycle is Grace's use of the character named Dotty Wasserman (also called Dorothy and Dot), who appeared in one of her first stories, "The Contest." In that story, written in the fifties, first published in *Accent*, and included in the first collection in 1959, Dotty is one of the two major characters. She is "Jewish, which is often a warm kind of girl, concerned about food intake and employability. . . . A medium size girl, size twelve, a clay pot with handles—she could be grasped. . . . On Sundays she'd come out of Brooklyn with a chicken to roast" (LDM, 67–68). Dotty wants to marry; her boyfriend does not. She makes strenuous efforts to change his mind and acts in decidedly bad faith throughout most of their relationship. Freddy's final offer is only "a great opportunity to start on a more human basis" (77), which does not include wedlock. She leaves him.

Dotty appears again in "Faith in a Tree," written in the middle or late sixties and included in the second story collection. There she has become Ricardo's refuge and is cited in a letter from him that does not include inquiries about his children or enclose a check for child support but instead complains, as Faith reads aloud to their mutual friend Alex Steele:

"I am not well. I hope I never see another rain forest. I am sick. Are you working? Have you seen Ed Snead? He owes me $180.

Don't badger him about it if he looks broke. Otherwise send me some to Guerra Verde c/o Dotty Wasserman. Am living here with her. She's on a Children's Mission. Wonderful girl. Reminds me of you ten years ago. She acts on her principles. I *need* the money." . . .

"Dotty Wasserman!" Alex says. "So that's where she is . . . a funny plain girl." (ECLM, 82–83)

Dotty next figures prominently in "Love," written in the late seventies and early eighties and published in the third collection. Her character has changed again, and she is not the same as either Freddy's Dotty, Ricardo's, or Alex's. What is notable here is that Grace has used her to connect "Love" and *Later the Same Day* with "The Contest" and *Little Disturbances* and to play with connections among autobiography, "real life," and fiction.

In "Love," the I-narrator's husband, relating a list of his romances, includes Dotty in his most recent—"that is, the past fifteen years or so"—list of lovers. "Hold on, I said. What do you mean, Dotty Wasserman? She's a character in a book. She's not even a person. O.K., he said" (LSD, 4). The wife immediately makes up a little story-within-the-story, and in it she creates a fictional lover who turns out to be her husband—just as he had appropriated the fictional Dotty Wasserman: "I used to be in love with a guy who was a shrub buyer. . . . [in] the downtown garden center of the city." Her husband asks, "How come I don't know the guy?" and she can only comment disgustedly, "Ugh, the stupidity of the beloved. It's you, I said" (4). Then she asks:

what's this baloney about you and Dotty Wasserman?

Nothing much. She was this crazy kid who hung around the bars. But she didn't drink. Really it was for the men, you know. Neither did I—drink too much, I mean. I was just hoping to get laid once in a while or maybe meet someone and fall madly in love. . . . She was also this funny mother in the park, years later, when we were all doing that municipal politics and I was married to Josephine. Dotty and I were both delegates to that famous Kansas City Meeting of Town Meetings. N.M.T.M. Remember? Some woman.

No, I said, that's not true. She was made up, just plain invented in the late fifties.

Oh, he said, then it was after that. I must have met her afterward.

He is stubborn. . . . [They spend the evening together, make love, sleep, and wake.]

In the morning he said, You're some lover, you know. He said, You really are. You remind me a lot of Dotty Wasserman. (LSD, 4–7)

Grace Paley was a "funny mother in the park," and Bob Nichols, the landscape architect who designed the park, is the model for the "shrub buyer" from Vesey Street. Both Grace and Bob are storytellers, writers who appear here fictionalized, telling stories to each other within a story Grace is telling us; these identities turn on the hinge of the Dotty Wasserman character, first invented twenty-five or thirty years earlier and identified *as a character* within these texts. Complex in its faceted metafictionality, this story is about writing/ telling stories as much as it is about its other themes and ideas.[12]

In this way, the stories insist on demonstrating that they are texts, explaining the narrator's choice of words, questioning the truth of any given narration, presenting two or more versions of the same story, or several stories that conflict, to describe the same situation and people. "The Immigrant Story" in *Enormous Changes* is an example: the "story" of Jack's parents is told twice, with two different plots, in two different voices—one a source of anger between Faith and Jack, one a revelation of tenderness for them both. Grace Paley's narratives cultivate self-explanation and self-examination in the reader, soldering the connection between her work as a writer and her work as an activist. In both arenas, she insists on revelation, eschewing mystification, denying power to traditional, canonical, institutionalized forms, demanding active participation from readers and citizens.

Strikingly—but not contradictorily—Grace also makes frequent literary allusions, which display her extensive knowledge of the canon in English and American literature (and her great affection for that canon), as in this passage from "Dreamer in a Dead Language":

I was once a pure-thinking English major—but, alas. . . .

What poet did you think was so great when you were pure?

Milton, he said. He was surprised. He hadn't known till asked that he was lonesome for all that Latin moralizing. You know, Faith, Milton was of the party of the devil, he said. I don't think I am. Maybe it's because I have to make a living.

I like two poems, said Faith, and except for my father's stuff, that's all I like. This was not necessarily true, but she was still thinking with her strict offended face. I like, *Hail to thee blithe spirit bird thou never wert*, and I like, *Oh what can ail thee knight at arms alone and palely loitering*. And that's all. (LSD, 14–15)

Though that knowledge and affection connect Grace to the educated classes and the elite (of both writers and readers) in literary history, her style and subject display her cultivation of the grass roots. In her desire to be understood and to understand a greater range than canonical fiction in English generally attempts, Grace is like the Romantic poets Faith quotes.[13] Grace Paley's reader might well be a woman surrounded by more diapers than daffodils, but like that of the Romantics, her writing is born of the same impulse as her politics; she seeks illumination. Art serves, she explained at Northwestern University in 1984, the same purpose as justice: to divulge "what isn't known." It is "the lighting up of what is under a rock, of what has been hidden." She argued that writers— especially those whose voices have not been heard before in Western literature—begin by saying, "I've got to light this up, and add it to the weight and life of human experience" (Gibbons, 234).

Her stories repeatedly assert that the attempt to distinguish between right and wrong is essentially the attempt to see clearly. Her characters, like Grace herself, strive to define and maintain an ethical base in their lives; they deliberately engage—if not embrace— the moral complexity of daily life, choosing to live consciously and analytically. Grace Paley seeks illumination for the sake of revelation and revelation for the sake of the action it inspires. Often nearly rabbinical in her rhythms and themes, she is a practitioner of the art of the question—the question asked, answered, re-asked, and re-answered, as in this contemporary response to the Socratic dialogue from "The Expensive Moment":[14]

Nick: For godsakes, don't you understand anything about politics?

Richard: Yeah, and why does Israel trade probably every day with South Africa?

Ruth: (*Although her remarks actually came a couple of years later*): Cuba carries on commercial negotiations with Argentina. No?

The boys at supper: Tonto (*Softly, with narrowed eyes*): Why did China recognize Pinochet just about ten minutes after the coup in Chile?

Richard (*Tolerantly explaining*): Asshole, because Allende didn't know how to run a revolution, that's why. (LSD, 184–85)

The answers to such questions—formed in the reader's mind as well as Richard's—are the truth Grace Paley seeks in writing her stories. Her characters query each other and their readers so that we all have a chance to answer.

When the first story collection was complete in 1959, Jess Paley delivered the stories to Ken McCormick's office at Doubleday. The editor read them all with much excitement and, wanting to know if there were more, called the Paley's apartment. Jess, who answered the phone, says that he lied—instantly and enthusiastically saying that there were dozens more. In fact, however, Grace's next story collection was not to appear for fifteen years, and individually published stories were scattered among several different literary, political, and academic journals over those years. That fifteen-year period spanned the rise of the civil rights movement, the antiwar movement, and the women's movement—all of which fostered Grace Paley's evolution as a political activist and fed the well of consciousness from which her stories continue to be drawn.

6

Enormous Changes

Though Grace Paley never stopped writing, and the publication of her first book demonstrated that she was in fact "a writer," her energy turned increasingly to political activity after 1960. Her desire to remain outside the literary world was abetted by her interest in the growing peace movement. She was one of the neighborhood people who founded the Greenwich Village Peace Center in 1960–61, and peace work became her political center in this decade. Additionally, in 1965 she began to teach fiction writing to college students, which altered her view of the literary community by urging her further into it—an ironic turn for a nonacademic artist and activist.

In fact, her growing reputation as a writer—which burgeoned in the mid-seventies and beyond—was fostered by the extraordinary circumstances of her first book's being reissued, by two different publishers, in 1968 (Viking Press, hardcover) and 1973 (American Library's Plume Books imprint, paperback). The more obvious effects of this practically unheard-of situation include the fact that new generations of readers came to know her work, keeping her as current as if she had published new collections; in addition, she began to make a living by her art. A less felicitous result was that she was misunderstood, perhaps even held back in her development. The reading public expected her, as late as 1973, to be the woman—the authorial persona—who had written "A Woman, Young and Old," when she was actually generating a new conclusion for "Faith in a

Tree" and creating "The Long-Distance Runner," two stories that reveal extensive development of political consciousness in their author.[1]

In that same vein, Grace was disappointed and irritated to find that her book's subtitle had been inverted and its preposition changed. Her own full title—carried on the original edition—was *The Little Disturbances of Man: Stories of Women and Men at Love.* The new edition read *The Little Disturbances of Man: Stories of Men and Women in Love.* Not only was her inversion of the genders ignored, but her prepositional suggestion of the adversarial quality of emotional relationships between women and men, a central theme in almost every story of that volume, was erased. Republication was not an unmixed blessing.

Her next stories, collected for *Enormous Changes At the Last Minute* in 1974, were all written between—or during—meetings, actions, classes, and readings. By the end of the fifties, the American Friends Service Committee had begun to fund small neighborhood peace groups. Naturally, their first contacts were with those who had political experience, people like Grace and her friends, who had already begun to oppose the proliferation of atomic and nuclear weapons and to educate against militarism. The Quakers' method was to seed small neighborhood organizations by sharing information, paying the rent on an office for the first six months, and encouraging each group's autonomy.

The Village Peace Center was such a group, begun largely by PTA members from PS 41. Many people who became Peace Center members in the early sixties were already working on the General Strike for Peace or attending small local meetings on neighborhood issues. These included Mary Perot Nichols and her husband Bob, who would later become Grace's lover and second husband; Mary and Bob were separated by mid-decade, Jess and Grace shortly afterward. Bob and Grace met in the struggle to close the roadway through the park; he had been very active before she came into the fight as a representative for the third grade of PS 41. (In 1960, Bob Nichols rode in the last private car to drive through Washington Square.) The Nichols and Paley families knew each other and had friends in common, though the three Nichols children—Kerstin, Duncan, and Eliza—were several years younger than Nora and Danny Paley.

Grace says that what she learned in this period from nonnative New Yorkers like Mary and Bob, people who had lived in other cities and in small towns, was that "you *can* fight city hall"—and win. Bob Nichols concurs, in ironic military metaphor: "We were very successful. Almost every war we waged, we won. All of our local campaigns were successful, with rare exceptions." This nearly all-win, almost no-loss record, gained in the park and the school, working on neighborhood issues, could not hold in the larger arena of national and international struggles, but it did strengthen Grace and her companions, encouraging them for the larger "campaigns" ahead. That was part of her education; she learned that if small groups of local people take action, they can win. To those who fear such local victories will only make people unrealistic, Grace says that's not so—"It happened, didn't it? It was real. We knew that you could do it, if you could just hold on, you could prevail. When you sit down in the park, if you stay there, you can win." Grace's personal stubbornness was intensified by what she learned in city and neighborhood politics, which fostered the tenacity necessary for organized resistance.

Other members of the Peace Center soon included Sybil Claiborne, by then a close friend, and Karl Bissinger, who came down from north of Fourteenth Street to join the group. Karl, who also became a personal friend, worked closely with Grace at the Peace Center, and later in the War Resisters League, for over two decades; he says it was at the Peace Center in the early sixties that they all began to understand that the Vietnam War "was really being run from Washington. How innocent we all were!"

Grace remembers that when she began to work in the Village Peace Center in 1960 or 1961, they fought civil defense drills in schools and protested atomic and nuclear bomb testing. "It was totally absorbing. I always had a certain amount of antiwarness in me. That was true even when I was in high school. Even in elementary school." At the Peace Center they also did "a certain amount" of civil rights work; they tried to work with people in Harlem, an effort which grew out of a home base that also fostered antiracism. Grace was also interested in the city itself, so that her consciousness grew beyond the block, beyond the neighborhood: "I was really interested in what we came to call 'ecology,' the whole thing about the parks and the piers and the rivers and the land that was New

York, that was Manhattan, that was the islands and the boroughs around it."

Sybil, who has done political work with Grace for nearly thirty-five years, says there is a notable difference between the central role her friend played at the beginning of the Peace Center and Grace's current situation. In the early years, Grace was really "in the middle of" the organizing; she had a lot more to say about what was to be done. Many of the actions and policy decisions that came out of the Peace Center were strongly influenced by Grace, but "over the years," Sybil observes, "she has stepped to the side." Now, in similar groups, while she may offer suggestions of a focus for action, she seldom initiates. Sybil assumes that Grace's new posture is one result of having become "famous"—she doesn't want to dominate the meeting—as well as the fact that "Grace is a genuine listener, a very careful listener." She listens well, to learn before she decides whether to speak. "Over the years she has taken more and more of a backseat."

In 1961, when Grace Paley was one of the new group's most active members, the Peace Center arranged a sizable demonstration at City Hall to protest the municipal air raid shelter program. Their success led almost directly to frequent actions against U.S. policy in Vietnam. Bob Nichols says the group's "specialty" was neighborhood vigils; he remembers being out on the street in the snow in front of a City Planning Board meeting and feeling strong support from the community when "people we knew all came by and said hello." When the war was recognized and its origins more fully understood, as Karl explains, Grace became one of the people (she may have been the originator of the idea) who read aloud the names of the war dead at vigils, urging that U.S. troops be brought home and the draft ended. Throughout the Vietnam War years, she was one of a group that picketed the court house every Saturday or Sunday, carrying signs that read "Not our sons" and "Stop This War." They never missed a weekend, no matter what the weather was, in eight years.

These demonstrations were part of the growing national movement against the Vietnam War and the draft and demanded a tremendous amount of Grace's energy and time. Her children, strongly affected by her activities, are truly "children of the sixties" in that they were themselves participants in protests against the war and racism and in the street culture that flourished throughout the period. Like many high school students, they struggled with those elements in their own lives—the inadequacy of the schools, the adolescent drug scene, their parents' growing disaffection—which replicated massive social upheaval throughout the United States and Western Europe.

The Paley children's adolescence produced at least one mirror reversal of the conflicts found in the "typical" American family. Most sixties parents despaired of their children's sudden revolutionary inclination, but Danny Paley says that at the age of thirteen or fourteen he became very conservative for about a year, "simply because everyone else in my family was so liberal." He hung up huge pictures of Lyndon Johnson in his room and displayed them in his windows. He says he did it because he knew that "it annoyed everybody. The more it annoyed them the more I put the pictures up." Furthermore, he "insisted" on visiting the capitol and the White House, as an exercise in citizenship and patriotism.

Despite that brief period as a right-winger manqué, Danny never strayed so far from home that he actually joined the opposition. Grace recalls with pleasure that he always—even in grammar school—loved neighborhood actions, especially when politics came right to the family's door. Nelson Rockefeller visited PS 41, as did Ed Koch before he became mayor. "And Danny loved that," Grace says. "He loved the fact that it was right there, next door, on the block, on the street." During the middle and late sixties, he and his friends were active in antiwar demonstrations, several of which he remembers as "really violent." Now, though his judgment stands allied with theirs, Danny Paley does not often engage in the political activism of his mother and sister.

Nora thinks she seemed awfully radical to her kid brother, maybe even more radical than their mother. As a child, Nora had had basically the same politics as Grace, but she recalls that "Danny was a little different." She feels that his stance had more to do with his reaction to her than to his mother, because he was the younger child. Alluding to Danny's "patriotic period," she remembers that even in the fifties, he would tease her by saying, "Oh, you just like Castro because he has a beard." He was near the mark there, Nora laughs: "That was probably true; when I saw someone with a beard

I did like them, because they looked familiar to me. Every man in the Village had a beard, and no one anywhere else did."

Like her mother and later her brother, Nora Paley rejected high school. "I wasn't not interested in learning. I was passionately interested in learning." But unlike Grace, who attributes her "failure" to succeed in high school only to herself, Nora developed a political critique of the school system. Along with many high school students of that time, some of whom organized teach-ins, published independent newspapers and magazines, picketed their schools, demanded changes in curriculum, and dropped out in great numbers, she understood the hypocrisy of the system and was very angry at being "forced to be in a place where we did nothing all day." She railed against the racism and class discrimination inherent in the tracking and grading systems. "All my friends were Puerto Rican. They were all being put in these vocational classes." Nora remembers the struggles of her good friends who were not allowed into the college-prep track, even when they asked to be placed there and demonstrated they could do the work.

She feels that Grace, who had always believed in the public school system, "just didn't know" about the daily reality of the average city high school. Sharing her mother's perspective in theory, Nora points out that "it isn't that I wanted to go to a private school; that isn't what I wanted. I just wanted to not be in a school that was as wrong as those [schools] were." Indignant about the schools and powerless in her youth, she held her mother responsible: "I was mad at her. I didn't think she was respecting me. I thought she should have had enough respect for me to let me quit high school and do these amazing things I had in mind. So it was a hard time between us, a very hard time."

Nora attended three different high schools, with three different ethnic and racial communities, before she finally graduated. The family prevented her from dropping out, which she passionately desired to do. Her disgust and boredom finally led to a total rejection of school. Like Grace at Hunter College, she made no formal statement. But she began to wonder what would happen if she didn't take midterm exams, or pick up her report card, or even show up for classes. She had never considered any of those possibilities before. When they occurred to her, she realized that the probable consequences of such behavior no longer mattered to her. She and her friends began to cut school, take amphetamines and ride the subway, speeding all day beneath the boroughs of New York City. Resembling the adolescent Grace Goodside of an earlier era, Nora was, she says, in "an extreme mode and an extreme mood."

She finally attended a school in Brooklyn, where her aunt Jeanne was a guidance counselor, and says that she only graduated because Jeanne "picked me up everyday in a car and took me there, which I hated—I *really* hated." Actually, her aunt Jeanne was the one who pushed Nora through the school system. Grace thought that because Nora loved her aunt—Jeanne and Nora have always been very close—she enjoyed going to school with her, and Grace knew that those rides ultimately helped to keep her daughter in high school. Since Nora didn't want to finish school, she naturally had a different view. She says—replicating her mother's assessment of her grandmother Manya's anxiety—that Grace simply didn't know what to do. She was worried about her daughter but didn't really understand Nora's situation. Her daughter knows—and knew then—that Grace did everything she possibly could, but, like her own mother before her, she was confused by a daughter who was thinking with a new kind of mind.

"Grace says now that she should have let me drop out of school," Nora points out, and Grace agrees: "I made a mistake. I should have let her leave school when she wanted to." The wisdom gained in that crisis with Nora was useful when Danny came to the same conclusion less than two years later; Grace changed her policy and allowed her second child to leave school.

Despite the apparently unique ferment of the times, both of Grace's children had high school experiences strikingly like their mother's. They started out as very good students, and then (echoing some of Grace's exact words), Danny says, "All of a sudden instead of school being important to me, girls became important, and my friends. I really went straight downhill for a number of years." Danny—more like his sister here than his mother—also recognizes the cultural aspects of his scholastic decline, viewing his shift from books to peers as typical—"like most teenagers"—and seeing the cultural and political upheaval of the time as a source and cause. As Grace would say, he was strongly influenced by the currents of his time and place in history. "I started taking a lot of drugs during that period of time," Danny says. "Nothing addictive, not heroin or anything, but enough to really kill me in school." Like Danny's maternal grandparents, who had been equally in the dark about their daughter, Grace and Jess had no idea what was going on in their boy's life; he can barely recall their presence during that period. Sooner than his mother, but right in line with his big sister, Danny became disaffected, and "finally I dropped out of high school."

But he too was subject to family pressure and finally graduated from a private school uptown, Robert Louis Stevenson, to which "rich people sent their kids so they could graduate from high school without having to do anything. It was a joke school; a lot of famous people sent their kids there." He was able to attend Stevenson because both of his parents were finally making some money. Not only was Jess getting a number of good assignments, but Grace had also begun to teach college classes, so the Paleys had at least one steady paycheck coming in.

Like most children, Danny Paley perceived his mother's increased activism and time spent at her work as his personal loss. "By the time I was a teenager—of course it may have been as much my fault as hers—I felt like she wasn't always there when I needed her." Now that he is a father, he views her chosen methods critically, suggesting that she should have been more directive, should have offered him more guidance. "I was doing a lot of stupid things, hanging around with the wrong people, and letting school get away from me. [But] she had a different kind of philosophy than in fact I would have as a [teenager's] parent. She felt she could trust me, and she wasn't going to interfere. . . . luckily it worked out all right. (It might not have though, because I had a lot of friends who didn't even live—you know, who O.D.'d on drugs or something [else] terrible.)"

At one point, when he *was* close to danger, his mother's intervention was dramatic and effective. "I was taking amphetamines in powder form, and somehow my mother became aware of it—I guess it was obvious because I wasn't sleeping at all. And then she got real angry—it was almost the same anger I had seen with that cop. And it affected me the same way." She yelled at him. She didn't mind about his social life, or his grades, or the hours he was keeping, "but," she declared, "*this* [taking amphetamines]—if you do *this*, just don't even come back here; I just don't even want to see you." "I never did it again after that," he says, "because I knew, when I saw that side of her, just like that cop must have known that day: Don't do it! And if a cop with a club and a gun knew not to, then *I* certainly would know not to."

Nora and Danny Paley's disinclination to accept the system is striking in terms of their mother's educational history.[2] When Nora was a teenager she never once considered the resemblance between her own behavior and her mother's earlier experience. It never occurred to her to make the comparison during that time because Nora, like most adolescent girls, was thinking of Grace as her mother—solely in terms of the maternal role—not as an actual person, a woman who had been a girl, a girl who had once had the same kind of life experiences she was having. Nora now thinks that the fact that she was repeating her mother's pattern—even if unconsciously—"might have been why I was mad at her. [I probably felt that] she, having had that experience, should have known better, should have understood, should have been able to deal with me and help me." Like Grace, who had resented the same responses in her own parents, Nora was angry that a mother who professed a radical analysis of society and its institutions would not apply that analysis to her daughter's life.[3]

While the children were growing up and out in miscellaneous directions, Grace too was changing. Thinking about the so-called empty-nest syndrome, she comments, "In my view, nobody really ever goes away; they're always coming back—they come back a lot. When I went away with Jess, I didn't put my family behind me. I wrote letters, they wrote letters, we were in touch. We always had contact. I didn't take myself away from them." She points out that when Nora and Danny were leaving home, she was leaving home too. "So it was very complex, very complicated. I was really too busy to worry whether they left or they didn't leave. And it seems to me that all their lives they keep coming back. So I think it's a big thing that psychologists just made up."[4]

Like much of American society, the Paley family rearranged itself through the decade of the sixties. While her personal "neighborhood" enlarged—extending her network of local and family ties—Grace reshaped or created new emotional alliances and connections, some of which provided essential sustenance for years and continue to do so today.

Among the people who gradually grew more intimate with Grace, and more important in her life, was Bob Nichols. Bob was a political ally, working at the Peace Center and taking part in various neighborhood demonstrations. By the mid-sixties, around the time Grace began teaching, Bob says that she "more and more did serious work in the basement of the Washington Square Methodist Church," where the resistance movement and draft counselors had office space. He says he frequently "went on actions and often stopped to hang around and wait for her—or we'd all go out for espresso." Bob's and Grace's lives coincided beyond political commitments. While continuing to practice as a landscape architect, Bob was a member of the Village Poets in the sixties; in addition to writing poetry, he wrote "about twenty" plays that were performed off-off-Broadway or in the streets.

One of his plays, typical of much urban street theater of the time in its community base, was an adaptation of *Everyman,* in which many neighborhood and Peace Center people took part. Sybil Claiborne remembers that Grace asked her to sew the costumes.[5] As in other towns and cities in the United States in that period, the community not only was engaged in critical analysis of federal and local governments and organized action against their policies, but also was coming together in pleasure—people enjoyed themselves. They brought passion and laughter to their serious business; they made art that was play and play that was streetwise education.

In that atmosphere, Grace Paley and Bob Nichols spent hours and days together—indeed, they worked years together, their camaraderie growing into friendship and love. Bob's marriage was over by the mid-sixties, and he had had liaisons with a few other women before he and Grace became a couple. Her own marriage had been relatively static until the early years of the decade, when the gaps between her and Jess opened painfully.

Though Jess had encouraged her to write stories and was enthusiastic about them when she did, he did not so actively cultivate his own art. This had not mattered in earlier years, when Grace had not yet published, but it may have begun to make some subtle difference after the late fifties, for she had become "a writer," regularly working at her craft. After 1960, and certainly by 1965, when she had begun to make new friends who were writers and teachers of writing, Jess was no longer in the center of her life. At the same time, as her political involvement increased between 1960 and 1965 and began to take her out of the neighborhood—or to jail—her closest attachments developed among those who shared that experience. Though Jess certainly held a similar world view, would probably have voiced many similar opinions, and must have pulled the same levers in a voting booth as Grace did, he never became an activist.

Additionally—and ironically, given his encouraging influence in her early story writing and his sporadic absences due to assignments out of the city—his frequent presence in the house may have lessened her opportunities to write. Karl Bissinger explains that when Jess wasn't working on a film, like a husband in early retirement "he would be around a lot. He would start at nine o'clock in the morning, and ask Grace to have cups of coffee with him through the day, and there was no time for her to write. It simply didn't occur to him that he ought to leave her alone. He was always there. As an artist she had no room to function."

When he did work on films, his assignments took him away from his family for long periods. In fact, Jess Paley was on his way to Southeast Asia when *Little Disturbances* appeared at the booksellers, and he missed the public's reception of his wife as a writer. He wasn't there for the excitement of the reviews or the thrill of seeing the book in stores. While Grace didn't necessarily resent his absence in all the major areas of her life, she regretted it. Regret seems to have been the overriding tone of her slow, difficult separation from Jess Paley. She regretted their lack of mutual interests and activities. She regretted his absences. She regretted that her steadily increasing success as a teacher and writer was occasionally concurrent with hard times in his own work. She regretted his lack of commitment to action for social change.

Like many couples then, the Paleys didn't break up so much as come apart; they moved in different directions. Or, perhaps more accurately, Grace moved away from where they had been together, and Jess, no matter how much he traveled, stayed there. The Paley divorce, which didn't actually occur until 1972, was not an unusual one. It produced all the requisite pain and doubt; it included the grief of the children, disillusionment on both sides, disagreement about who would leave the family home, and the complication of at least one new lover.

Grace and Jess's marriage was subject to the cultural and political circumstances that broke open so many American marriages in the sixties. The Paleys were actually among those most likely to come apart: they had married young, in a period of national stress and uncertainty; the husband had been deeply affected by his war experience, professionally and emotionally dislocated; the wife was eagerly moving beyond the immediate concerns of a traditional wife and mother, and she was changing while her husband's projects and interests remained static. Moreover, after years of "crummy" part-time jobs, she had finally begun work that would make her financially independent. In previous eras, such women rarely worked for (good) pay, generally suppressed their interests, and arranged themselves around their husband's and children's needs and desires. But Grace Paley's natural obstinancy and determination were explicitly encouraged by a decade of rapid, intense sociopolitical change.

Grace's own mother had remained—long after necessity, until her death—in a family household that was far removed from her ideal; Grace's aunt Mira—eventually as bitter as she was beautiful—did the same. Neither woman had acted decisively in her own behalf. Grace defined her mother's situation in "Mom," first published in 1975: "Her life is a known closed form" (86). Beyond the cautionary models of her mother and aunt, we can look to the character of Grace herself. Her friends say that one of the reasons she took so long to leave the marriage is that she doesn't really believe in divorcing anybody. Jane Cooper, who came to know her just as the separation began, says, "Relationships that have been family to Grace, that have been really close over the years—those she never really lets go. Those people are always her family. So [the separation] must have been not only excruciating for her, but also really really hard to understand; it took a great deal out of her. I think it actually tore her apart, truthfully. But finally she got to the point where it was necessary to separate; there was no question about that."

Whereas some of Grace's people found Jess remote and preoccupied, even narcissistic, Grace never seems to have blamed him. Karl Bissinger explains that "Grace is loyal. She's in it for the long haul. She doesn't take on anything lightly. My sense of [their relationship] is that there was a whole lot going on" that no one but Grace and Jess would ever know. Karl did feel that he could see Grace was "driven to the point where she decided to call it a day.... it was clear that Grace *had* called it a day."

Whatever was difficult or painful between Grace and Jess Paley, everyone who knew them understood that the issue was not initially a loss of love. Once Bob Nichols entered the scene, having to choose was all but impossible for Grace. Sybil Claiborne says that in the late sixties, when both men figured prominently in Grace's life, she probably would have liked to be married to both of them, holding both of them dear as she did. "Wants," a story Grace wrote at the end of the sixties and published first in 1971, is narrated by a woman who—prompted by an encounter with the man to whom she "had once been married for twenty-seven years" (ECLM, 3)—ponders the kind of romantic and realistic considerations Grace must have weighed in those years: "I wanted to have been married forever to one person, my ex-husband or my present one. Either has enough character for a whole life, which as it turns out is really not such a long time. You couldn't exhaust either man's qualities or get under the rock of his reasons in one short life" (ECLM, 5).[6]

The chasm between Grace and Jess was not the result of her attraction to and growing love for Bob Nichols. Bob could only have moved into a life where there was room for him, and that room had already been provided by the Paleys' divergence. At first, they did the sort of thing many couples do in such straits: Grace traveled to Europe to join Jess on an assignment in 1966; he photographed her looking beautiful in a gondola on the Grand Canal in Venice. He remembers that one afternoon they discovered a copy of *Little Disturbances* on a tiny marble table in the hallway of their pension in Florence. Though of course she accused him of planting it there, he still insists he was as astonished as she to find it.

But they continued to grow apart. In the face of increasing intensity in the antiwar movement, one of the major problems between them had to be that cynical as he was about government policy, Jess still did not choose to take action. Some of their friends and family felt that because he had no apparent substantial political convictions, he resented her expense of energy in that direction and even sometimes doubted the sincerity of her commitment. He often expressed annoyance with her; he complained about feeling neglected. His personal unhappiness and disapproval of her activities constrained Grace. He refused to take part in the life she and her friends lived. He eventually refused to go anywhere with her, her sister recalls, though sometimes Grace would cajole or plead with him to come. Finally she stopped pleading and went, Jeanne says, "on her own."

In this period she began to be arrested for various forms of civil disobedience. One of the first big actions (which brought out lots of people, garnered good media coverage, and created an impact felt by the authorities) was in that same year of 1966; Grace and Bob were among those who rushed out into the street and sat down under the Armed Forces Day Parade's rockets and missiles on Fifth Avenue. Carrying daffodils, the demonstrators sat down to register their objection to the celebration of the military and its weapons. Their refusal to allow the parade to continue led to their arrest and removal; that was the first time Bob Nichols and Grace Paley were arrested together. So, in the same year as that romantic sojourn in Italy, Grace was sent to the Women's House of Detention, causing a separation that was a more appropriate emblem of her relationship with Jess than the gondola ride had been.

Naturally, the children were affected by the antipathy between their parents. Danny remembers his father's growing anger toward his mother and a general increase of tension in the house:

> until it got to the point where I couldn't stand to be there anymore—although I was at the age where I didn't want to be there anyway. Beyond that, it was a kind of drifting apart—it just seemed to happen. The splitting up period lasted a few painful years. I guess it started when I was about fifteen, and by the time I was eighteen, they were pretty split up. When they finally did get divorced [in 1972] it was a relief to me, because I thought that was something they certainly needed to do. By that point it was pretty clear.

He suggests that "some of it had to do with my mother's own life taking away a lot of time, probably [time] that my father felt he was losing. She was spending more and more time writing, which was part of the argument [between them] I think. And the Vietnam War was in full swing; she was spending most of her time involved in that. I'm sure there were other things I didn't know about, but that was one thing I was aware of; there was a lot of tension about that." Those times, he recalls, were "painful for everybody."

His sister concurs. Talking about difficulties between her mother and her from 1963 to 1967, when Nora was moving from school to school, disgusted with the absence of useful alternatives, she recalls that those were also years of grief between her parents. Nora was nearly eighteen when Grace finally left Jess, and she says she felt upset and angry even though she understood the split was a good thing, certainly for Grace. Like Grace explaining that life in an extended family is good for children but not for grown-ups, Nora points out that her parents' divorce was ultimately good for them though it initially made their daughter miserable. Like many adolescents in that situation, she took on a burden of responsibility; she worried about both of her parents and her brother. She remembers resenting Grace's relationship with Bob; she knows she didn't want anybody to replace her father. Referring to this now as a "childish and typical reaction," she explains that she accepted the new family configuration only after several years.

In 1967 Grace moved out; Jess insisted he would not leave the apartment. Karl remembers that "she was floating; she was literally living out of paper bags, staying with friends. Yes, she packed her overnight clothes in a paper bag," and she stayed days and weeks at a time with Del (Adele) Bowers and with Mary Gandall, both pals from the old playground days, when all their children were small. Clearly Grace thought the apartment on Eleventh Street was hers; she made no effort to find a new home and waited for Jess to leave, which he finally did—though no one seems to recall exactly when.

By then she was able to support herself, working at Sarah Lawrence and making "decent money. Not great, but decent." She was "all right" financially; "yeah, I didn't have a high rent, the rents weren't high there and then." Asked if, like so many wives, she might have stayed married to Jess too long because she was economically unstable, she says, "No, not then." This answer suggests that such a situation might have obtained at another time—maybe early in the marriage, early in their lives. Visiting Chicago in 1987, she recognized landmarks near the corner of Halsted Street and Chicago Avenue. "Look at that. That's where we had that big fight [during World War II, when he was stationed just outside Chicago]. If it had ended differently, my whole life would have been different. Might have been, might have been."

Exhilarated by her community's commitment to political action— and its frequent mobilization—Grace was among those who experienced an accelerated rise of consciousness that matched the swift change in the society. The intensity of national and international political movements fused with her own excitement. This is not to say, as we might of so many Americans in that period, that she was radicalized. Grace was already a radical thinker; her analysis of the place and time in which she found herself was always politically rooted. She had been conscious for some years of the mutual impact of citizen and state and had long before developed an analysis of the complicated relationships among capitalism, racism, and imperialism.

The civil rights movement, the peace movement, and the developing coalition to end the Vietnam War were readily absorbed into her world view. Now, however, she began to make some new connections. Her emotional life, her sexuality, and her maternity had not yet been consciously integrated into her world view.[7] Nor had they been spontaneously absorbed once the women's movement demonstrated that the personal is political. The rising of Grace Paley's feminist consciousness—its fits and starts, fears and regrets— may be traced in her stories.

Feminism requires more than a clearly demonstrated consciousness of inequity, more than an artist's accurate—even staggeringly truthful—description of the phenomenon of male supremacy. Feminism demands deliberate opposition to that phenomenon and overt struggle against the power dynamics of patriarchal culture. Readily traced in Grace Paley's stories is a movement from exceptionally clear descriptions of patriarchy, and characters' conscious acceptance of—or collusion with—it, to outright challenges to the power dynamics of the status quo.

Examining the early years of her political development, scholars might be led to consider Grace Paley feminist in her early portrayals of women and children. The stories are indeed distinctively radical in their placement of women and children at the center. Her characterization of mothers is especially notable: they struggle with the disparity between the patriarchal institution of motherhood and their lived experience.[8] Her other women are also unusual in fiction; witness the tenacious self-control of Dotty Wasserman and the integrity of Rosie Lieber in her first two stories. These are characters whose lives had been left out of canonized literature or had been depicted solely in terms of their connections to men—lovers, fathers, sons, husbands. Women and children are remarkable in

Grace Paley's work for the fact that they appear in stories about their own lives.

Not until after 1970, when she was nearly fifty years old, did Grace Paley's stories begin to display a feminist consciousness, however. Though the women in her earlier stories often laugh at or seem to ignore patriarchal power and display attitudes and behavior markedly different from those traditionally presented by both male and female writers, they are nonetheless complicitous in their own oppression, for they do not actively challenge the status quo. In fact, Paley characters and narrators often echo their author's reluctance to politicize self-definition in their lives. Faith describes (her own) single motherhood, in "A Subject of Childhood," but denies the sociopolitical analysis manifest in her generic situation: "I have raised these kids, with one hand typing behind my back to earn a living. I have raised them all alone without a father to identify themselves with in the bathroom. . . . It has been *my perversity* to do this alone . . . " (LDM, 139, emphasis added).

However grudgingly or wittily—and sometimes quite happily —Grace's women accepted and played out the roles defined for them by men. Until recently, they still sang a song we recognize as the lowdown blues of women in a man's world. Singing a song of fathers, sons, and husbands, her women croon and moan, *Oh yeah honey, I know he's no good, but I love him*—and variations on that theme. Grace Paley's version of these blues is written repeatedly into her early stories. In "The Used-Boy Raisers," for instance, Faith's narration includes this self-assessment: "I rarely express my opinion on any serious matter but only live out my destiny, which is to be, until my expiration date, laughingly the servant of man" (LDM, 132).

Who is "man" to these women? Rosie Lieber (created around 1952–54) knows that her lover Vlashkin—who would have her travel with him "on trains to stay in strange hotels, among Americans" but not be his wife—is "like men are. . . . till time's end, trying to get away in one piece," but she still believes that "a woman should have at least one [husband] before the end of the story" (LDM, 21–22). Young Josephine and Joanna (around 1954–56) get mixed—as well as garbled—messages from their mother, a battered daughter, and their grandmother, an abandoned wife. Marvine and Grandma continue to take care of or lust after men, even as they acknowledge that "it's the men that've always troubled me. Men and boys . . . I suppose I don't understand them. . . . [My sons are] gone, far away in heart and body" (LDM, 28).

In "Faith in the Afternoon" (1958–60), Faith's wandering husband Ricardo is described as the quintessence of exploitive masculinity, but she misses him, feels sorry for herself in his absence, and weeps for her loss when she thinks about friends who have also lost their husbands—though all are unappealing or present tragic liabilities. Dolly Raftery (mid-1960s) denies and sidesteps her anger, explaining, "Men fall for terrible weirdos in a dumb way more and more as they get older; my old man, fond of me as he constantly was, often did. I never give it the courtesy of my attention" (ECLM, 17).

There is one exception, and that is the brief flash of hilarious satire in "The Floating Truth" (around 1957–59), in which the "career" possibilities of a young single woman are considered and detailed on a phony résumé. Résumé entries include a description of her traveling around the country "for five months by bus, station wagon, train, and also by air" to "bring Law and its possibilities to women everywhere"—with the purpose of urging women to increase their consumption of legal services. Another entry on the bogus résumé is a stint writing "high-pressure" copy for "The Kitchen Institute Press's 'The Kettle Calls'" (its title a Yiddish-inflected pun), which was designed "to return women to the kitchen" by means of such fear- and guilt-producing slogans as "The kitchen you are leaving may be your home." On radio and television, and in ads in "Men's publications and on Men's pages in newspapers (sports, finance, etc.), Men were told to ask their wives as they came in the door each night: 'What's cooking?' In this way the prestige of women in kitchens everywhere was enhanced and the need and desire for kitchens accelerated" (LDM, 183).

That this character, a young woman seriously seeking work—whose only actual employment in the story is pointless, a waste of her time and mind—should be ironically represented as an agent of the duping and oppression of other women is an unmatched phenomenon in the early and middle years of Grace's writing. With the young woman's anger and dissatisfaction articulated in the text— though deftly displaced onto another woman—this story displays a startling recognition of women's socioeconomic condition;[9] it even includes an incident in which sexual intercourse substitutes for cash payment.

That this story is one most readers and scholars find stylistically disturbing, even incomprehensible, is neither accident nor coincidence.[10] The eruption of feminist politics and the extremely frank, even bitter, view of young women's life choices are disguised—buried, really—by the extraordinary style and breezy tone of the narrator's voice. This I-narrator/major character is never named, which makes her difficult for readers to identify with. Her employment counselor is called by at least ten different names, including Lionel, Marlon, Bubbles, and Richard-the-Liver-Hearted, all of which render him comic, masking his exploitive relationship with her. Notwithstanding the fact that he mocks her desire to work for social change "in a high girl-voice" (176) and that his final appearance is an image of him standing in the street to "pee . . . like a man—in a puddle" (189), his nastiness is less notable than his amusing conversation and especially his sympathetic and fascinating situation: he lives in a car—which, years ahead of its time, has a phone—and he keeps houseplants on its back window ledge. Despite his failure to earn the payment she has made in the backseat, the protagonist is "not mad" at him (188). Nevertheless, "The Floating Truth" was unique among the collected stories of Grace Paley for many years, stylistically and politically ahead of its time and, in relation to her later development, even ahead of its author.[11]

Not until the early seventies, in three stories ultimately published in *Enormous Changes*, did Grace Paley's women openly begin—in words *and* actions—to question the necessity of the traditional power dynamics and social arrangements between women and men. In the late sixties and early seventies the choices and definitions in Grace Paley's life were strongly affected by society, just as they were in the late forties and early fifties, when the socioeconomic position of women in the United States was in flux. In the earlier period women's position had been deliberately manipulated by such forces as government policy and the spread of rapidly calcifying psychological theory; this time it was shaped by women themselves, organized for social change *as women*.

"The Immigrant Story" and "Enormous Changes at the Last Minute" were originally published in 1972 in *Fiction* and the *Atlantic*, respectively, and "The Long-Distance Runner" appeared in 1974 in *Esquire*. All were written late in the period preceding the publication of her second book—that is, after 1970—and all contain evidence of a newly rising feminist consciousness. We may contrast them with the original version of "Faith in a Tree," which was published in 1967 as "Faith: In a Tree" and did not include its final episode yet.[12] As it first appeared in *New American Review*, the story concludes with Faith's interest still focused on a potential male lover—whose interest has unfortunately just turned from her to her friend Anna. The addition of the final section about a demonstration against the Vietnam War and its effect on the people in the park, which is the now-familiar conclusion published in 1974 in *Enormous Changes*, shifts Faith's consciousness decidedly. Her own enormous change at the last minute lessens—even discards—the effect of her emotional dependence on men.

These three stories provide a clear indication of the future development of their author's feminism. In "Changes," Alexandra deliberately chooses to raise her child without a father-in-residence and to do so in concert with her young pregnant unmarried clients (who have previously been less important to her than "the boys").[13] In "Story," Faith—as character and narrator—openly refuses to accept masculinity as definitive.[14] When Jack says of his mother and father, "Bullshit! She was trying to make him feel guilty. Where were his balls?" she declares, "I will never respond to that question. Asked in a worried way again and again, it may become responsible for the destruction of the entire world. I gave it two minutes of silence" (ECLM, 172). In the final story of *Enormous Changes*, "The Long-Distance Runner," Faith wishes to create a bond with Mrs. Luddy that will transcend their romantic and sexual attachments to men. When the two women discuss men, Faith expresses the opinion that men don't have the same creative "outlet" as women, adding, "That's how come they run around so much," to which Mrs. Luddy replies, "Till they drunk enough to lay down." Faith answers, "Yes. . . . on a large scale you can see it in the world. First they make something, then they murder it. Then they write a book about how interesting it is." Mrs. Luddy concurs: "You got something there" (189).

Faith and Mrs. Luddy come to almost the same conclusions as Mrs. Grimble, who is the narrator and central character of "Lavinia: An Old Story." First published in 1982 in *Delta* and then included in *Later the Same Day* in 1985, "Lavinia" was actually written at the end of the sixties. Grace says she "lost it for a long time," but it is also possible she might not yet have been willing to go public on some of the issues raised in that story. Just as she undermined her sharp burst of feminist consciousness in "The Floating Truth," she might have simply buried it. In any case, Mrs. Grimble goes even further than the other two women: "What men got to do on earth don't take more time than sneezing. . . . A man restless all the time owing it to nature to scramble for opportunity. His time took up with nonsense, you know his conversation got to suffer. A man can't talk. That little minute in his mind most the time. Once a while busywork, machinery, cars, guns" (63).

It is striking that as she grew more overtly political/feminist in her writing, Grace put such strong statements about men's place and purpose in this world into the mouths of Black women. There is a difference between the way her white women characters and her Black women characters talk about men. Did she think that Black women have a more negative view of men than white women do? Did she think that Black women are more clear-sighted, and more capable of articulating what they see, than white women? What does it mean that the "mama" Faith finds and learns from when she goes home to her old neighborhood is a Black woman? Had Grace Paley fallen into romanticizing Black women's strength and their struggle against multiple oppression? Had she fallen into the habit of making Black women the caretakers of us all, Black and white, women and men?[15] Or is she offering respect and admiration here? Is she suggesting that a history of racist oppression, combined with sexism, has given Black women a deeper understanding of the power dynamics of gender than white women have? There are too few Black women characters in the collected stories to answer these questions usefully, but the questions—especially in the light of contemporary Black women's social and literary criticism—nonetheless must be asked.[16]

These stories presage the further development of their author's feminist consciousness and the erosion of women's acceptance of male dominance in her work; they also serve to illustrate the beginnings of that erosion in her own life.

7

An Irrevocable Diameter

At the same time Grace was leaving her marriage, writing more stories, and working against the Vietnam War, she was becoming a teacher. In 1964 she was asked to lead a discussion group—six or eight women, as she recalls. They met in each other's homes; as the teacher, Grace "read short stories, and commented on them." She began formal teaching in 1965 at Columbia University, where she had done all that typing. She had gotten the typing job through her friend Ellen Currie, a writer who now teaches at Sarah Lawrence College but who then worked full-time in Columbia's offices. Grace is vague about the circumstances, but she recalls that the first class was "in general studies or something," and she got it because they "just gave me a chance." She says, though, that that doesn't count as "a real job," like the one that began the next year at Sarah Lawrence up in Bronxville—half-an-hour's drive north on the Hudson River Parkway.

From the fall of 1966 through the spring of 1988, Grace Paley taught fiction writing in her office and classroom in Bronxville. "Some years I taught in two schools.[1] I got paid very little when I began to teach, but at least I made a living at Sarah Lawrence. I got Blue Cross and all of that."

She usually taught part-time, though in several years, like the years when Nora was a student there, she would teach full-time to make more money. She explains:

I'm not thrifty; I never have been. Sometimes we had money and sometimes we didn't. We lived like sailors. I've never been cautious about money, and I think it's because when I was a child my family was pretty well off, and my father was very generous. He never said, "Boy, did we used to be poor"—which they were when my brother and sister were growing up. If you asked him for a dime he gave you a quarter. He reveled in the fact that he could do that. And so [saving money] really has not been important to me.

Saving money has not been an issue, but making enough to live on—enough to write on—has definitely mattered. Danny Paley points out that his mother was very lucky to get that job at Sarah Lawrence, since she had never graduated from college herself: "There she was, getting a job at the most expensive girls' school in the country; her writing got her that job, and really made her more secure." As Grace has told her interviewers for years now, she began teaching "for the same reason that many creative artists do: to make money. Her teaching job ... was taken to subsidize her writing, not to sustain and nourish her as did the writing itself" (Darnton, 65). But she found, as the best teachers always do, that teaching enriched her life and thus her writing: " 'Young people read different books and think about different things; [this is important as a resource for teacher-writers] because as a writer one of your jobs is to bring news of the world to the world. . . . To me, teaching is a gift because it puts you in loving contact with young people. You don't get that from your children's friends, and your children go ahead and grow up on you, so it is a present that these eighteen-year-olds come into your life' " (Darnton, 65).

Though college classrooms and teachers are virtually absent from Grace's stories,[2] young people—roughly aged sixteen to twenty-five—are frequently featured as subjects of older characters' conversations or as characters in their own right. These latter are often Richard and Tonto, Faith's boys, but after the mid-sixties[3] include Dennis, Alexandra's lover in "Enormous Changes"; the title character in "The Little Girl"; the boy and girl in "Conversation"; Cynthia in "Runner"; Mickey in "Friends"; Zagrowsky's daughter Cissy; and the young soldier in "Listening." Like Faith's sons, these characters are circumstantial representatives of the ideas and movements of their times and places. Even the tragedy of Juniper in "The Little Girl" may be read as a sociohistorical case study of white youth in the "hippy" period of the sixties:

> Why Carter seen it many times hisself. She could of stayed the summer. We just like the UN. Every state in the union stop by. She would of got her higher education right on the fifth-floor front. September, her mama and daddy would come for her and they whip her bottom, we know that. We been in this world long enough. We seen lots of the little girls. They go home, then after a while they get to be grown womens, they integrating the swimming pool and picketing the supermarket, they blink their eyes and shut their mouth and grin. (ECLM, 157)

Grace Paley felt that "these eighteen-year-olds" and the job itself were "a present," since she never applied for a position at Sarah Lawrence College. She was invited to teach there through the recommendations of writer-teachers Harvey Swados and Muriel Rukeyser and was probably welcomed not only because of her writing, but as a result of her participation in a series of Teachers and Writers Meetings, which took place in 1965. Jane Cooper, who remembers those meetings clearly, believes that the decision to hire Grace was much influenced by the impression she made on one of the college deans in those discussions.

Jane met Grace Paley at the first of the Teachers and Writers Meetings. These were gatherings at which writers from outside the academic community came together with teachers of writing to suggest "various ways in which writing could be made more attractive" to students. The opportunity for this program and its government funding were a result of the trajectory of Sputnik-caused dismay about the supposed ignorance and incapacity of U.S. youth in science and mathematics; by the early sixties school administrators had added to their anxiety by "discovering" that American students could not read or write.

The purpose of the meetings was to define ways teachers and writers could cooperate and ways to open up the standard writing curriculum. At Sarah Lawrence, certain staff members were chosen to attend the series of meetings; Jane Cooper, though not a delegate (she hadn't yet published her first book), was the secretary at each meeting and kept notes of all that happened. "There was quite a lot of ire eventually, and a lot of it seemed to be going off in all directions. You couldn't imagine how anything was going to come out of [the series]," she recalls. Anger and chaos notwithstanding, several successful programs did come out of that series of meetings, including the popular Poets in the Schools.

There were about forty people at the first meeting—writing teachers, delegates from national and state organizations, and members of small community groups. Most were writers, some were arts organizers and neighborhood group leaders; Grace Paley was among the latter. Jane says that she particularly noticed Grace, who "was one of my heroes of the meeting":

> there was this wonderful woman, and every time she opened her mouth she made sense. Everybody else was sort of windy, and then Grace would speak and she would say, "Well, I really care about my neighborhood. I don't think you can do these things unless you think about what your neighborhood is." And she would say, "Now, at P.S. 41 we're doing such-and-such." And the sense that I got of her was that she was not only a remarkably honest person, but someone who dealt in grassroots politics, [always] asking the question, "how do you [meet] the exact needs of my street, my block, my neighborhood?" Everything she said was pithy, to the point, and humane. I was struck by her; as I was writing up [my notes] I kept coming back to things that she had said.

When Grace began to teach at Sarah Lawrence, she and Jane "immediately became friends." Twenty-two years later, Jane says that their intimate friendship "still seems to me so unlikely—so unlikely. Grace and I couldn't be less alike."⁴ The truth is, though, that they came together out of apparently diverse but actually somewhat similar backgrounds. One a Jew from the Bronx and the other a Southern/East Coast WASP (Florida, North Carolina, and New Jersey), they were middle-class girls only two years apart in age. Raised in families where political discussion was one of the dishes on the dinner table, both grew up in the Great Depression and experienced World War II. When they were young women, their lives were filled with soldiers and youthful speculations about war. Both had surprised their families with unorthodox responses to education and career choice.[5] Jane Cooper and Grace Paley came together at Sarah Lawrence College and formed a friendship that nourished and encouraged their writing and teaching. "We laughed a lot," Jane says.

Together the two writers played an important role in the creation of the unique and nationally prominent undergraduate writing program now in place at Sarah Lawrence College. Though a poet, Jane had been teaching story writing "for years and years and years." When Grace came into the department, Jane was still teaching fiction writing, so they shared some of the early students in the new program.[6] At that time there were five writing teachers, three for fiction and two for poetry. The writing department began to grow; they created a senior seminar in which each of the teachers would take two senior students in conference courses and see them an hour a week. "When anybody had any work that seemed finished, it would be dittoed up for all five teachers and all ten seniors, who would then meet together and discuss it," Jane recalls. Several students who had already worked with Jane later worked with Grace, so the two women had many reasons to confer at work— creating a professional partnership that remains a strong component of their friendship. "We've always worked very well with the same people. Though teaching in different ways from different points of view, I think we had a common sense of what teaching should be doing," Jane says.

Grace's teaching has, naturally, the same political base as her other concerns do. Just as she presented a "grassroots" perception in the Teachers and Writers Meetings, she perceives student writers as generators of their own style and sensibility. Literally unschooled in academic style and presentation, her classroom ethics the same as those that increasingly made her a conscientious objector to the social and political status quo, Grace was a catalyst even for her colleagues. Jane recalls that as soon as she began to work with Grace, to teach with her, she felt a radical shift in her perception of her own course, "which had been a very good course in the well-made story. I suddenly wanted to blow it to bits. It just didn't make sense to me anymore to think in terms of the well-made story. I really heard, in what Grace said, ways in which people were going beyond the well-made story. And this was terribly important to me, and it became very important to the way my poetry was moving also."[7]

Despite Grace's being "technically brilliant," Jane explains that in class Grace "always says the humane thing. She's very capable of criticizing a student's story without demolishing anything. The core of the story still is absolutely alive, and that's a wonderful thing to witness. Underneath the technicality, there is [always] the moral vision. Students who have worked with her will tell me how she would send them back and back and back with the same story to go over it again—and go more deeply," which is Grace's own way of writing, her way of finding her stories.

Her classes were popular almost immediately; her reputation as a valuable and exciting teacher was generated in just a few terms. Not only other students, but other teachers would tell young writers to be sure they had at least one course with Grace Paley. Always there were many more applicants than openings for her classes. Many student writers are grateful for Grace's criticism—a combination of sensitive questioning and thoughtful, frank commentary. Certainly there have also been those who did not flourish with her teaching; but these are a minority, and their complaints are mostly about her lack of time and the crush around her. Her skill brought her many invitations; she began to teach summer writers' workshops, traveling to Iowa, California, and North Dakota. In more recent years, she has joined the visiting professor circuit and teaches full terms at colleges and universities, giving readings and interviews in the school's community. She increasingly accepts offers to be a visiting professor; in 1987, for instance, she taught the spring term at Stanford, and in early 1989, she took a two-week seminar assignment at the University of California at Santa Cruz.[8]

Students recognize in Grace the combination of a questioning contemporary mind and a romantic passion for the beauty and truth of the classics. For years she maintained a schedule of small group meetings in her office or a nearby classroom, where she and her students would read the classics out loud. Among her favorites is Milton, which sometimes shocks critics who shortsightedly assume that her politics would dictate his exclusion or a taste for only more recent writers. Often she begins her classes by calling on students to recite memorized pieces they have chosen from the works of traditionally taught writers. One spring morning in 1988, when Grace had to miss the meeting, students simply went on without her, reading aloud their planned selections from the book of Genesis; the class opened with a young woman's recitation of lines by Emily Dickinson. Grace, who went to school when memorization was a primary pedagogical method, believes that it "clears your brain; it's like taking a bath."

Much of what Grace learned and taught in her first few years at Sarah Lawrence has remained central to her philosophy of teaching and to her own writing—and this is simply because it embodies her essential world view. She has never changed her style to adapt to the academic world, nor has she taught her students to do so. In 1970, the year in which she received an award for short story writing from the National Institute for Arts and Letters, she contributed "Some Notes on Teaching: Probably Spoken" to Jonathan Baumbach's anthology *Writers as Teachers/Teachers as Writers*, listing "about fifteen things [she] might say in the course of a term" (202).

Among those "things" is a recurring emphasis on the writer's consciousness of language; she emphasizes the importance of "the language that comes to you from your parents and your street and friends." Of course this emphasis is a result of her own discovery that literature could be written in one's real voice and could then move into the voices or language of others. In this essay she writes that she would ask her father to tell her stories and that she tries to remember her grandmother's stories; she urges her students to do the same, asserting that "because of time shortage and advanced age, neither your father nor your grandmother will bother to tell unimportant stories" (203). She entreats students to be open and to "remain ignorant"; she warns them "to remove all lies" from their work, naming—like the recitation of plagues at a seder—the lie of "injustice to characters," the lie of writing to another's taste, the lie of "the approximate word," the lie of "unnecessary adjectives," and even the lie of "the brilliant sentence you love the most" (205).

Years later, she continues to insist on the primacy of honesty: "The story is a big lie. And in the middle of this big lie, you're telling the truth. If you lie [there], things go wrong. You become sentimental, opaque, bombastic; you withhold information" (Darnton, 66). At the heart of her teaching is the memory of her own early work. She remembers the beginning of her love of language and how that young love sometimes blinded her to excess or led her to imitation.

She remembers the teaching she received—when it was wrong, like the teacher who expelled her from class for using "inappropriate" language or subject, and when it was right, like Auden telling her to write in her own voice. She knows that all artists imitate the masters when they are young in their craft, and she respects the youthful passion that bathes itself in words for their own sake, for the sake of their delicious sound and thrilling sense.

Grace insists that fiction writers and poets should read their work aloud, that poems and stories must not be left to "just lie there in books on a table." And so she became the primary organizer of Sarah Lawrence's now-traditional Tuesday night readings, at which both students and faculty read from their work. She felt that the readings would continue only if students eventually took them over—which would be fine—but that if the students didn't take them over, the readings would die—which would be appropriate.

Jane, who resisted the idea at first because their workdays were already so long (Sarah Lawrence's professors spend time outside of class, one-on-one, with all of their students every week of the term), remembers that "Grace said she thought it was really important that students share their work through reading it, and learn how to read it. So every other week a faculty member would read with three or four or five students—and it became a very important program, a very important influence within the writing program." Grace insists that Jane helped to start the program, but Jane's memory is different: "I guess, in effect, I went along because she believed in it. I thought I'd [just] stay the first year, support it [and see what would happen]. But I was very dubious."

In 1988, the first September after both Grace Paley and Jane Cooper had retired from the campus, students were still reading their poems and stories aloud to each other, their writing teachers, and their guests on Tuesday nights. It turns out that Jane and Grace were both right; the Tuesday night readings are a success, and they certainly do make for a long day's work. Jane Cooper's last day on campus, when she retired after thirty-seven years, was on a Tuesday. "And it was a typical Tuesday at Sarah Lawrence," she says. "Fourteen hours."

This rigorous academic life—by no means a vague, aesthetic entanglement in ivy—encouraged Grace's tacit entrance into the literary life, and neither sensibility was ever really separate from the life of political activism. In 1967, the year after Grace Paley joined the faculty in Bronxville, student protesters held a major demonstration at Columbia University, and many Sarah Lawrence students took the train into Manhattan to join them. In 1968 there was a substantial antiwar demonstration at Sarah Lawrence itself. And in 1969 Grace Paley went to Vietnam.

That journey, which she has since referred to as one of the most important events of her life, was obviously a result of her increasing activism. She had been active all along in the neighborhood, at the Village Peace Center, and by now was working also in Resist and the War Resisters League, both national networks. Once again among the boys—as in the army camps of World War II—Grace now studied the military from another perspective. All that she had learned in years of political readings and meetings was augmented by the antimilitary, antidraft, antiwar struggle of the sixties and seventies.

Many members of Grace's neighborhood organization took Quaker training in draft counseling, and during most of that long war, they counseled "about a hundred kids a week," Sybil Claiborne estimates. Karl Bissinger remembers that "on some nights in the summertime we would have kids lined up clear around the block waiting to get free counseling. Of course, every tenth person was an FBI informant, but that didn't matter. We cheerfully counseled them too." The group also helped to set up the national Medical Committee for Human Rights and assisted those men already in the military who were seeking medical justification and documentation to get out. Center members eventually created and maintained a support program: they found jobs, homes, and even doctors and dentists for all that young army who'd rejected the Army.

Grace was one of the organizers of The Women's Vigil (the weekly demonstration that lasted eight years), which was staffed by members of the center and their friends. Angry Arts—artists for whom political action was integral to the creative process—and a lot of street theater were also generated or supported by the Peace Center, which offered desk space, or phone use, or just an address. Even the fledgling women's health movement got some assistance from the center;[9] though Grace never worked on reproductive health issues in those days, "in the very first abortion speak-out (in the late sixties) I was there, and I did talk about my abortion, and the Peace Center gave some desks to the new Abortion Rights Center."

Through this period, Grace Paley still thought that she had to make a conscious effort to keep "politics" out of her fiction, though much of the success of her earlier work is due to the failure of that effort. One of the most notable aspects of her fiction is that it offers the inescapably political quality of daily life without dogma or polemic. Nonetheless, in her pre-feminist years, the obvious political nature of antiwar work kept her from deliberately placing it, as subject, at the center of her writing when she worked at the job called "literature."[10] Because feminist politics were not so clear to her then, she felt no compunction about writing and publishing "Politics"— one of the rare explicit presentations of "politics" to appear in Paley stories composed before 1972[11]—a somewhat ironic picture of community action as a process born of maternity (ECLM). Not until "Listening" in *Later the Same Day*, written and published in the eighties, would she directly address soldiers' lives per se—in a short story she had worked on extensively and included in a collection.[12]

Instead, throughout the sixties and into the seventies, Grace wrote essays, stories, and articles for political journals and little magazines with overt movement sympathies.[13] Journalism has been, historically, a strong influence on the American short story form, and perhaps its content as well, since the nineteenth century when Bret Harte and Mark Twain wrote for newspapers and then published (sometimes expanded) versions of those stories as popular literature. In the 1920s, 1930s, and 1940s, Ernest Hemingway was a correspondent, Dorothy Parker wrote reviews, and Kay Boyle and Katherine Anne Porter sent dispatches back from war zones for international magazines and U.S. newspapers. Though academic criticism had begun to move the short story in other directions by 1950, the journalistic aspects of the short story—immediacy, realism, stripped-down prose, non-Romantic subject matter, and political perspective—were never cut out.

One of Grace's first such ventures was the publication of "The Sad Story About the Six Boys About to Be Drafted in Brooklyn," which appeared twice in 1967.[14] "The Sad Story" is not so polished as those in her collected fiction, but, as the following excerpt shows, it contains many of the now-classic Paley trademarks. Like a number of her stories, it is shorter than most short fiction; its language is unusual in its quickly executed images and occasionally bizarre sentence structure; and both the framing and phrasing of the story remind the reader, visually and rhythmically, of poetry. The story is funny, ironic, and terribly sad in its essential truth (except for an amusingly pivotal foray into Lamarckian theory), and it offers hope in a sweetly utopian conclusion.

I

There were six boys in Brooklyn and none of them wanted to be drafted.

Only one of them went to college. What could the others do?

One shot off his index finger. He had read about this in a World War I novel.

One wore silk underpants to his physical. His father had done that for World War II.

One went to a psychiatrist for three years starting three years earlier (his mother to save him had thought of it).

One married and had three children.

One enlisted and hoped for immediate preferential treatment. ("The Sad Story," 18)

Her choice not to publish such fiction outside the movement did not prevent her from admiring the art and appreciating the social impact of mainstream work that did focus on war, the life of soldiers, and the military mentality. She remembers being at a meeting with students during the war when Joseph Heller was present—perhaps as the invited speaker. Someone asked him if he thought that *Catch-22* had anything to do with people not registering for the draft or with the spread of antimilitary feeling in the country. He said no; he didn't see any connection. Grace was surprised, disappointed, irritated, and maybe angry. She stood up and said, "I think they have everything to do with each other. I think they're very closely connected. I think *Catch-22* has been a tremendous influence, and I think you should be proud of that."[15]

Her own antiwar work remained outside the classically drawn literary sphere, within that apparently ragged but actually quite well-defined arena called "the movement."[16] Peace movements in the United States have always been made up of a multitude of organizations, loosely joined in coalition for national and international action. Grace's decade of work, developing out of neighborhood resistance to shelter drills in the fifties and growing into nationally coordinated antiwar organizing and action in the late sixties, constituted her membership, her credentials.

Though her family was disturbed by her actions and their consequences, they became accustomed to their steady increase. Isaac Goodside, despite—or because of—his own political history, was angry about her radicalism, and they argued frequently. Jeanne Tenenbaum was frightened the first several times Grace went to jail, but finally the sisters had a long conversation in which Grace explained that imprisonment was sometimes part of the action and that, while inside, she continued to work; she told Jeanne that in jail she had an opportunity to learn from women she could never have known otherwise and that she actually enjoyed going to jail sometimes, for those reasons.

The first time Grace was in jail, she was only one block away from home, in the old New York Women's House of Detention.[17] The proximity and familiarity made Nora feel that her mother hadn't really been "sent away." In fact, the teenager was "excited," because throughout her childhood she had seen and heard all the people on the sidewalks calling out to women on the inside: "They would be out there yelling and screaming at the tops of their voices, out on Sixth Avenue, but you could never see the people up in the windows. So it was real exciting when Grace was actually in there, in this place I was so interested in."

But Nora, like her aunt and grandfather, also feared for Grace in the streets of the later sixties and seventies. At one huge demonstration, a march down Fifth Avenue that was lined with almost as many observers and police as there were participants, she and Grace were marching with the Bread and Puppet Theater. Their group had a big puppet of Uncle Sam, all suited up in red, white, and blue and smoking a fat cigar; like the famous Camel billboard, the puppet puffed steam from its stogie. It was a giant figure, with two people inside the puppet and more holding it up and maneuvering it from the outside. At one corner, where the march was turning down a side street near Central Park, a gang of men with baseball bats waited behind the police line. When they saw the Uncle Sam puppet, they became enraged; here was the reason they'd brought their bats. A tiny mob, they broke down the police barrier and surged toward the Bread and Puppet contingent.

Grace immediately moved to meet them, putting her arms out wide in a holding gesture to stop them. Nora couldn't tell if she actually stopped every one of them, but the angry group halted. And nothing happened to Grace. Later, to her daughter's passionate—and angry—protests, Grace replied, "Ah, they wouldn't hurt a middle-aged lady." For Nora, "it was the most terrifying experience for me to see my mother do that—just step right into danger. She would do these little brave acts, and I would really be angry that" she was endangering herself. "I didn't want her to do it—but I was also proud of her. I wasn't afraid she would go to jail; I was afraid she'd get hurt."

Grace Paley was, in some ways, typical among movement activists. Grace was among the urban guerrillas who protested the rapidly rising number of Americans killed in Southeast Asia; that group planted 360 crosses in a park near City Hall, creating over-night a field of symbolic graves for the GIs killed in one Easter week. She sat down with hundreds of friends in the middle of dozens of streets and avenues in New York,[18] and she joined those who took small boats out into the river for a blockade of the navy in New Jersey. She was one of the regulars who turned out in public support, with banners and posters, when young men refused induc-tion at the local draft board, and she traveled the crowded buses from New York to Washington for repeated demonstrations of citi-zen anger and disapproval.[19]

In other ways, however, Grace Paley was an exceptional candi-date for public work. Out of the PTA and into the streets, she had developed into a charismatic speaker and organizer. Like the voices of her fictional narrators, her own voice is compelling. In the gritty charm of its Bronx cadence and pronunciation, Grace's voice is easy to understand, compellingly sincere, simple and intimate, revela-tory and explanatory without being directive; her public style is no less personal than her immediate presence. A live model of the feminist axiom—the personal is political—Grace Paley often cata-lyzes and embodies the thoughts and feelings of her audience as she speaks.

By 1969, though she never got caught in the kind of notoriety that dogged—and damned—some women who were antiwar activists,[20] she was prominent enough to be chosen to represent the nonviolent branch of the nation's antiwar movement in a small delegation that traveled to Hanoi to receive three prisoners of war and bring them home. Other members of the group were Rennie Davis (representing the New Mobilization to End the War in Vietnam), Linda Evans (from Students for a Democratic Society), and Jimmy Johnson (of the Fort Hood Three). These antiwar activists represented the people of the United States, not the U.S. government. They were accompanied by three members of a movement film collective called Newsreel, who documented their travels.[21]

Recognizing the positive value of such a mission, especially in the face of its own failure to effect many prisoner releases or exchanges, the State Department made propaganda, if not hay, out of the occasion. Of course, almost no mention was made in the media of the role the peace activists had played in the return of these prisoners—all bomber pilots. Credit went to the State Department. Moreover, despite governmental assurances to the contrary, Newsreel's film was impounded immediately by customs agents when they returned to the States, and all of the delegates' papers and personal belongings were examined exhaustively.

On the home front, Grace's children were in much the same position they had been in since the mid-fifties—worried about their mother, amazed by her, and working out a stance that could encompass their conflicting feelings. Now aged twenty and eighteen, they had long understood her purpose and certainly felt both pride and respect, but they also felt a consistent low level of anxiety and fear. Danny was opposed to her going: "I thought it was really dangerous, which—obviously—it was." He was always, in fact, worried about her physical safety, especially in the streets. He kept thinking that "something would happen—maybe some cop would be brutal." But in the face of her intense commitment, he gave up trying to stop her. Nora recalls that people were always astonished when they learned her mother was in Hanoi; they literally couldn't believe it.

When she returned, Grace spoke and wrote about her experiences; we have those recollections in her nonfiction prose, which weaves her fascination with language into her interpretation of the culture and people she found in Vietnam. She loved their names, and she recited lists of villages and cities in her speeches: "our interpreter Nhan said, 'Grace, if you would stay another two weeks, I could teach you the tune of the language.' Speaking is singing—a lot of up and down anyway. The word *Hoa* means flower, *Hoa* means harmony. The tune's important" ("Report from the DRV," 5). In her articles Grace displays the same clarity and economy we find in her fiction, so that one line, one image, one brief remark can tell the whole story in miniature, a microcosmic mirror within the larger text:

> The woman who called before I left for Vietnam was a pilot's wife. She had not heard from her husband in 2½ years.... [When Grace returned with no word of the man] I had to tell her this. She asked me why the Vietnamese insisted on keeping the pilots. I explained that they were considered war criminals, who had come 10,000 miles to attack a tiny, barely armed country in an undeclared and brutal war. She said, "Well, they're airmen. They're American officers." I told her about Nien Trach, Dong Hoi, Vinh Linh, the dark tunnels, the people seared by napalm, shattered by pellets, the miles of craters, the bloody mountains. She said, "Oh, Mrs. Paley, villages and people! My husband wouldn't do that." Before my eyes filled with tears in sorrow for my country, I said, "Oh? Well, I guess it must have been someone else." ("i guess," 33)

With the same kind of images and punctuation before us, with a "real" voice in our ears like the voices we hear in her stories, we read the nonfiction, in which—as a war correspondent of sorts—Grace struggled to understand and interpret the war and to define her country's responsibility: "well of course it's a war and they are bombing communication, transportation. It's true, they are overkilling the Vietnamese countryside and the little brooks, but that's America for you, they have overkilled flies, bugs, beetles, trees, fish, rivers and the flowers of their own American fields. They're like over-grown kids who lean on a buddy in kindergarten and kill him" ("Report," 7).

Throughout her magazine writings and speeches, as in her fiction, she includes children, alludes frequently to motherhood, and makes metaphors of mothering and childhood. In an edited speech transcription published soon after her return, she describes a place "near the sea," where an American pilot named Dixon is buried, and says that the Vietnamese have marked it with a cross "in case his mother should want to come see it after the war" ("Report," 8). She considers the proliferation of "military targets" and muses: "the next thing a logical military brain hooks into is the fact that [in a people's war] every person is a military target, or the mother of a military target . . . " (8). Much later, when the war was over and her energies had been further invested in antinuclear and related environmental activism, she recalled her Vietnam work in a similar mood:

> In another time, my friends and I vigiled every Saturday afternoon for eight years on Eighth Street in Manhattan. . . . One day, an old lady stopped me as I was giving out leaflets. I loved her at once, because she reminded me of my own mother and several aunts. . . . [The two women converse about the importance of supporting resisters in prison.] I remembered my job. . . . "Could you give me your name? We're a local group." "Yes, certainly," she said. "My name is Sobell. I'm Morton Sobell's mother." I said, "Oh, Morton Sobell. Oh. . . . " Then, without a thought, we fell into each other's arms and began to cry, because her son was still at that time hopelessly in jail and had been there for years, all through his young manhood. And the sons and daughters of my friends were caught in a time of war that would use them painfully, no matter what their decisions. ("Living on Karen Silkwood Drive," 12)

This emphasis reflects not merely Grace Paley's nurturant consciousness, but her preoccupation with the global need for taking care, for mothering-in-the-world, which is reflected in the preponderance of her stories. Of the forty-five collected stories in three volumes, twenty-two have motherhood as a central focus, and at least eight others include it as a major issue.

Grace believes that going to Vietnam in 1969 was of tremendous importance in her life; being there "deepened" her thinking. For the first time she went to "a place that was *totally* different," not different like California, or different like Europe, but an utterly unfamiliar culture in which even the alphabet, her major resource, was unknown to her. She notes, too, that she went to a place that was being assaulted, systematically destroyed, by her own people.

And, "another thing was that then I saw war. You know, I had been through the Second World War, but I hadn't seen it. There I saw war."[22]

Out on the road, traveling from Hanoi into the countryside, the American peace brigade saw that every city they passed had been destroyed. On that journey, she writes that because "we were not military men, not even people who'd been to wars, we weren't bored by the repetition; we didn't even get used to it" ("Report," 6). She compares Dong Hoi to Pompeii—historically the site of "a great, grass-terraced open theater" and a "thousand year old wall." Dong Hoi was once home to 33,000 people, but in 1969 it was a ghost city of white doorsteps, "as though Baltimore had disappeared into the grass" ("i guess," 31). Grace crawled through the tunnels of the province of Quanh Binh, called The Land of Fire, where the people lived completely underground because of the constant bombing—day and night, for more than two years.

She met soldiers again, talked to American soldiers in prison—the ones she had come to bring back home, and the ones who weren't getting out. "I learned a lot about the military, about the people in the military, about what it really is," she says. She was touched by the fact that men who were in prison "weren't cold to us at all, even though they knew we were from the peace movement; they really did talk to us." Grace particularly remembers one man; he had been among the first Americans sent to Vietnam, and in 1969 he had been a prisoner of war for six years. All the pilot-prisoners were officers of course, and many had signed on to stay because they needed a little more flight time. They had made career decisions in taking repeated Vietnam duty; "they wanted to go from major to colonel. And before my very eyes, when we brought this guy home in the plane, they turned him from a major into a colonel."

Many of the military men Grace spoke to on that trip and back in the States engaged her affection or interest; very few were like one of the POW's she negotiated for—who was "a complete and total shit." Most were what Grace calls "perfectly nice guys." She flew back to the United States in conversation with a perfectly nice guy who said, "Gee, Grace, I don't know what I'm gonna do when I get home. I just don't know what I'm gonna do." She suggested, "Well, you know how to drive an airplane; you know how to fly a plane. You could do that." He looked at her when she said that, and answered, "That's like driving a truck. That's not interesting." Then he said, "I'm sorry to say this, but I really liked bombing; it was very exciting." You can see, Grace says now, "how I learned a lot. Here's this perfectly nice man telling me this"; he was no doubt the sort of fellow Marvine, in "A Woman, Young and Old," would have called a "soldier of the Republic" (LDM, 30).[23]

After her late summer expedition in 1969, Grace spent much of the fall speaking about what she had learned in Vietnam and working toward the big November march on Washington. There were several actions planned for that demonstration, demanding various levels of commitment; for some protesters, the Pentagon was again a major target, as it had been in the first major "siege of the Pentagon" in the fall of 1967. Grace was there with friends, and to their surprise, they met Nora, who had come by herself on a bus from New Hampshire, where she had just started school at Franconia College. With no knowledge of each other's presence in the city—after the chaos of a long night of struggle and confusion among the National Guard, District of Columbia police, and the thousands of demonstrators who had come to protest the war—mother and daughter met at the doors of the Pentagon.

Arriving alone and knowing no one else there, Nora had sat through the night on a cold staircase with hundreds of others, huddled together for body warmth. Their sitting had been declared illegal by the District of Columbia police, who were pulling demonstrators off the steps and taking them away throughout the night. Nora was near the front when the morning light came, for many people had already been carted off. In the dawn Nora could clearly see the soldiers in their riot gear, up on the roofs, out in the streets, and right there on the stairs, their guns pointed at the people—and she was frightened. As the sky continued to lighten and faces emerged from the shadows of the crowd, Grace appeared. After a dark, cold night of anxious uncertainty, in the dawn of drawn bayonets, suddenly *her mother* appeared—what a story!

Her own fear was immediately dispelled, but not so much by the classic "flood of relief" as by the resurgence of that old anxiety: please, Grace, don't do anything dangerous! That was all Nora could think about in this scene, a grotesquely enlarged version of what she had experienced throughout her childhood and adolescence—this time there were thousands of armed riot police and soldiers wearing gas masks. On such nights in Washington, the air was nearly palpable, toxic with tear gas and exhaust from the thousands of vehicles jammed into the capital. Ironically, the big buses that brought protesters into the city from half or more of the states in the Union waited to take them home with their engines running, clogging the streets with noxious fumes that mixed with spreading tear gas and Mace in the cold wind.

The two women spontaneously generated a classic mother-daughter duet. Nora says that her desire to protect Grace, to keep her mother away from the most dangerous action, was what made her brave. Grace remembers being so worried after meeting Nora that she determined to take on nothing extraordinary because she needed to protect her daughter. As the police worked over the crowd, grabbing, clubbing, often injuring the people they "arrested," Nora forced herself to be calm. She saw her companions of the nightwatch being beaten, dragged across the cement, and tossed into steel trucks, "literally lifted and thrown into the trucks"; when it was her turn, the pretty, white-skinned, redhaired college girl was hustled very quickly but quite decently—almost solicitously—into a truck by "a cop who was protective of me!" Grace—who had seen girls and young women beaten on their breasts and pregnant women punched in the belly—was as amazed and relieved as Nora. Like mother, like daughter; tough—and lucky.

Karl Bissinger, who was in the streets with Grace many times in those years, speaks of her courage as a kind of intelligence of emotion. He and Grace were in Washington together during the 1971 May Day Protest, another demonstration that led to thousands of arrests. They began their day's work at five in the morning; they left the apartment of a local family that took in visiting demonstrators for every major march and rally, and they went down to the Capitol. One plan was to cut off the city of Washington, or at least isolate the center of government, by keeping traffic out and letting no one leave. Karl and Grace were in a group whose tactic was to sit down and stop traffic on a bridge coming over the Potomac. The simplicity of this plan cannot begin to predict the reality of the action. "It was really a scene out of the Inferno. I'd never seen anything like this," Karl remembers.

The police came through with tear gas, throwing canisters directly at the people; they threw the tiny bombs sometimes called "poppers," making a terrible noise to confuse and frighten "the enemy." Soldiers wielded drawn bayonets, and police brandished billy clubs; "people were getting their heads cracked right and left. They were trying to round us up and the arrests were beginning. And I was scared. I was really, physically, scared." Karl looked around at Grace and saw that she did not appear frightened: "Grace was alert. Grace was with it—she was remembering what you should do, but she was not physically scared. And I was sort of knocked out by that, because Grace has more imagination than I do; Grace knows better than I what's gonna happen." The demonstrators had, of course, anticipated and prepared themselves for the arrests that followed. There were thousands arrested on Mayday, and the area jails were literally overflowing. Grace was one of hundreds kept in the Washington football stadium, home field of the Redskins. She was there for three days, sleeping on the ground; people repeatedly walked the round of the stadium to keep warm in the late spring chill.[24]

Karl points out that the qualities he saw in his friend Grace that day in Washington are rooted in the same dignity—masked by her simplicity of style—and the same patience—refined from simple stubbornness—with which she had moved from place to place at home, carrying her nightgown and toothbrush in a paper bag. Her life was now so complex that its personal and political aspects were interwoven too tightly to distinguish and separate. The children's growing up and graduating from high school, the escalation of the war and her resultant education and activism, the development of her consciously political writing and speaking, her position as a teacher of writers and a designer of curriculum, her emergence as a well-known writer, her struggle with the dissolution of her marriage—plus visits with Jeanne, Victor, and Isaac and the maintenance of an intricate network of friendships—all of these things together defined the essential character of the mature Grace Paley.

8

An Interest in Life

In 1972 Grace and Jess Paley divorced; in that same year, she married Bob Nichols. The following year, in which her father would have celebrated his ninetieth birthday, Isaac Goodside died. In those years, Grace began to travel again, so that her 1969 trip to Vietnam became the first of several important visits to distant places; between 1972 and 1977 she went to Chile, Russia, and China, as well as Puerto Rico. Before 1969 Grace had lived by the movement adage to "think global, act local," which was personally strengthened by her twin desires to stay in the neighborhood and avoid the literati. Now, though she carefully maintained her connections on the block, the center of her life was no longer that extended family of park, playground, and PTA; her territory had expanded.

Her father's death changed her relationship with the Bronx; the real streets were so much altered that the old place—though the house on Hoe Street still stood intact—was located now in memory rather than family life. Even the oldest folks who lived there in the late sixties and early seventies had never gone to Dr. Goodside with their aches and pains or seen little Gracie running up and down the block, and the younger ones hadn't grown up watching the teenaged Grace rush in and out with her friends. Moreover, at the other end of Manhattan Island, her own children had begun to make their way, in fits and starts, to and from different addresses. Grace herself was now "based," so to speak, in Bronxville as well as the Village. Bob's Vermont house, and the towns and land around it, were beginning to become yet another home to her, and her work on the national level—as organizer, writer, and teacher—had begun to develop an international component.

In these years, one decade giving way to the next, Grace's stories still did not overtly depict her movement work, but their characters are clearly drawn from the metamorphoses she was undergoing; her title for the second collection, published in 1974, suggests both the impact of such changes and their felt rapidity.[1] The first and last stories of *Enormous Changes at the Last Minute* offer narratives of careful introspection and keen observation that lead to personal transformation in the context of a changing world. We might consider the creation of all three collections to be a means of organizing the past, a sophisticated filing system that orders, integrates, and analyzes what the author has learned over time.

Their publication, then, is a statement: what has been learned in the chaos of experience as "fact" has been transformed and is now deliberately arranged in sequence and published as "fiction." The creation of sequence is part of the writing; it does not replicate, but represents or evokes, "real life." Even if a story has been published earlier, separately, its new public appearance in a collection —often altered—indicates the writer's desire to place it in a context that instantaneously constructs new meaning.

It is also true that like any thoughtful editor, Grace makes decisions about the placement of individual pieces for the sake of balance, in terms of tone and (likely) emotional impact; she tries to effect a change of pace and staggers the order of sad or funny stories when she can. These are practical matters; she also arranges stories by length—she wants the very short ones distributed throughout, to avoid the effect of several long stories together. Such concerns do not diffuse considerations of theme, political consciousness, or character development. They may instead create that same sense of "reality" within the collections that the individual stories suggest. It is also accurate to say that the collections move through an effective, if not strict, chronology. If we consider both style and political consciousness and track her stories through all three collections, we would begin with "Goodbye and Good Luck," which is relatively straightforward and direct in both areas, and come eventually to "Listening," which is an exceptionally complex story, thematically and structurally labyrinthine.

Grace chose to open *Enormous Changes* with "Wants," a story in which the (Faith-like) narrator encounters her ex-husband in the street; because they were married for twenty-seven years, she feels justified in greeting him, "Hello, my life"—but he rejects the definition: "What? What life? No life of mine" (ECLM, 3). In the midst of their rapid meeting-cum-argument—which takes place in and around the public library—she decides to reread Edith Wharton's *The House of Mirth* and *The Children*, which she says "is about how life in the United States in New York changed in twenty-seven years fifty years ago" (ECLM, 4). Having thus placed herself in a literary/historical context, the narrator concludes her story with a self-assessment: "when a person or an event comes along to jolt or appraise me, I *can* take some appropriate action" (ECLM, 6).[2] This collection, we understand, is going to be about the coming of such persons and events and the actions taken in their wake. *This* book, we come to see, is also about "how life in the United States in New York changed in twenty-seven years."

The concluding story, "The Long-Distance Runner," is narrated by Faith, who announces that "one day, before or after forty-two," she became a long-distance runner. Though she admits to being "in many ways inadequate to this desire," she still "wanted to go far and fast . . . round and round the country from the seaside to the bridges, along the old neighborhood streets a couple of times, before old age and urban renewal ended them and [her. She] had already spent a lot of life lying down or standing and staring. [She] had decided to run" (ECLM, 179–81). Faith is very close to Grace here; she wants to make an accounting of the past, to see where it has gone and to understand how she carries it inside her. Grace Paley's marriage is over; her father is dead; her children are practically self-sufficient. The world is at war again—or still—and now the writer has lived more than half a century. The examination of time and age and their relationship, their almost physical joint history, is a favorite subject in these individual stories and thematic in the collection as well. Often whimsically introduced, these issues are always interwoven with examinations of family, of generations and relations. In "Faith in the Afternoon," we learn Faith's antecedents when the narrator says that she is "seasick with ocean sounds" because "her grandfather, scoring the salty sea, skated for miles along the Baltic's icy beaches, with a frozen herring in his pocket. And she, all ears, was born in Coney Island" (ECLM, 31–32).

In "The Long-Distance Runner," Grace recorded both the remembered past and the changing present by describing the rearrangements time makes in the lives of houses, families, and cities. Faith returns to her Jewish family's former apartment and lives there for three weeks with four Black children and their mother, Mrs. Luddy, who answers the door when she pounds on it in terror, screaming "Mama! Mama!" Faith concludes her story by trying to explain to her own children, her lover, and eventually her readers what happened: "A woman inside the steamy energy of middle age runs and runs. She finds the houses and streets where her childhood happened. She lives in them. She learns as though she was still a child what in the world is coming next" (ECLM, 198).

The selection and arrangement of stories for *Enormous Changes* were part of that process for Grace Paley. She looked back over her years of changes—and all the years of changes that had led up to them—and tried to see what was coming next. A good deal of what was coming next—a new home, some new family, and an ongoing in-house dialogue about political theory and action—would come to her in the person of Bob Nichols.

Bob Nichols's family life and background are notably different from Grace Paley's. Born in 1919, Bob grew up in the town of Worcester, Massachusetts, and in rural Vermont, where his father had a house built as a retreat from urban life. An only child, he went to boarding schools from the age of ten through adolescence and spent only short periods with his parents after that. Robert Nichols grew up with inherited money; he has always had a private income, as had his father. In 1987—when the money had dwindled considerably —he said that he was "just beginning to understand what it means to live a life in which money is not taken for granted." His parents divorced when he was seventeen, right around the time he went off to Harvard.

He says that his father "was something of a loner," who designed his Vermont house to get away from the upper-middle-class social milieu he had grown to disdain. As his son would be in later decades, Bob's father was interested in the people of the Vermont countryside and towns, but unlike his son, he maintained a distance from the people who became his neighbors; he called them "characters" and rather romanticized them. Bob's mother had what her son calls "a pretty unhappy life" during her marriage but enjoyed herself with both friends and suitors when she moved away after the divorce. Unlike her husband, she had not sought isolation, and when he moved her to Vermont, she missed the family and community life she had had in Massachusetts.

After his parents' divorce, his own years at Harvard, and many months on duty in the South Pacific during World War II—like Jess Paley and Victor Goodside—Bob spent only a few more seasons in the Vermont house; he married and moved to New York City in 1952. He stayed in Manhattan over twenty years, working as a landscape architect. Bob was one of the city planners who urged the creation of "vest-pocket" parks in the city and designed playgrounds—including the one in Washington Square Park in the Village—with children's safety and imagination in mind. He was one of the originators of the now-popular, large-scale log installations with chain-hung tires, unpainted wood, multilevel platforms, and tunnels. His full-time residence in Vermont began in the late seventies and early eighties; he just came up one time and stayed on, he says. He hadn't necessarily expected or planned to stay, but he's been there ever since.

Bob was politically active; like Grace, he became involved in neighborhood organizing in the parks and then "ban-the-bomb" and peace work. Also like Grace, he began to take his writing seriously in the fifties; his early work included collections of poetry published by small presses in artist's editions and several plays. His street productions were often done in concert with a loose repertory company of neighbors.[3]

His wife Mary Perot—a member of what he calls "the impoverished upper class" of Philadelphia—is a former editor of the *Village Voice* and has directed the office of public relations for the mayor's office in New York City. She had three children, two girls and a boy, before she took on such work and before the marriage began to falter. At the time of the divorce, Bob and Mary's children were not yet teenagers. All three Nichols children went to private schools. That difference would have been one of the few major philosophical and practical disagreements between Bob and Grace in the late fifties and early sixties; she would have disapproved of that choice, but in those days she was not a close enough friend to have argued it out with the Nicholses.

The families were casually friendly. Danny Paley remembers visiting Bob's Vermont house one summer: "In fact, my father helped him build the pavilion, which is a little building" next to the house. Bob and Mary separated before the mid-sixties, and Bob and Grace had neither a romantic nor a sexual attachment until sometime after that. Danny says that when Bob became a good friend to Grace, "I never really thought of it in romantic terms, you know, between my mother and him. . . . later on it gradually occurred to me that they were going out together."

Bob's marriage was well over by the time he and his neighborhood pal and movement comrade came together as a couple. When Grace left Jess and was staying with various friends, she began to see Bob more and more often. In those days, Karl Bissinger remembers, Bob "always looked like Ichabod Crane—his hair sticking out to here, his shirt torn and [pulled] out. And I know that he could afford Brooks Brothers clothes. [At the same time,] Bob was the kind of artist that Grace could respect and understand" because of the work he wanted to do: he was serious about his writing, and he construed his art in political terms. Bob Nichols was a visibly eccentric fellow, whose art and politics were so consuming that his disheveled appearance was of no concern or even notice to him. Grace Paley found him charming.

Bob was, even with his Brooks Brothers shirt tucked in, an exotic for this Bronx Jew. Though Grace has never been exploitive or condemnatory of Jews in her stories like her Jewish brothers-in-print who often attach the unfortunate effluvia of twentieth-century American materialism to Jews (and especially Jewish women), Grace's Jewish women nevertheless often couple with non-Jews. From young Shirley Abramowitz's tolerance, through Faith's two Catholic husbands[4] and brief dalliance with Nick Hegstraw, to the newest autobiographical figure in the cycle, Ruth Larsen, who has taken the Christian last name of her husband Joe, Grace's Jewish women exhibit not only an acceptance of, but a romantic interest in, *goyim*.

In her poetry, which she has always acknowledged as being closer to the bone than her stories are, Grace has explicitly depicted herself as one who suffers because she has forgotten Jerusalem and has coupled with a Gentile.[5] "Even my lover, a Christian with pale eyes and the barbarian's foreskin/has left me," the speaker realizes in "A Warning" (LF, 24). The speaker in another poem, untitled,

Grace Paley with her children, Danny Paley and Nora Paley, probably in the park in the Village, circa 1952.

Grace Paley at a conference in New York City, 1974. (Photo by Dorothy Marder)

Grace Paley marching with Allen Ginsberg, Vera B. Williams, and the Bread and Puppet Theater in New York City, 1979. (Photo by Dorothy Marder)

Grace Paley at the Women and Life on Earth Conference, Amherst, Massachusetts, 1980. (Photo by Dorothy Marder)

Grace Paley at the Women's Pentagon Action, 1980. (Photo by Dorothy Marder)

Grace Paley at a Wall Street demonstration, 1984. (Photo by
Dorothy Marder)

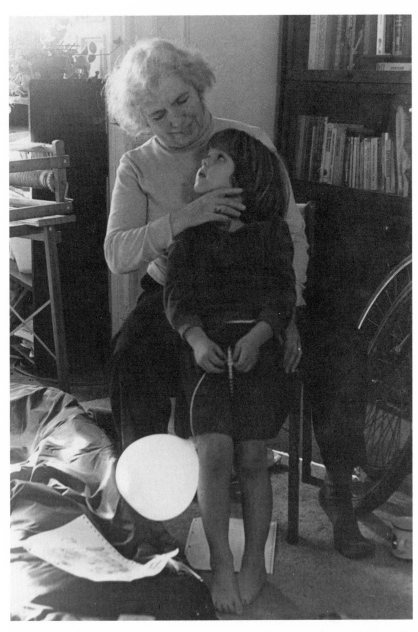

Grace Paley with her granddaughter, Laura Paley, at Laura's home in Brooklyn Heights, circa 1986–87.

Grace Paley and Bob Nichols, her husband, in their Vermont garden, circa 1987.

Grace Paley explaining her position against the Gulf War at a press conference in 1991. (Photo by Linda Eber)

admits that she "cannot keep [her] mind on Jerusalem" and wonders what will happen "when the Lord/remembers vengeance/(which is his)/and finds me" (LF, 43).

Though her sexual and romantic interest in the Christian "other" might be construed as similar to that lust for "blondies" we find so often in fiction by Jewish men, it is also based in her lifelong, laissez faire acceptance of whatever her companions may be and especially her desire for an ongoing cultural, ethnic, and racial mixing and blending of peoples. Grace Paley has been mining that symbolic vein in her stories and has worked into it the related issues of difference, otherness, and, especially, Jewishness. Thinking globally is not an axiomatic exercise for Grace; she understands the world in ecological terms, as one entity made up of inextricably related and interdependent, though variously exploitive and supportive, elements. Her stories repeatedly present both metaphoric and actual racial blends and mixtures.

On the metaphoric level, she offers cultural exchanges, like the ones that occur in "The Long-Distance Runner," when white Faith returns to her old Jewish neighborhood and stays in her family's apartment with Black Mrs. Luddy—in what has now become a Black neighborhood—for three weeks (ECLM); in "Enormous Changes," when the middle-aged Jewish social worker, Alexandra, has an affair with—and a baby by—a young non-Jew, Dennis the cabdriver, who shuttles back and forth from his commune to his rock band and her bed (ECLM);[6] in "The Expensive Moment," when Xie Feng comes from China and visits Faith at home (LSD), and in "Listening," when straight Faith is confronted by lesbian Cassie (LSD).

She has also written stories in which skin color per se figures as a major theme or issue. Babies who are born to parents of different colors, or are being raised by a mother whose skin doesn't match theirs, are found in at least four stories, and in each the babies bring satisfaction, pleasure, contentment, and higher consciousness to the adults around them.[7] In "Northeast Playground," first published in 1967, one of the characters is Leni, a young, white, Jewish street whore whose baby, acquired from a john in payment of a debt, is "dark brown" (ECLM, 146). Becoming Claude's mother has pulled Leni off the streets and into the playground, where she is more than happy to raise her son on Aid to Dependent Children.

"At That Time, or The History of a Joke," first published in

1981, offers a young woman who receives "a uterine transplant" and "almost immediately" begins "to swell, for in the soft red warm interior of her womb, there was already a darling rolled-up fetus" (LSD, 93–94). When the child is "unfurled," it is revealed to be "as black as the night which rests our day-worn eyes" (LSD, 94). This would hardly be notable if the young woman were not white.[8] The child is hailed as a messiah, "a virgin born of a virgin," and her birth is a sign of goodness, even redemption, for much of humanity: "Throughout the world, people smiled" (95). (The narrator is careful to note, however, that "certain Jews who had observed and suffered the consequence of other virgin births" are less than delighted with the symbolic value of this baby.)

"Ruthy and Edie" was first published in *Heresies* in 1980 but was lengthened to include this theme by the time it appeared in *Later the Same Day* in 1985. Sara, the daughter of Ruth (who is probably Jewish and is married to Joe Larsen, who is probably not), is married to Tomas, whose name suggests that he is Latino. Letty, their daughter, is her grandma's darling. The child Letty embodies two aspects of this theme. She not only is a child of her parents' own rainbow coalition—and thus represents hope for an end to racism—but, as a little child in need of both freedom and safety to grow up, also represents the urgent necessity for adults to protect the world for her, for the future of humankind: "Letty began to squirm out of Ruth's arms. Mommy, she called, Gramma is squeezing. But it seemed to Ruth that she'd better hold her even closer, because, though no one else seemed to notice—Letty, rosy and soft-cheeked as ever, was falling, already falling . . . onto the hard floor of man-made time" (LSD, 126).

In "Zagrowsky Tells," published singly in *Mother Jones* (as "Telling") in 1985 and collected in *Later the Same Day* the same year, Grace presents Emmanuel, the five-year-old son of white Cissy Zagrowsky and a Black gardener who worked at the mental hospital in which she has been a patient. Emmanuel, in whom the suggestions of Claude's, Letty's, and the unnamed baby girl's situation are developed fully, is "a little boy brown like a coffee bean," a "brown baby. An intermediate color," his grandfather says, just a little lighter than "a chocolate popsicle" (LSD, 159, 170, 173). His name—insisted upon hysterically by his mother—means Messiah in Hebrew, and he is indeed the harbinger and catalyst for Izzy Zagrowsky, whose garden-variety racism has receded considerably since his grandson's birth.

Emmanuel is a material result of his mother's institutionalization, but he also serves to heal the grief and misery in his family, embodying a bond that holds the generations together. The baby's name, his situation, and his grandfather's commentary on his life and character all emphasize this theme and its positive values. Grace began to work with the theme in the mid-sixties, when she moved further out of her neighborhood and often worked closely with many different kinds of people—including Bob Nichols—creating a cultural exchange of her own.

Bob remembers moving into the Eleventh Street apartment with Grace in 1969; he had been separated from Mary and living in his office since 1966. Once they became a couple, Grace began to go up to Vermont with him for the summers. There was no New England idyll for the radical writer-lovers; rather, a typically gendered arrangement evolved between them. The first time Grace went, Bob's young daughter Liza came to stay with him—and when Bob didn't take up the necessary mothering, Grace did. She took the child swimming every few days, arranged to meet some women with children Liza's age, and slid back into the role she had just been growing out of. Writing stories, organizing against the draft and the war, involved in a serious love affair, her own children nearly out of the nest, Grace had "really [been] looking forward to the next few summers alone" with Bob, but she found that her life remained as complicated in the country as it ever had been in the city.

Both of them tell stories about Grace patiently brushing the summer tangles out of Liza's long hair every day, pulling the brambles out one at a time. Bob remembers the scene with sweetness and nostalgia, gratified at the warmth between his child and his lover; Grace remembers it as a reluctant but deliberate resumption of mothering. Certainly it must have been necessary for Grace and Liza to come together as friends in Bob's house. Grace, a newly single, sixties woman was moved by old patterns, nurturant compassion, and good sense. She may have thought—even then—that she would marry Bob Nichols.

Danny Paley recalls that he and his wife Debbie were the only other people present at Grace and Bob's wedding. Debbie and

Danny may actually have provided a contemporary version of her friends' influence in 1942: the young couple had just gotten married themselves in October of 1972.[9] They happened to be present when Grace and Bob, after some conversation about whether or not to marry, decided "to just get it over with." The newlyweds accompanied them, as Danny recalls, to the appropriate civic offices, but the line of waiting couples was long; neither Grace nor Bob was willing to stand in line. Bob said, "Well, forget it then, forget the whole thing." She agreed: "All right, forget it. I don't care anyway." But they were both visibly upset. Though they had been casual about the decision, the snag in the timing became a snag in the feeling; even though they had been determined not to acknowledge its importance, this wedding was—after all—major business.

Then "someone," Danny says, suggested going over to Judson Church on Fourth Street, one of the Village gathering places for activists, to ask Al Carmines, the pastor, to marry them. Al Carmines was a composer—he had done the music for one of Gertrude Stein's New York productions—and a peace activist, but he was also an ordained minister, though Danny thinks he probably hadn't made a wedding in twenty years: "We went over there and he just did it on the spur of the moment as a favor to them." This odd little church wedding, with its renegade pastor officiating, took place on November 26, 1972, just a few weeks before the bride and groom left to spend two months in Chile.

Grace says that she and Bob got married because of historical circumstance; in "my generation," she says, "that's what we do." Besides, "[we] were traveling around together, we were together all the time. So we thought we should [get married], and we did. And the truth is that then we forgot to change our passports anyway" when they went to Chile at the end of the year. Sybil Claiborne asserts that the timing of Grace's decision to marry was circumstantial: "She might have felt differently ten years later. But at that time people were marrying each other."

Actually, despite the line of waiting couples, this is not exactly the case. At that time—early in the seventies—people were divorcing each other, in greater and greater numbers. Grace and Sybil seem to believe that the decision to marry was almost no decision at all, that the Paley/Nichols marriage was bound to happen—a cultural accident; but in such thinking they are rejecting the histori-

cally left/bohemian call to "free love" that echoes back beyond
Emma Goldman in favor of the bourgeois standards adopted by the
immigrant Goodsides. Both women are speaking in the present, out
of considerably different standards—born of their feminist activism
of the past fifteen years—than they would have had in 1972.

It is, then, interesting to see that Faith's second marriage, to
Jack, is hard to find in the texts of the stories. She might be
married to him in one story and might be living with him in
another; in others, she might not be either, but he's still near the
center of her life. The ephemerality of Faith's marriage in the fiction
is a good reflection of the vagueness, and certainly the unorthodox
arrangement—maybe even some embarrassed denial—of Grace's
own marriage.

Jeanne Tenenbaum saw her sister's marriage as an old-fashioned
love match and imagines no problems stemming from the couple's
differing backgrounds and ethnicity. Nora Paley too makes little of
Bob Nichols's being a Christian and a monied New Englander. She
says she never thought of Bob as being particularly different from
Grace, because he was, after all, "a guy from the Village, one of the
people around." He was a poet, and Nora had known him for years;
if she had thought of him as a New Englander, she might have
considered him an outsider, but that was never his identity. She
says that Bob, in doing street theater, writing plays for one of the
local churches, and doing a lot of antiwar work, was simply one of
the Village family. Danny also saw him this way, acknowledging
that Bob is indeed different from Grace in terms of ethnic, cultural,
and religious heritage but insisting that he is "really in a lot of ways
very much like her," because "he comes from the same kind of
Village bohemian fifties New York City background—and they've
really got a lot in common in their politics."

They have also got a lot in common in their eccentricity of
personal style and the impact of their physical presence—which is
considerable. Grace has cut off her long hair, which she used to
twist round the crown of her head as it grew grayer and grayer.
Now the visual drama of her appearance is supplied by a small cloud
of silvery white waves and wisps that emphasize her wide rosy face
and dark shining eyes. Like her mother, she is a short, round,
buxom woman; her big smile remains slightly cockeyed because of
uneven front teeth, but it is—really—dazzling. She always wears

sensible clothes, but in surprising colors or with earrings and scarves that provide the pleasure of color and light. She chews gum—and snaps it—when she makes speeches and reads her stories aloud to audiences. She writes at a board table, seated on a wooden chair with a small pillow on it; her electric typewriter is a concession to the end of the twentieth century, but no computer will replace it on those boards.

Despite all those years in the city, Bob looks as if Norman Rockwell had been commissioned to invent him: the Vermont man. He wears thick heavy boots, scruffy pants, plaid flannel shirts, and hooded sweatshirts. His face is ruddy and seamed; his hands are rough and cracked, knobbed like pine branches. His eyebrows, crowning supraorbital ridges like cliffs, are wild, tangled black and white in contrast to his absolutely white hair and beard. He makes no small talk, but he engages in big talk about politics or books and enjoys argument as exercise. He gets up every morning at five to write in his upstairs room, with its long, high window facing Grace's garden and the White Mountains across the valley. Though he doesn't farm the land around his house, Bob does raise some sheep; their social behavior, he explains, is just what everybody says—even outside of metaphor.

When they left for Chile with their passports unchanged at the end of 1972, they were energetic and hopeful, excited by the prospect of visiting a socialist country working to educate, feed, and rebuild itself. Their two-month visit, spent with no prescience of Allende's impending death and the militarization of Chile, encouraged them enormously. They stayed for six weeks at a student boardinghouse and attended socialist party meetings; they met people who spoke freely to them—truck drivers, newsvendors, people in the cafés and on the roads—telling them about their lives, before and since the coming of socialism. They traveled around the countryside and read about the internal politics of the revolution in fourteen different newspapers they were delighted to find in the capital. By no means an accomplished workers' paradise, Allende's Chile was in conscientious struggle with its own revolution; Grace and Bob brought back with them a strengthened belief in the possibilities for personal and social change they saw there.

When they returned, they published a series of articles called "Chilean Diary" in the War Resisters League journal, *WIN*. Appearing over both their names, the series was actually written in the first person by Bob, after he and Grace had discussed and wrangled over their memories, judgments, and decisions about what should be reported. The style of the series is identifiably Bob Nichols's; in diction, syntax, and point of view, it is much like the quartet of politically and stylistically visionary short novels he published at the end of the seventies.[10]

In the series, the narrator is "I" and, rarely, "we"; Grace is cited by name once in the text. Her presence is otherwise distinguished from Bob's by a classical division: as they appear here, her interests and his are predictably gendered. Bob's narrating voice establishes itself as masculine immediately, early in the first installment of the series; describing the well-dressed crowds of people in Santiago's modern central district, he says, "The women are all in miniskirts and look absolutely wonderful" (6). This remark is exactly the sort Grace criticized in "Midrash," written in 1983–84: Faith had "democratically *tried* walking in the beloved city with a man, but the effort had failed since . . . he had felt an obligation, if a young woman passed, to turn abstractedly away, in the middle of the most personal conversation or even to say confidentially, wasn't she something?—or clasping his plaid shirt, at the heart's level, oh my god!" (152).

A different sort of comment about women (and children) might well have been prompted by Grace's interests, like descriptions of young Gypsy beggars in the city and women's relationships with men in the countryside, while other passages are probably born of Bob's special interests, which include agriculture, the technology of energy, and locally based political structures. We cannot, however, be absolutely certain who noticed or commented on what. For instance, the comparison of Chilean peasant landholdings with those of the North Vietnamese in the second installment of the series might well have been made by Grace (11). What we can see, though, is that when the narrator is plural or when Grace is named, the subject is women or family life, as in the third installment, when she is absorbed in conversation with a Quillota mother and daughter (10).

Despite these effects of gender socialization, this couple is one in which the wife is often given public precedence over the husband. Grace and Bob, from the beginning of their relationship, have had to deal with the consequences of her growing reputation outside the neighborhood. Whatever effects her fame had on Jess Paley and on that first marriage, Bob and this second marriage were new when Grace was already on the way to becoming GRACE PALEY. So, though Bob did all the writing and much of the reporting for this series, Grace's reputation—even in *WIN*, where, presumably, the two writers were equally valued—dictated an inequity of credits. The blurb accompanying the first installment of the series reads, "Grace Paley is a widely known author of short stories and *WIN* articles. She teaches at Sarah Lawrence College and is active with the Greenwich Village Peace Center, Resist, the WRL, and other groups. She is married to Robert Nichols, who is a well known landscape architect, playwright and pacifist activist" (6).

By 1979, when Grace was featured in a photo essay in *People* magazine, Bob was accurately described as "a landscape architect and author" (22) and even noted for having "once protested the Vietnam war with a two-week fast" (23), but he is quoted as saying, with what must have been multilayered irony, "I'm here to take her phone calls and see that she gets dressed" (23). Granted, *People* had an interest in trivializing them and making Grace look cute—not dangerous—when they featured one of her major arrests of the decade. But this disparity is in fact a problem for them, as it is for other couples whose careers bring public recognition to one but not the other.[11]

After Allende's government was struck down, Bob wrote "Chilean Diary Revisited" in the first person plural. "Grace and I," he says, and "we." He mentions his wife when he refers to their trip or their earlier articles, but these are not writings in which Grace has taken part. This, and two more articles in which he analyzes the position of the left in Chile before the coup and discusses what may be learned from the Chilean experience, are thoroughly his own, as is the later series, "China Diary," which followed their 1974 trip.

Unlike Grace, Bob has always made progressive politics the obvious and intentional center of his fiction and much of his poetry, as well as his essays. In this period he encouraged her as she began to move the content of her political life into her fiction, where her consciousness was already in residence.[12] He had not read her stories before working with her in the Village Peace Center, but when he did, he asked about her second book and her plans for collecting the stories she had written since 1959. These questions, he says now, "were incomprehensible to her; she had very bad writing habits." She had no formal—or even informal—plans, though of course she was writing.

"At one point," at least, he thinks that he "did say to her—'you're doing a lot of politics, it's important to your life; better get some of these characters into your writing.'" Given his own experience, he had to say, too, that "'America dislikes it, but maybe you can find a way somehow.' Over fifteen years," Bob estimates, "this development [in her fiction] took place, to the extent that it came naturally," as all the elements of her life were integrated into the evolution of her story cycle. This was the period in which she wrote the new conclusion for "Faith in a Tree" and incorporated some of the slogans and images of the antiwar movement into her text.[13] Between 1971 and 1973—and especially in the fall of 1973, while in residence at Yaddo, the writer's colony in Saratoga Springs[14]—she also wrote "Enormous Changes," "The Immigrant Story," "The Little Girl," and "The Long-Distance Runner," all of which contain, and some of which focus on, specific socioeconomic and racial issues.

Isaac Goodside would not have approved of this development or the political aspect of art in general—his daughter's, his new son-in-law's, or even Pushkin's and Chekhov's. Nor would he have been inclined to even mention politics, except as an obstacle, in a discussion of literature.[15] Bob Nichols met Dr. Goodside in his last years, when Isaac had become, for his family, someone else. Bob liked and admired the old man and says that senile or not, Isaac was "very smart, very clever, and a very funny guy." But he understood that Isaac was not the slightest bit interested in him, the new man in Grace's life—not because he disapproved of Bob, or his politics, or the idea of his daughter *having* a new man, but because he simply wasn't interested. Isaac's own life was coming to an end, and Bob was just a bit player in the last act of that rich drama.

Isaac Goodside, like Mr. Darwin in the Faith stories, never saw his younger daughter enough in the war years; she was so busy all the time. Nonetheless, Grace and her father were close throughout his life; their bond remained strong. This was probably because she had been the baby of the family, certainly because Manya had died so early, and surely because—in their likeness—they continued to strike exciting sparks whenever they were together. Unlike the socialist Mr. Darwin, Isaac Goodside became very conservative in his later years and disapproved of his daughter's radical activities even more than he had in her youth.[16] He loved her no less of course—maybe even more for making their relationship so interesting and complicated—and always accepted her, but he expressed perpetual disapproval of her choices and regularly disagreed with her opinions, fighting with her at every visit until just before his death.

Everyone in the family believes, as Danny Paley explains, that his grandfather "was a very dominant figure" in her life and "had a profound effect" on Grace. Danny himself, like his sister Nora, always felt close to Isaac and corresponded regularly with his grandfather when he went to school outside of New York. The love between her children and her father pleased Grace enormously, and she gave it—so to speak—to Faith's son Richard and *his* grandpa in "Conversations." At the appearance of the contentious Richard (who is disgusted with his elders for the low level of their political activity), "his grandfather looked at him and nearly fainted with love. 'He looks wonderful, this boy,' he said. 'I like his hair long'" (15).

Isaac Goodside died in early 1973. When he retired from medicine in the forties because of his wife's death and his own dangerous heart condition, he thought he had only a few years left. By his mid-seventies, he had become an artist, painting portraits, still lifes, and landscapes, and he wrote stories and memoirs as well. In this new incarnation he lived another thirty years; he never had another heart attack, and he died quite peacefully.[17] In the last few years of his life, still living in the Bronx apartment his wife had died in, he had a stroke and became senile in what his grandson calls "a kind of wild way."

Becoming senile changed Isaac Goodside in what Danny Paley calls "unexpected ways," just as an accidental head injury to Alexandra's disapproving father in "Enormous Changes" made it possible for him to appreciate his daughter. The fictional old man "fell hard on the bathroom tiles, cracked his skull, dipped the wires of his brain into his heart's blood. Short circuit! He lost twenty years in the flood, the faces of nephews, in-laws, the names of two Presidents, and a war. His eyes were rounder, he was often awestruck, but he was as smart as ever, and able to begin again with fewer scruples to notice and appreciate" (ECLM, 134–35). Grace's father, the model for Alexandra's,[18] was rendered no longer conservative; he had gone back in his mind to the early days of the Russian revolution.

Nora remembers that her grandfather had "wild dreams" about the czar's children and that almost all his concerns after the stroke were about Russia. Even though he was senile and didn't recognize his grandchildren half the time, they enjoyed his company just as much at the end as they ever had. Nora says that the essential character of her grandfather was "still very much there, and I loved being around him. I was privileged to be with him in this time when he was in another dimension."

In those years, Dr. Goodside would walk with his cane but often forgot that he had been ill; his children hired a companion for him, but he would go out alone whenever he could get away. Jeanne says that he would bang the cane on the floor of the apartment or go to the door and try to get out. He would call out, "Let me out of this prison! Let me out of Siberia!" Then Jeanne, if she was present, would say to him, "Look, Pop," and show him the pictures he had painted—which would bring him back to the present. "Look, Pop, look at this painting. Do you remember you did this? Do you remember this one? (The whole house was full of his paintings.) And he'd say, 'Of course. I must be getting senile.' And he was."

When he could get out on his own, he would get on a bus and go somewhere, anywhere. He was in fine shape, an affable, intelligent old fellow who just happened to be talking about the czar of Russia. Jeanne says that he used his cane mostly for the visual effect and that he always wore a homburg and looked quite beautiful when he went out to stroll. His character and wit, his sense of humor, were such that strangers rarely suspected that there was anything "wrong" with him—and indeed, since he took on these adventures with great verve and strength, there apparently wasn't.

Once he disappeared completely, creating an indelible chapter in the family folklore. Everyone tells the story of how one day Dr. Goodside went out for a walk on his own and didn't come home. He was eventually picked up by the police, and when the family was finally contacted, he was in a rage because he had determined that the police were the czar's army, trying to impound him or press him into military service. When the family came to pick him up, he complained angrily that they had refused to give him any vodka.

Grace experienced a surge of writing in the fall of 1973 that was surely prompted by her father's death and her recollections of his life—which seem to have included a reassessment of her parents' marriage. She was, in terms of her slowly growing feminist consciousness, released by her father's death.

The collected stories, particularly when read in the order she designed for publication, display a deepening understanding of her relationship with her mother. Manya's long illness through the late thirties, her husband's dominance in the family, and especially her death when her younger daughter was not yet twenty-five had made it impossible for the two women to work through the welter of their complicated feelings. From 1975, when Grace first published "Mom" (her first story in which the narrative voice is clearly a mother's daughter's voice, woman-identified, as distinct from that of a father's daughter), to the present, the figure of the mother and the representation of mother-daughter relationships in her writing— especially when contrasted with her presentation of the father and father-daughter relationships—exhibit a definite pattern of change, reflecting a developing feminist consciousness.

In "Mom," she attacked what she recognized as "the mocking campaign" against mothers by male doctors and fiction writers; she gradually went on to make her mother/wives noticeably stronger and more seriously critical of (even well-loved) men. In the third story collection, published in 1985, the father-husband figure has been rendered far less sympathetically than he had been in Grace Paley's earlier stories. In "Dreamer in a Dead Language," Faith's father is associated with both her ex-husband, the irresponsible philanderer Ricardo, and her current lover, Philip, who is noticeably lacking in sensitivity. Mr. Darwin, still funny and smart but now a serious poet, has become arrogant, egotistical, tired of his wife, and utterly unable—as well as unwilling—to understand and respond to his daughter as the person she is.

In "In the Garden," the father of two kidnapped girls has made their return impossible by his arrogant response to kidnappers' demands. In "Lavinia: An Old Story," both Robert and Mr. Grimble are implicated as instrumental in their wives' failures to do useful work in the world. In "Friends," Selena's husband has dumped her for a younger woman, women's desire for and interest in men are defined—albeit jokingly—as symptoms of a disease, and women's longstanding friendships are ironically described as "at least" as important as their marriages to men. In "Anxiety," a young father is unable to see that his ego is more important to him than his little daughter's pleasure; he hurts her because his pride is wounded by her innocent silliness. In the strongly autobiographical "Mother," the author has created a portrait of her own parents' marriage: for the first time in her daughter's published writing, Manya's disappointment, her losses, and her worries are definitively fictionalized; both Grace and her father (who "appear" as the I-narrator and the husband) are sources of anxiety and sorrow for the mother in this story.

Not only are these men of the third story collection presented with less sympathy than their predecessors, but their wives, daughters, and lovers are less willing to put up with their failings and flaws than were Ginny, Anna, Rosie, and the rest in the first collection. The cynical skepticism of Dolly Raftery, Alexandra, and Mrs. Luddy in the second collection has developed into the repeated disappointments and acknowledged anger in Faith, Ruth, and their friends and neighbors. It is interesting to speculate about how these later stories developed in terms of the events of their author's family life (her father's death and her own divorce), political developments in the women's movement, and even the possibility that Grace deliberately waited to make them public.

While Grace Paley's stories reveal the political and creative release provided by her father's death, her poetry offers the grief, sorrow, and deep pleasure of her long years in loving struggle with him. After Isaac died, she wrote in "On Mother's Day":

> I am especially open to sadness and hilarity
> since my father died as a child
> one week ago in this his ninetieth year (LF, 34)

She has written of their relationship in various other poems as well. In one untitled poem, she alludes to the strong correspondence between her father and herself, that longtime identification between father and daughter:

> in my drowned father's empty pocket
> there were nine dollars and the salty sea

he said   I know you   my darling girl
you're the one that's me (LF, 41)

In two poems called "My Father at 85" and "My Father at 89,"
she traced the change in his consciousness from before the stroke to
after it. The first "quotes" him in four stanzas; he is passionately
addressing the political issues of the time, naming presidents Nixon
and Johnson, questioning the future of the United States. The
second, one brief stanza, also "quotes" him, but his focus is much
changed:

. . . . .he
asked us   children
don't you remember my dog Mars
who met me on the road
when I came home   lonesome
and singing   walking
from the Czar's prison (LF, 70)

Victor, Jeanne, and Grace could not remember the dog or the
road, never having seen them; but in October of that year, as a
delegate to the World Peace Congress in Moscow, Grace went to
Russia, spoke her father's language again, and felt some of what he
might have known there.

9

A Woman,
Young
and Old

By the middle of the seventies, her second book published, Grace Paley had undergone another series of major changes. Publishing sporadically over the fifteen years since her first collection had come out, she won a Guggenheim fellowship in 1961 and an award from the National Endowment for the Arts in 1966. Her teaching at Sarah Lawrence had provided entrée into a network of writing contemporaries, and her travels had introduced her to a global network of political colleagues. As an accomplished writer and a prominent activist, she had an international reputation in two spheres. Whether she wrote stories based in what she learned on the streets or was carried by her linguistic preoccupation into actions that were based in language, the two spheres were always combined in Grace Paley.

That combination was manifest when she traveled to the USSR. In the decades after World War II and before the recent political transformations in eastern Europe and the former Soviet Union, when U.S. citizens-in-the-street saw posters or heard speakers criticizing the policy of the United States, their frequent response was, "Go tell it to the Russians!"—or less civil words to that effect. After this had happened to Grace a certain number of times, she took their advice. At any rate, she took the opportunity when it came along. In October of 1973 Grace traveled to Moscow as a delegate to the World Peace Congress, representing the War Resisters League. This trip, sponsored by the League, was indeed business, but it provided certain extraordinary pleasures. Closest to her heart was the fact that Russia—not the USSR, but *Russia*—was "Mother Russia! Oh my country of my mother and father's childhood! Oh beloved land of my uncle Russya killed in 1904 while carrying the workers' flag! Oh country my own of storytellers translated in my ear! of mystics and idealists who sharpened my English tongue" ("Conversations in Moscow," 5).

With her father's recent death, all the immigrant family of her childhood was gone, and she was on pilgrimage to the homeland. Everywhere she went in Moscow, she heard the voices of her mother and aunts, saw the faces of her uncles. Every day, all day long, she heard murmurs and laughs and whole conversations in Russian, evoking her girlhood on Hoe Street in the Bronx. When she first arrived, she stood listening in the lobby of the Hotel Rossiya, with her "nose somewhat stuffed by sentimental remembrance of those dead speakers." Riding a bus "up Kalinin Prospekt," she saw "one lady looking like my mother" who "said of another lady who looked like my aunt, 'Listen to that one, she knows nothing, still, she teaches...'" ("Conversations in Moscow," 4).

Memory, stirred by language, was aroused in her; the past was suddenly present in the words, rhythm, and sound of her own childhood's talking: "Three times a day, in the dining room, my bones nearly melted. 'Please,' I said starting the days listening and answering, 'one egg only, but coffee now.' 'Oh of course my darling, my little one, only wait.' Day and night I received this tender somehow ironic address, full of diminutives, of words hardened by fierce consonants, from which the restrained vowel always managed to escape" ("Conversations in Moscow," 5). The wordswoman, the lover of language for its own sake, was surrounded by the sound of her birth tongue, the words that are roots in her life. This immersion in the past is curiously foreshadowed in two of the stories she completed before going to Russia, the last ones she wrote before collecting seventeen of them into *Enormous Changes at the Last Minute:* "The Immigrant Story," which is at least three stories, about turn-of-the-century immigrant families in the United States, and "The Long-Distance Runner," about the later fate of those immigrant Europeans and the African American families who came to walk the same streets. Both pieces focus on a people's way of talking—in both sound and sense—and on the importance of exchange in language: telling, listening, and retelling.

From another intimately experienced perspective, one that is far more contemporary than nostalgic, Grace was aware throughout the conference that, as a woman, she was in a minority among the delegates. In her long article, "Conversations in Moscow," she comments on the small number of women delegates from India and the Mideast and the greater number from African countries (10). When she describes meetings between Soviet dissidents and American activists, she includes descriptions of Yelena Sakharov and Angelina Galich talking about their grandchildren and whispering, contradicting, and interrupting each other and their men (7).

She acknowledges her own weakness of position and disposition. When she and Paul Mayer were both censured by their colleagues for their part in creating and presenting a leaflet criticizing both the USSR and its dissident intellectuals, "I was more contemptuously dealt with as a woman and a mere leaflet carrier" (6);[1] and when she was talking with the Russian intelligentsia, Paul Mayer suggested switching from Russian and English to a language in which he was fluent but she did not know—German—and she "foolishly defer[red] as is my habit" (7), and so lost much of the subsequent conversation.

None of these observations is unusual, since by this time radical white women's writing had begun to be published again by mainstream presses in the United States. Phyllis Chesler's *Women and Madness* and Shulamith Firestone's *The Dialectic of Sex* had already appeared, and Andrea Dworkin's *Woman Hating* was in the works.[2] But the deliberate inclusion of this kind of consideration in Grace Paley's writing is, like the beginnings of change found in her stories of this period, further evidence of her rising feminist consciousness. (She did, however, deploy at least one shot that qualifies as *argumentum ad feminam*—her slightly snide description of the angry women in her own delegation, whom she calls "American ladies" ["Conversations in Moscow," 6].)

The purpose of the Congress was, of course, to afford peace activists the opportunity to share ideas, learn strategies, and strengthen international networks. But Grace and Paul Mayer, who was one of several delegates from the Peoples Coalition for Peace and Justice, had taken on an additional task. They had, along with five other Americans,[3] created an independent statement to read and distribute in Moscow. The seven signers identified themselves in terms of their documented criticism of the U.S. government, condemned the Soviet government for silencing its people, and—in an unusual and surprising addition—called on known Soviet dissidents to join world protest against repressive and murderous actions by the Chilean and South Vietnamese, as well as the Soviet and U.S., governments. Some delegates immediately "corrected" or "excoriated" them, but many others approved ("Conversations in Moscow," 5). Notwithstanding that approval, Grace and Paul were both subject to harsh criticism in their own group; at least some of the angriest Americans—apparently forgetting the peacefulness of their mission—said they thought Grace should be shot, and Paul Mayer had to resign from his position as co-chairman of the American delegation.[4]

Grace and Paul had other extracurricular activities planned as well. They had arranged to meet with some of the dissidents whose critical voices they were encouraging. Paul had been working in Russia since April, planning the Congress, and had already met Aleksander Galich and Vladimir Maximov. In October, he and Grace, "welcomed [by the Russians] . . . with apples, sardines, tomatoes salted and unsalted, glasses of Georgian wine" ("Conversations in Moscow," 6), began a brief series of informal meetings with those two men and with Angelina Galich, Aleksander and Nellie Voronel, and Yelena and Andrei Sakharov.[5] They met, Grace writes, "in Moscow 70 years after my father and mother ran for their lives," in a home that was "in food, furniture, language, gesture—very like my own home in the East Bronx" ("Conversations in Moscow," 12). The Americans made their statement of urgent criticism, the Russians responded just as strongly, and so began a succession of mutual teachings and learnings, arguments and agreements, all offered and accepted in various languages—an exchange, one might say, also "very like" the sort that used to take place in the Goodsides' home in the East Bronx.

Grace writes about Russian Jews in her long essay "Conversations in Moscow" and notes that she "cannot write about the[ir] conversions"—a reference to the desperate attempts of post-Revolution Russian Jews to gain full status as citizens (8), their situation reminiscent of the *conversos* in medieval Spain. She cites her family's teachings about the role of the Russian church in fomenting Jew-hating (8), and she quotes a long, subtly anti-Jewish commentary as retold by Galich to "explain" the situation of Jews in the USSR (10). Galich, himself a Jew, had recently converted; this did not produce the desired effect, however—he was soon denied permission to emigrate (12).

More overt than her growing feminism, Grace's sense of her Jewishness is manifest in her essay about the Peace Congress. She records her delivery of an ironic commentary on repressive Soviet policies to Aleksei N. Stepunin, Secretary General of the Institute of Soviet American Relations who worked with her throughout the Congress, with this preface: "In the end I had to be true to my American creed which is to leave them laughing and to my Russian Jewish creed which is to leave them in a little pain at least" (11).

Unlike her trip to Vietnam, this venture provoked only positive responses from her family; maybe they too were responding to a pull on their roots. Jeanne says that she admired Grace for making the trip: "She had a lot of courage, that girl, I must say. A lot of courage." Danny, perhaps the most outspoken family critic of his mother's trip to Vietnam, was very proud of her. Unfortunately, some of Grace's extended family—including at least one longtime friend—did not share these views. When the trip was being planned, money was raised in the community, primarily by Karl Bissinger, to cover expenses for Grace and Maris Cakars, another delegate from the War Resisters League. The money naturally represented a pledge of support as well as plane tickets and hotel bills. When Karl called folks to ask for money, he didn't tell them that Grace would be distributing the controversial leaflet or that she was going to see the dissidents while in Russia: "I knew [that] on her agenda was [a plan] to break out of the regular thing and go see the dissidents. But you couldn't say that to anybody. You couldn't tell anybody that."

Given that situation, Karl says now, there were some people that he should not have asked, no matter how close they were to Grace. These were people who absolutely did not want to criticize or embarrass the Soviet Union, and at least one of these was a good friend of Grace who became "very angry, very aggravated"; she felt "betrayed," Karl says, because Grace "had taken some of her dough and gone and criticized" the Soviet Union. "And she didn't talk to [Grace] for a long long time," Karl says, feeling heavily responsible for the situation himself. He feels that his judgment was off in this case—that he should have known who to ask and who to skip over.

This episode—or the skeleton of it—is the basis for the central incident in "Love," written through the mid-seventies and first published in the *New Yorker* in 1979. Faith, who narrates the story, tells her husband Jack about an encounter she had on the street: "Suddenly my . . . eyes saw a fine-looking woman named Margaret, who hadn't spoken to me in two years. We'd had many years of political agreement before some matters relating to the Soviet Union separated us. In the angry months during which we were both right in many ways, she took away with her to her political position and daily friendship my own best friend, Louise—my life-long park, P.T.A. and anti-war movement sister, Louise" (LSD, 6–7).

This instance, one of the thousands in which we can specifically locate the use of fact in fiction, is a good example of the dynamic, integral relationship between "the life" and "the work." A story is not—cannot be—simply a replay of a "real" incident; after all, writers and readers cannot even agree on, much less replicate, *exactly* what happens or is. Writers make texts; the life thus produces the work. But then the work produces the life. Grace Paley's stories incorporate life, transform it, and then the stories, once written, rebound to transform her. As ideas and drafts, thought and written, they are known to the writer; as texts, printed words on paper, they are known to others, received by an audience that in turn acts on the writer.

Certainly the two women Faith calls "Margaret" and "Louise" saw themselves in the text and understood "Love." Karl, who knows both women, is witness to the fact that they recognized themselves. Whether they threw up their hands, dropped their copies of the *New Yorker*, and rushed to the phone to forgive Grace and speak to her with "Love" is not precisely the point. Whether the three women have ever spoken of this to each other or not, all have been changed by knowing that Grace wrote the story and by having read it; now they all must have even more complex feelings about those "matters relating to the Soviet Union" *because of this story*. Grace Paley, who makes art out of her life, has subsequently and repeatedly experienced her life as it was made out of that art. Oscar Wilde said that life imitates art, in a deliberate turnaround of the classical concept of mimesis, but imitation is not what is at issue here; the ongoing, organic process by which life and art are in constant relation—in a constant mutually influenced reflexive dynamic—is the point.

The specific effect of any one story is not the only way in which "the work" affects "the life." One of the most obvious changes Grace Paley experienced as a result of the publication of her stories was that by 1974, when Farrar, Straus and Giroux brought out her second collection, she had become not only a writer but a literary figure.[6] Despite her initial hesitation and fear, she accepted that appellation; it was, by 1974, a self-definition. She had, in her alienation from the literary establishment—both deliberate and by default—"sought for her form somewhere else," as Jane Cooper says, and she had found it. Now Grace wanted to be a writer among writers; she had had no writing community for almost thirty years.

In the Western tradition of letters, noted in the writing of scholars and critics, there is a false image of the lone writer as the clichéd poet starving in his small bleak room—in the United States this may be construed as the literary version of the lone wolf—passionately bleeding his ink into lyric. The writer in the image is male, solitary, an idealistic aesthete, frenzied with the burden of his gift—and so on. Though this scene has only rarely been enacted by canonized men of letters, patriarchal culture has always imposed a harsh measure of loneliness on its women writers.

Though most Western women writers have (literally) written on tables in the parlor or kitchen and most have been—like the majority of their nonwriting sisters—mothers, the few who have been canonized are those who come closest to the romantic male ideal. That is, most of these have not been women engaged in raising children and, even if they have lived with family, were in relatively isolated circumstances (like Emily Dickinson and Emily Brontë), or lived with a single companion, had servants, and moved among the social, intellectual, and aesthetic brahmins of their time and place (like Gertrude Stein and Virginia Woolf). When women writers *have* been able to realize professional community, to meet or correspond, they are—like their male peers—inevitably enriched and inspired.

Grace Paley's self-defined and self-imposed isolation as a writer is neither precisely nor exclusively the matter of personal taste she insists on calling it. Jane Cooper, considering Grace's finally coming in from the cold, speaks of all artists' self-doubt and specifically of women's difficulty in saying " 'I'm a writer. Yes, that's what I do; I write.' There's a great deal of difficulty naming that, saying that, and taking responsibility for whatever it means to say that to other people. But," Jane adds, very gently, softly—and accurately—"I don't think you find that so much with men, denying that they are writers."

Grace was not peculiar in her hesitation; whatever her individual reasons for shunning the literary establishment—the politics of elitism, critical emphasis on form, arguments about the importance of sociopolitical relevance, not to mention such treatment as Norman Mailer offered when her first book came out—she falls well within the recognized range of women writers as outsiders, as delineated and analyzed by, for instance, Joanna Russ and Tillie Olsen. Historically, few women have been able to define themselves as artists or writers, and fewer still have been able to sustain that definition and turn it into reputation, as Virginia Woolf explained in *A Room of One's Own* in Britain in 1929—and as scores of feminist critics and scholars continue to explain in the United States in the 1980s and 1990s. Grace Paley did not go so far as to change her name to George, but in the fifties she did send out stories signed G. Goodside and G. Paley, hoping to "at least get in the door" that way.

Though she never spoke of this in her earlier, pre-feminist, days, Grace always understood she would have an uphill battle as a woman and as a writer of short stories. She turned away from poetry and then, once she had published fiction, rejected the privileged form of the novel. Grace says that her attempt to write a novel in the seventies was "a mistake" and that she never should have let herself "get talked into it." That pressure was a result of the longstanding belief—in both aesthetic and academic circles in the United States—that the short story is an inferior genre, meant only to serve as an exercise for serious writers on their way to the big book, the novel.

As with her fortunate timing in terms of the market and audience for women's work, Grace's timing was serendipitous here too. Not only did she realize that the novel form was wrong for her (thus far in her development[7]), but also the reputation of short fiction had begun to rise by the end of the sixties. American publishers realized that people were buying collections of short stories, and critics began to see that virtuoso work was being done—as it had been for some time—within the genre.

The short story genre has been embattled from its beginnings, usually marked in the United States by Washington Irving's tales from the early 1800s.[8] By the turn of the nineteenth century, only a few critics in the United States took it seriously, though American writers had embraced the form. Their enthusiasm may have been rooted in the fact that the storytelling tradition is honored in all of the various racial and ethnic backgrounds of this patchwork society. Indeed, this equality of access may be the reason critics labeled the form "minor," but the attention of scholars did begin to increase.[9] Rigid formality (i.e., "the well-made story") was considered crucial—perhaps to gain credibility—and scholars' prescriptive definitions stood side by side with their reluctant recognition of the great variety among stories. Everyone admitted that, unfortunately, the sketch, the tale, the short story, the novel, the novella, and the romance all overlapped at their boundaries of definition. In fact, the form has always stimulated experimentation, innovation, and variety. The line from Washington Irving to Grace Paley would hardly be straight as the crow flies.

In the modern period, specifically in the decade after World War I, narrative time sequence, cause and effect, motive and act, intention and consequence, and the relationship of the individual to society and its various cultural myths all changed, as Virginia Woolf chronicled in *A Room of One's Own*. The forms of experience had been altered, so fiction altered too. Critics realized that writers had to discover new ways of writing to suit new ways of being, and they eventually endorsed the burgeoning variety they had found so disturbing.

In 1933, when Grace Goodside was eleven years old and just about to leave off being a darling prodigy, the Oxford English Dictionary Supplement finally introduced the term *short story* as a designation of literary form, thus conferring the term's admission to international literary vocabulary in English. Those critics who favored the genre were emboldened and grew expansive; they began to write about the relationships among the short story, cinema, and photography—all rapidly rising art forms—claiming that short fiction was a visual, fluid form, cut loose from the weight of the novel. They not only dared to suggest such alliances with new, quickly developing arts, but also claimed music, painting, sculpture, and poetry as analogues to and sources for the short story genre.

By 1950, just as Grace Paley was on the verge of writing her stories, American critics had begun to divide story writers into two broad categories: those who (basically) maintained the traditional form and those who (mostly) experimented with it. Plotting does not occur in real life, the more radical critics and writers said; things just happen, and we move along by fits and starts, not on an Aristotelian track. Writers began to write stories that approximated or represented that allegedly more realistic movement through time and space—or created utterly fantastic movement—abandoning or altering chronology and jettisoning clear-cut characterization as well. A few lines, an image or two, would suffice for a character by the mid-sixties—no more details of dress and body were necessary. Plot was pronounced old-fashioned and relegated to ancient history, along with Edgar Allan Poe and O. Henry.

American stories in the second half of the twentieth century are born of the antiplot movement and raised in sociopolitical disillusion. In a sense, all short fiction since World War II is politically motivated, consciously social in content; writers can no longer pretend their characters and events exist separate from the horror of contemporary life.[10] Correspondingly, postmodern short story writers have done away with both denouement and resolution; their conflicts are no longer reconciled. Stories go on, beyond the words on the printed page; characters continue their lives. Readers are let into some few episodes in those lives and then let out again. For decades, readers had been trained to expect endings that would tell us what stories are "about"—even Henry James usually did us that favor. Modern stories too were more or less closed. But now the open ending is standard, and we are forced to accept ambiguity and possibility in short fiction, as in the other arts.[11]

Grace Paley is a master of the swinging door that lets us in and shows us out of her character's lives. Reading her cycle, entering her characters' neighborhood, we may go in and out several times in one volume. Her work is not so fragmented as Donald Barthelme's or so blatantly self-conscious as John Barth's; she is a technical innovator who is comparable both to them and to the modernists Edith Wharton and Sherwood Anderson. Her kinship with earlier, fundamentally moral, canonical writers like Joseph Conrad or even Charlotte Brontë is not mitigated by her similarities to her contemporaries.

In "A Conversation with My Father," first published in 1971, which is perhaps the most overtly metafictional—and certainly the most analyzed—of all Paley stories and which she readily acknowledges is autobiographical, the narrator takes a theoretical, philosophical antiplot position. The father asks his daughter the narrator to "write a simple story"—which she construes to be "the kind that begins: 'There was a woman . . . ' followed by plot, the absolute line between two points which I've always despised" (ECLM, 161–62). Actually, Grace Paley insists that *she* does not despise plot and quite naturally, of necessity, uses some whenever she writes a story. Things do happen in her stories, but since those things rarely happen by moving from A to B to C, and since she dislikes transitions and avoids natural chronological order, her texts, like Robert Altman's sound tracks, offer us contemporary naturalism. That is, sometimes they are more like life than they are like the traditional literature/cinema we have been schooled to recognize.

Moreover, as the narrator explains, her aversion to plot is not "for literary reasons, but because it takes all hope away. Everyone, real or invented, deserves the open destiny of life" (ECLM, 162). Her motive is social—indeed, political. In that same story, the narrator goes on to espouse the open-ended text and to relate that choice to social circumstance: "I had to say, 'Well, it is not necessarily the end, Pa. . . . It doesn't have to be. . . . it's a funny world nowadays'" (ECLM, 166–67). The last phrase is essential Paley; it points to her reason for choosing the open-ended structure. She seeks a form that will accommodate personal and social change, both evolutionary ("later the same day") and revolutionary ("enormous changes at the last minute"). Though she loves language, plays words like music, and might be described as making metaphor like a verbal sculptor, she is essentially about the business of meaning; a writer who believes that art should offer truth and serve justice, she is not interested in structural design for its own sake.

Like many of her late-twentieth-century colleagues, Grace Paley is not interested in symbolism either; she wants only to say what she is saying, just one thing at a time. That one thing may be complicated and important and may reverberate throughout her story cycle, but it is itself only—it does not stand for something else. Likewise, linear narrative is less and less prominent in her stories over the past thirty-five years; readers' responses and perceptions tend to be diffused throughout the stories, rarely epiphanic. This is not to say that the texts are utterly realistic; her stories have always had at least a hint of the unreal and fantastic about them (which is one of the father's complaints in "A Conversation with My Father"). Is Faith really up in a tree? Are her two husbands really there together at breakfast? Did Eddie really believe that Itzik was his half-brother, and could the cockroach segregator really have worked? The surrealism—maybe even cubism—of "The Floating Truth" and the bittersweet fantasy of "At That Time, or The History of a Joke" belie the possibilities of realism, but they never attempt allegory.

With the publication of the second story collection, Grace Paley took her place among postmodern American fiction writers, just when her position as a political figure was becoming more and more a part of her culturally defined—and widely known—persona. Grace's commitment to a conscious politics of art places her work outside of current theoretical definitions. Isolation, anomie, and alienation are the antithesis of Grace Paley's characters' situation; their location within both her story cycle and their neighborhood emphasizes the complex interconnectedness of their lives. Many postmodern characters are awash in a self-consciousness that denies connection to—or even the existence of—the material world. Grace Paley's characters, however, never leave the material world; if anything, they bring their self-consciousness to it. This is the Paley stance: her stories are designed to meet the commitments of consciousness, the need, especially in contemporary society in the United States, to locate and anchor the self in urban chaos.

Grace Paley lives in social criticism; she keeps it on the surface of her life—and on the surface of her stories. More and more often, her characters talk about the front-page issues of daily life. Children are kidnapped. They go mad. They are raped. They become addicts and die far away from home. Marriage is forever fractured, despite heterosexual attempts at love and romance. Friendship is a source of sustenance, nurturance, inspiration—and sometimes pain—for women. Motherhood is still basic in most women's lives; the patriarchal nuclear family, though, is under fire from all sides. War is constant. The purchase of food is an issue. The drinking water is an issue. Abortion is an issue.

Many contemporary short fiction writers practice the newly

celebrated art of interruption, by suddenly appearing in the middle of their own paragraphs, calling attention to the artifice—the createdness—of literature. Grace Paley, in contrast, opens up the act of storytelling, revealing her manipulation of language, but—like the master magicians Penn and Teller when they "reveal" the mechanics of their tricks while stupefying audiences by performing those very tricks—she has integrated that manipulation so that her narratives are both story and voice. No intrusive external consciousness or voice "interrupts" her narration, for the voice is always present. Her stories present the illusion that the teller is the tale, the illusion that the tale is, in effect, autobiography.[12]

Annie Dillard has made an argument that bears interestingly upon Grace Paley's work in her discussion of "the very short story," which is sometimes called "the 'prose piece' "; Dillard prefers to call these "short prose objects." Grace Paley has written many such pieces[13] and has found that some readers, unwilling to perceive and judge them as anything but short fiction manqué, simply dismiss them as unfinished, incomplete. Dillard, however, recognizes the form and comments that "fiction in this century has been moving closer to poetry in every decade"; she considers "the very short story" evidence of that movement.

When Dillard asserts that poets write the best "short prose objects," we recall that Grace herself wrote only poetry until around the age of thirty—but the critic insists that the "intentions" of such works "can only be aesthetic," for "no sentimentality of subject matter interferes with their formal development" (114–15). She argues that the form is almost wholly concerned with technique, despite its occasional references "to the world" (114–15). Notwithstanding that critical pronouncement about "the very short story" form, Grace Paley's "Mother," written in the late seventies and published in 1980, is both a renegade and a fine example of the subgenre; it has a complicated three-part skeleton and three basic structural elements which turn on a hinge, a pivotal paragraph in the center of the story. Though we would hardly call it sentimental in the old pejorative sense of the term, it is absolutely concerned with sentiment, with feeling; moreover, it is strongly autobiographical and is about emotion—the narrator's longing to see the dead mother, the love and pain flowing between the narrator and the mother, and the thwarted tenderness between the mother and father.

Annie Dillard also—perhaps contradicting herself—insists, "Fiction keeps its audience by retaining the world as its subject matter. People like the world. Many people actually prefer it to art and spend their days by choice in the thick of it" (78). Here she sounds very much like Grace Paley, but when she asks, in her discussion of students, critics, and writing, "who is writing fiction these days who has not been to college?" (94), we see that the space between Annie Dillard and Grace Paley is a gulf.

Nevertheless, Dillard again approaches Paley when she designates what she calls the "crank narrator" in contemporary fiction: "a prose style so intimate, and so often used in the first person, that it is actually a voice." This voice is "a character outside bourgeois European culture; so is its creator. These writers either derive from peripheral countries, or are Jewish, or émigré, or are in some other way denied access to mainstream European culture" (108–9). Her choice not to name writers who are women and/or not white does not exclude them from her last phrase; the omission only makes that choice—like the concept of *peripheral countries*—come screaming off the page. She has here, in her delicately retrograde style, usefully described Grace Paley's narrators.

Though Dillard unfortunately eschews overt expression of the political conclusions her analysis calls for, she does finally decide that artists are among the proper interpreters of the world, and she suggests that sentences of plain prose exist to refer to the world (146). That world is with us in the plain prose of Grace Paley's stories. In "Ruthy and Edie," Ruthy's wish on the candles of her fiftieth birthday cake is "that this world wouldn't end. This world, this world, Ruth said softly" (LSD, 124), whispering the chorus of Malvina Reynolds's "Love It Like A Fool."

In "Friends," when Tonto accuses his mother of optimism ("Next thing, you'll say . . . the world is *so* nice and round that Union Carbide will never blow it up."), Faith first asks why, to the unhappiness caused by her friend Selena's death, "did Tonto at 3 a.m. have to add the fact of the world?" (LSD, 88). Tonto's "world," she says, "poor, dense, defenseless thing—rolls round and round. Living and dying are fastened to its surface and stuffed into its softer parts. He was right to call my attention to its suffering and danger. He was right to harass my responsible nature" (LSD, 89). Faith insists that considerations of the world must always include the "private" facts of people's individual lives. This is the dynamic synthesis of Grace Paley's fiction as it has evolved within the conflicting aesthetics and politics of the postmodern era.

Grace Paley's fiction is like that of many other women writing fiction in English now in that she is translating her life—"the world"—into her stories. What Maxine Hong Kingston calls "talking-story" is what Grace Paley does in her work. These writers are willing to dissolve right through the usual boundaries of time, space, and fictional speaker. The marginalization of women and nondominant ethnic and racial groups explains autobiography in the fiction of these people. Since Western critics historically recognized all white Christian male work in English as the norm, they did not consider its fiction to be autobiographical and were thus able to segregate "autobiography" into a separate, lesser, genre. In their andro- and ethnocentric bias, the critics thought that Herman Melville, Nathaniel Hawthorne, D. H. Lawrence, and Joseph Conrad were writing "everybody"'s story and hence expressing "universal" truths. Others, however, have finally managed to get published in greater numbers; they too write about themselves and their own kind, in a new autobiographical fiction that many critics have decided is not literature, or surely not "universal," at any rate—all these tales of dark and female people.

But it is not only the skewed perception of white Christian male critics, which ghettoizes and negates the value of such work, that sees long-oppressed peoples telling their stories autobiographically. From a different perspective, such fiction is of considerably higher status than traditional critics are willing to acknowledge. These stories *need* to be told. They have been missing, and telling them is an act of restoration, of joining together, making whole the fabric of world literature. These people have had their hands raised a long time, waiting to be called on, waiting to be recognized. When they are called on, they pour out generations of energy in words; their texts are fountains of passionately released language. They seek, in their stories, not just recognition of the self, the individual, the one who finally got called on and got into print, but also recognition of the group. They are representative. They are signposts, flares and beacons to the rest. Those markers are necessary, for the openness of contemporary forms is particularly appropriate to those whose presence calls canonical principles into question or even obliterates them; previously "a closed form," as Grace wrote of her mother's life, these lives are now open-ended.

The story, perhaps more than the novel, lends itself to the open ending; most postmodern novelists writing in American English—Mary Gordon, Larry Heineman, and Susan Dodd, for instance—tend to put the past into the past and, despite some back-and-forth movement, advance through the present toward a foreseeable future. Even such a dreamlike, lyrical novel as Marilynne Robinson's *Housekeeping* offers some conclusiveness in its conclusion. Those writers who have wrested the novel away from closure (like Toni Cade Bambara in *The Salt Eaters* or Maxine Hong Kingston in her two "memoirs") do not include Grace Paley. Success with her first book in 1959 led to the then-inevitable critical pressure to progress according to formula, to write a novel. She "failed" at that attempt, as she had "failed" in high school and college: the form was not appropriate. She tried to make Faith's family the center of a saga, generations and connections that would weave their stories together into the requisite big book, but it didn't happen.

Three of the more obviously linked stories, "Faith in the Afternoon" (ECLM, written in 1959–60), "Faith in a Tree" (ECLM, written in the mid-sixties), and "Dreamer in a Dead Language" (LSD, written in the early to mid-seventies), were part of that attempt, but instead of becoming a novel, they provide—through their presentation of the same characters, their intertextual references, and their mutual history and world view—a good example of the kind of connection Grace's story cycle offers in place of the novel. She says that whenever she tried to spin out the plot, she would realize that she could achieve the desired effects in a shorter form. Why "make it longer," she asks, when you already have what you need in a story?

After that brief capitulation to critical pressure, which frustrated her and made her angry at herself, Grace may have felt justified in having kept the literary world at arm's length so long. She was enormously relieved, however, when she learned that she could be part of the writers' world without engaging in what she considered artificial stylistics or bad faith. Like teaching, her work at the PEN[14] American Center in New York—where she is a member of the Freedom to Write Committee and the Women's Committee[15]—has helped bridge the gap she feared between politics and literature. PEN's membership includes a substantial number of other writers who are concerned about the social impact and responsibility of writers and the treatment of those who write and speak out against government policy in their home countries—such cases as Margaret Randall's long struggle to regain her U.S. citizenship and the terrifying Rushdie affair. It is rumored that Grace has occasionally indulged in deliberate recruitment to be sure that that continues to be true.

When she thinks about having become "a literary person," Grace agrees that the transformation took place over a long period and was almost imperceptible. She rarely speaks of the long time it took for her to define herself as a writer, but she willingly generalizes from her own experience to comment on how difficult it is for women to be taken seriously—even in the midst of success. In 1984, at a Northwestern *Triquarterly* symposium, Grace addressed this issue, "saying that her stories were considered nice, little unimportant stories about domestic situations. As if to prove her point, an article in the Chicago *Tribune* about the conference referred to her as an 'intellectual version of Erma Bombeck.' "[16]

Nevertheless, she minimizes the process of that long-deferred entry into the literary community, formalized through membership in PEN, by telling the story this way:

> It's just that I really like people, and I'm a person who believes in working with others. I come from a union family. A lot of Americans, now, they're not accustomed to working with other people. They may be more individualist. But I'm an organizational person, so I naturally would join a writers' organization. It would be natural for me to do that. Just as it would be natural for me to join a teachers' union. So therefore I get to know the people. I get to like some of the people. And then they get to be my community too. So I have the teaching community, the writing community, the political community— and in many ways they overlap. Like Esther [E. M. Broner] is in my teaching and writing community.[17] And Sybil [whose first novel and first collection of short stories were published in 1989] is in my writing and my political community."

This new community, a congregation of writers as friends and colleagues, was instrumental in the publication of *Enormous Changes*, which she finally put together when she got back from the USSR. For several years, certainly since the mid-sixties, everyone close to her (and many of her readers and critics) had been urging—maybe even scolding—her to create another collection. Her family believed that her work during the war kept her from writing, but we would be wrong to assume that she was simply so pressed or so exhausted that she could not write. The fact is that she chose to do the one thing rather than the other, though in some sense—musing in a back corner of her mind, scribbling notes here and there, spending an occasional afternoon doing two pages and putting them away for three years—she was always writing.

Danny Paley remembers "bothering her to spend more time writing. I was worried that she wasn't writing enough, and god knows how long the war might drag on." He says she was unwilling to discuss her writing with him, though he often asked what she was working on or what a particular story was about. He would "always" ask her when the next book was coming out, but she would answer "in as few words as possible." He gradually asked her less and less and finally realized that he wasn't going to get the answer he wanted. "A few times I was tempted to look in her manuscripts, but they were so filled with corrections and revisions that I couldn't read them; I wouldn't even try to read them," he says.

The late Donald Barthelme, who lived just across the street, was another who urged Grace to create a second book. He insisted, despite her denials, that she must have enough stories for a collection (her first one contained only eleven, after all) and nagged her—in the right way, of course—until she searched around (her filing system has never been what most would call efficient) and found he was right. He read and commented on all the stories, as did Andrea Dworkin, who read over the whole collection when Grace finally began to work on arranging it. She says that Andrea "was really a big help" in defining the order and in proofreading.

Many of the stories she read aloud to Jane Cooper, who remembers the process because it was part of their longtime exchange of critical listening and reading: "She would read them to me and I would really listen very hard. And then I would say something like, 'Well, the end just doesn't seem quite right yet,' or 'Wait a minute, there was a point way back at which my concentration left you. Could we get back to that place?' or 'Somehow this doesn't seem right' or 'Could you work a little more on this page?' or 'Here's a section that doesn't quite work for me.' Both of us do this very well in oral terms, but then I would usually look at the thing afterwards to identify those spots."[18] Some of the stories they worked on together finally did "turn up in the book," and Jane says she thought she'd never read them before in her life, so changed were they from the versions she had heard or seen in that preparatory phase.

Finally, at Barthelme's consistent urging, Grace took a batch of manuscripts to Roger Straus at Farrar, Straus and Giroux. They published the collection of seventeen stories she named *Enormous Changes at the Last Minute.* Eleven years later, they published the next seventeen as well.

By the time *Enormous Changes* was prepared for publication, two first-person narrators who sound a lot like Grace Paley and Faith Darwin had been identified as writers—in "Debts" and "A Conversation with My Father." (In the third collection and in uncollected texts, Faith is unquestionably defined as a writer.) The final story in *Enormous Changes,* "The Long-Distance Runner," depicts Faith facing several of the issues and circumstances that confront her author. Her children are nearly grown and mostly gone: "I kissed the kids goodbye. They were quite old by then. It was near the time for parting anyway. . . . I told them they could take off any time they wanted to. Go lead your private life, I said. Only leave me out of it. . . . I said, Goodbye. They said, Yeah, O.K., sure" (180).

Her new man, Jack, is on the scene, and she wants the kids to accept him: "Why can't you be decent to him? I asked. It's important to me" (197). She has said goodbye to "the whole house of her childhood" (184) by visiting her former home and declaring her mother dead, and by finding a nascent sisterhood with the "mama" who saves her by taking her into the old apartment.

Faith is moving off home base; after a long time in one place, she has "decided to run" (181), and she is trying to understand and explain what these transitions mean to her. But, "What are you talking about?" her elder son demands. "I don't know what she's talking about either," says the younger. "Neither did Jack, despite the understanding often produced by love after absence. He said, Tell me again. He was in a good mood. He said, You can even tell it to me twice. I repeated the story. They all said, What?" (198). Though she was satisfied with what she had learned, with what she had taken into herself from the world, Faith apparently has more to learn and further to go before she can make herself understood. Grace Paley's travels too had only begun to produce stories that would move outside the neighborhood.

10

Goodbye and Good Luck

The decade from 1975 to 1985 is marked by two kinds of movement in Grace Paley's life, both of which fostered continuing change in her political perspective and activities. First, she began to spend more time in the country, planting a garden and growing herself into the New England countryside—its towns and people were becoming a second home for her, and her politics soon included their needs and interests.[1] Her family preceded her there: Nora, first living in New Hampshire and then settling in Vermont, had become a New Englander some years before, and in 1980 Bob gave up New York City entirely and went to live on his land.[2]

Second, Grace continued to travel, both within the United States and to other countries. This period included a number of trips to colleges and universities as visiting author or speaker, and of course there were deliberately political journeys as well. She made various notable trips to Washington, D.C., visited the Women's Peace Encampment at Seneca, New York, and ended the decade by traveling to Nicaragua and El Salvador. Both *Leaning Forward*, her first published poetry collection, and *Later the Same Day*, the third story collection, were published in 1985, and they offer the accumulated knowledge and understanding born of going outside the neighborhood and bringing it all back home.

The introduction to that decade of movement was noteworthy: Grace and Bob toured China for three weeks in the spring of 1974 with a group sponsored by the *Guardian*. Her previous year's trip to the USSR had been paid for by the movement, as had the trip to Vietnam in 1969, but Isaac had left Grace "a little bit of money," and "that's how we got to China."[3] Like most movement progressives and leftists in the United States at that time, Grace was enormously impressed with the revolution in China and admired the ongoing courage, strength, and dedication of the Chinese people. Her enthusiasm and knowledge even turned Jeanne Tenenbaum around on the issue of family-size restriction as practiced in the People's Republic of China; Grace was eloquent in defense of the one-child limit, arguing that the Chinese had no choice but to restrict their birthrate in the face of their slowly developing resources and enormous population. Like the tour group members in "Somewhere Else," Grace Paley was "in love with the Chinese revolution, Mao Zedong and the Chinese people" (LSD, 48). In 1974 China had not yet experienced the division so clearly represented by the passionate student demonstrations and bloody government reprisals of 1989; this was unimaginable in the early seventies.

In Beijing, Grace bought a jacket of the sort worn by Chinese workers—in an effort, Bob thinks—to be inconspicuous ("China Diary I," 8). As she has been since her childhood days in the Great Depression, Grace was sharply aware of the obvious distinctions money makes; being an American tourist in China complicated the issues of class, race, and privilege, making her supersensitive. Naturally, she wrote this consciousness, with its built-in criticism, into her China story. Ruth Larsen (who, in the third collection, is almost as autobiographical as Faith is) thinks that Frederick J. Lorenz, a member of her tour group, "should have been spoken to," because in "this China, where all the grownups dressed in modest gray, blue, and green, Freddy wore very short white California shorts with a mustard-colored California B.V.D. shirt and, above his bronze blue-eyed face, golden tan California curly hair. She didn't think that was nice." She is challenged immediately by the caustic Ann, who asks, "Who are you, Ruth? The commissioner of underwear?" (LSD, 50). Like Ruth, and despite her good intentions, Grace was foiled by the long-standing, though counterrevolutionary and manifestly impractical, institutionalization of sexism in China: she bought a jacket with pockets—which only men wore then in the People's Republic—thus calling attention to, and perhaps embarrassing, herself by appearing to flaunt American feminism.

Grace and Bob both wrote about their trip, he in series of diary excerpts, as he had done in collaboration with Grace when they returned from Chile, and she in the story called "Somewhere Else."[4] They were interested in many of the same issues, and both chose to focus on one incident, the behavior of two members of their tour group and the results of that behavior. When Bob writes that he and Hank de Suvero took off for "an hour's stroll through some 'real' section" ("China Diary II," 8)—that is, out of Central Tientsin and off the recommended path for tourists—they are on their way into both adventure and Grace's fiction. Like the women who became Margaret and Louise in "Love," Bob and Hank are transformed into Joe and Freddy, accused by their guide of transgressions against the Chinese people in "Somewhere Else."

Bob's diary descriptions of the pleasure he took in solitary rambles and discoveries, as well as his now-international fascination with noodle factories—"Mr. Wong ... [Joe says,] I'm crazy about your street noodle factories" (LSD, 52)—in conjunction with Grace's having made her character a playground builder, reveal Bob to be Joe's original, just as Bob's published details of the incident on their tour reveal Hank de Suvero to be the original of Grace's Freddy.[5] Like Hank in Bob's diary, Freddy is accused of taking a photograph without asking permission and "invading" a noodle factory. There are, of course, incidental differences, like the fact that on the *Guardian*'s China tour no one admitted taking such a photograph; Hank may have been accused unfairly. In Grace's story, the narrator makes it clear that Freddy, as well as several other members of the group, might indeed have taken the photograph Mr. Wong describes.

Here is a place where, because we also have the text of Bob Nichols's diary, the transitional space between life and story is nearly transparent. With Bob's text as our lens, we can observe the writer's choices. This is true even when we grant the impossibility of faithfully rendered "reality"; Bob Nichols intended "nonfiction" in his diary, but we may choose to take his perspective as a different version, rather than a perfect copy, of "reality." Grace's purpose, unlike Bob's, is not to create a lengthy report for interested folks back home or to tell anecdotes from and make an analysis of her trip to China. The two authors' differing intentions must have dictated even such simple distinctions as their descriptions of the moment of accusation. Bob's Mr. Ho, in the present tense, is "sitting in the middle of the sofa smoking cigarettes" when, after a "long generalized speech. . . . He raises his finger and points dramatically at Hank" ("China Diary," II, 8). Grace's Mr. Wong, in the past tense, is sometimes paraphrased, and his accusation is interrupted by many paragraphs of the first-person narrator's description, commentary, and explanation and the other characters' dialogue. "Mr. Wong pointed his political finger at our brilliant comrade Frederick J. Lorenz" (LSD, 49).

In keeping with her belief that every story is at least two stories, Grace has set the China episode in juxtaposition to another, which transforms the first by becoming its other half. The second story takes place in the South Bronx and another, less blasted, section of New York City, probably the Village. To go beyond the implications of the specific incident—the accusation itself—to explore its meaning and come to understand what Grace would call the truth of the event, she offers two "somewheres" and demonstrates that "else" may mean "other."[6]

Though Freddy is the accused, both parts of the story are about Joe, the unaccused guilty party who finds himself in similar situations in both parts of the text. Joe is twice accused of invasion and theft—the essence of imperialism—and the story calls up the old notion of the camera as thief of the soul. Despite the fact that his interest in the lives and culture of the "others" he encounters is neither born of narrow self-interest nor dulled by unconscious ethnocentrism, Joe is ignored and rejected by his accusers when he wants to be seen, accepted, and known by them. In both cases, Joe wants to be understood as himself—an individual—rather than as a member of his class, nation, or race; but both times he is defeated by history. Too many who look like him have come before him— Michelangelo Antonioni, cited in the text, and all the other Western artists and powers that have created "the Orient" in China and U.S. colonial governors in Central and South America, plus the closed hierarchy of New York City governance in the South Bronx.

Joe wants the Chinese people and the young men of the South Bronx to believe in his willingness to put sincere effort into their cause—with some vanity perhaps, some ego, but not very much. He is a student in the Chinese world, seeking entrance so he may learn from it; in the Bronx he offers himself as a skilled assistant, a teacher with the goal of giving up power to his students. In his job, working with young people, and in his chance encounter with the young men on the front porch, he tries to put both the technology and the opportunity for creative expression into their hands; he is acutely aware of his dual position in that community, realistic and ultimately defensive about making "a big Marxist deal about it" (LSD, 59).

But in both China and the South Bronx communication is hampered because Joe does not share the people's language, culture, class, or race.[7] In both places they disarm him, rejecting his professed purpose. He knows it, and he understands their rejection of him. Joe Larsen's struggle to understand and integrate all the story's issues—about film and cameras and "taking" people—is at the thematic heart of "Somewhere Else." Grace worked on this story for a long time; she kept going over it and changing it, especially the ending.[8] Finally, she chose to have the China tour group come together for a reunion, where they would watch slides of their trip. The first one they see is of an old man holding his grandchild; and though the slides belong to Martin—who took over four thousand pictures—it is Joe who remembers where the pictures were taken, demonstrating the value he has given them and the careful quality of his own "taking" of the people of China. Joe is struggling; his consciousness of these contradictions is visibly rising in the course of the story.

Grace Paley's own consciousness was visibly rising in the decade from 1975 to 1985. Though most peace activists at first refused to see the relationship between environmental work and antimilitary actions and considered such efforts to be counterproductive or much less important, a major shift began when the Vietnam War ended. Grace was one of those who broadened her sphere of activity. Her personal knowledge of the devastation of the Vietnamese countryside and the herculean energies required to empty the soil of poison and bring it back to fertility informed her work as an environmental activist in the States.

Her realization of the interconnectedness of the various "issues" that often escaped—or fragmented and stalled—movement people was fostered by her travel to other countries, by her new life in rural Vermont, and by her growing involvement with women's groups, whose actions were based in an integrated analysis. Many peace groups, certainly those dominated by male leadership, had ignored or deplored women's organized actions throughout the sixties. Progress away from that low level of consciousness can be traced in the pages of movement publications like the War Resisters League's *WIN*, in which women battled their "brothers" over basic feminist issues. The published evidence of these battles suggests that Grace Paley, an occasional contributor, was not one of those who challenged the male power structure within the movement in those earlier days.

The Village Peace Center, which had developed a strong single focus on antidraft work, was closed in 1974, when the draft was halted. Many of its members, like Grace Paley, Sybil Claiborne, and Karl Bissinger, had already become active in the international War Resisters League (WRL), which is, as Grace likes to point out, one of the few large pacifist organizations that is secular. Grace traveled to Paris as a WRL representative in early April 1975 to meet Vietnamese ambassadors at the international peace negotiations. Her brief report on that experience, published as "Peace Movement Meets with PRG in Paris" in *WIN*, is more journalistic than most of her earlier nonfiction but still presents people as characters, complete with dialogue—which always interests her most. That same year she published a passionately argued essay against the baby airlift, in which Vietnamese children were flown out of their country and given to U.S. families and agencies to arrange adoptions ("We Were Strong Enough"). At the end of the year, "Mom" appeared in *Esquire* magazine—a piece that defies categorization: short fiction, essay, autobiography, memoir, collage.

Across that range of work we find evidence of Grace Paley's ongoing concern with language—its use and abuse, its environment and employment. The opening line of the PRG article informs us that Madame Binh's greeting was a *"taped"* one—though "warm"— and goes on to discuss ambassadorial "conversations." The article about the Vietnamese children, interlaced with quoted conversations and interviews, turns on definition and expression, particularly of the word "orphan." "Mom" is prime Paley, offering—in less than two pages—references to literary figures, immigrant reverence for the English language in the United States, the importance of individual sentences, the variety of languages available in one neighborhood, the mystery of naming (including the case of the ineffable name of God), and storytelling.

In the second half of the seventies, Grace actually took on a brief assignment as a journalist—she wrote a regular column[9] for the impressive but short-lived magazine *Sevendays*. Her column had two names in its brief life: it began as "The Demystified Zone" and soon became "Conversations." The former was a declaration of her insistence on writing as revelation, and the latter—defining language intercourse—has been a constant theme in her work.

In that column she published "Living on Karen Silkwood Drive," in which she tells the story of the occupation of the Seabrook construction site in New Hampshire. Here, as in her fiction, she tells two stories, enlarging the history of the proposed 1,150 megawatt nuclear reactor by pointing out the immutable connection between this demonstration—a camp pitched by two thousand people in the parking lot of the reactor site—and the Women's Vigil against the Vietnam War and the draft.[10] She looks at the land around the site, which has been scraped raw out of a lush tidal marsh, and she thinks of Quang Tri. The article offers the perspective of an older person who finds herself (as she often does now) among mostly younger proponents of a cause to which she has dedicated a good portion of her time and strength.

These young folks, she relates, appear at first to be somewhat the same as the sixties variety; discussing the supplies they have brought for their stay at the camp or in jail, Grace compares granola ingredients with a young woman. But these young people, perhaps having learned from women's movements, have developed "a new democratic process"; there is an "almost continuous parliament of Spokespersons sent from each affinity group to bring views and initiatives to the Decision-Making Body—the DMB" (11). Grace records how they discuss, among other things, whether to go limp or stiff when they are finally carried off—as they know they will be—and how to deal with arrest, bail, and court pleas; they want to operate in consolidation, and they seek consensus. As had others in the not-so-distant past, these people benefited from Quaker teachings —though Grace admits that she's too interested in what everyone else looks like, and in what they have to say, to personally match the Quaker model.

Official removal of the antinuke activists began in the afternoon of May Day 1977, and at seven-thirty in the evening, with her husband and twenty-five others, Grace Paley was "arrested"—that is, "picked up and dumped into an army truck," where they "remain[ed] sitting or organized into sardine sleep" throughout the night (12), on an icy metal truckbed that Bob Nichols remembers quite physically. More than fourteen hundred people were finally arrested, including many other members of Grace and Bob's small Vermont affinity groups, who have remained attached to the Clamshell Alliance in its long battle against the building of the Seabrook plant.[11]

The following year Grace took part in another sort of occupation, this one relatively brief and numerically tiny, but engendering a governmental response even more heavy-handed and tactically questionable than the New Hampshire governor's decision to instigate mass arrests and interminable snarls in his state's courts. The War Resisters League arranged for a dual action on Labor Day, September 4, 1978; teams of demonstrators appeared at exactly the same time in Red Square and at the White House (5 P.M. in Moscow, 10 A.M. in Washington). Each group unfurled a banner urging the superpowers to disarm.[12] Grace and Karl Bissinger were on the hometeam, inevitably dubbed "the Washington Eleven" by the press.

The seven Americans in Russia[13] went individually to the giant GUM department store, crossed from there to Red Square, and began handing out leaflets as they pulled open their banner. The banner was ripped down in less than thirty seconds, and they were arrested. The plainclothes police, who rushed from all over the square to cut off the action, took a little longer to scurry around collecting the leaflets, which had been tossed into the air when they couldn't be offered politely. Four of the seven were taken away, and the three left began calling out "Mir Y Druhzba"—Peace and Friendship—until uniformed police convinced them to leave. All seven were frightened, and some had visions of dank prison cells and harsh inquisitors. They were all reunited by seven that evening, however, and told they could continue their interrupted itinerary. Their guide took them to a Moscow nightclub, where they indulged in vodka, caviar, and champagne toasts to peace and freedom. Learning of the less pleasant circumstances of their eleven colleagues at home, the group quickly decided to leave for New York. They got back just as the others were released.

On the home front, a few minutes before the appointed time, the eleven[14] had joined other tourists waiting to see the White

House and then stepped out of line at ten to open their banner on the lawn and distribute leaflets. (These had the same text as the Russian-language leaflets being passed out in Moscow.) The U.S. Secret Service was not so quick as its opposite number had been in Red Square, and there was enough time for some leaflets to be distributed—and even for one good photograph to be taken of the eleven with their banner open and easily read.[15] The White House security agents' inefficiency was made up for by the District of Columbia's constabulary and the judiciary branch. The pacifists were charged with illegal entry, booked, and jailed for thirty hours (Karl says the charge was really "trespassing in the garden of the presidential palace"; Grace says they were accused of "stepping on the grass"). They were threatened with a six-month to one-year prison sentence and a $1,000 fine, but, after a full jury trial—which took place three months later and lasted eight days—they were eventually put on probation for three years, with the proviso that if any of them were arrested during that period, they would spend six months in jail.

The strong contrast between the Soviet and American responses to the demonstration was ironic—if not absurd—in light of the far more rigid constraints on spoken and printed dissent in the USSR, and there was a swirl of publicity around the case, much of it prompted by the presence of well-known artists and writers among the defendants. There was international coverage because of the dual action, and most of it was critical of the U.S. government's handling of their "half" of the demonstrators. Surprised despite her experience, Grace said, "It's as though in the midst of the terrible noise of impending war, someone dropped a feather and the Administration said, 'Did you hear that? Arrest those guys.'"[16]

That winter when the trial took place, photos show Grace outside the courthouse bundled in wool, with a dusting of snow on her shoulders. She was probably on her way to invade yet another sacrosanct national preserve: the Library of Congress. Jane Cooper had been invited to read her poems there, and the reading was on December 4, the first day of the Washington Eleven trial.[17] At a luncheon in honor of the people who were reading that evening, Jane spoke privately to her old friend, William Meredith, who was then poetry consultant at the Library of Congress. She told him that after lunch she was going over to watch the trial of the

Washington Eleven and that she planned to "mention it" that night at her reading. "I'm going to talk about it," Jane said, knowing that the Library of Congress was taping the reading and that the tape would be available for high school use. "Bill looked a little taken aback, but I must say he rallied nobly and said, 'You can do anything that you have to do.'"

She did. At the beginning of the reading, Jane dedicated her reading to the Washington Eleven and then explained who they were and why they were on trial. She had just read the first line of the first poem when the Washington Eleven walked into the reading room. The tone of the reading had been one of propriety and high decorum (the audience sat on little gilt chairs, and there were antique musical instruments in glass cases) "when suddenly in walked this mob of somewhat less decorous folks." They arrived in time to hear Jane give her first public reading of the entire text of her Rosa Luxemburg poems.[18]

Jane used her work further to benefit the Washington Eleven. She conferred with Jan Levi, whose Flamingo Press was just beginning to consider such projects, and they acted so quickly that the first edition of the Luxemburg poems appeared as a small pamphlet just three weeks later, at a reading fundraiser. Then another, bigger, reading was held, and the first printing of five hundred sold out, as did a second run of five hundred shortly afterward. By donating her work to raise money for the Washington Eleven, Jane probably could have kept that little Flamingo chapbook in print indefinitely. Bob Nichols speculates that the number of rallies and benefits to raise money for bail, defense funding, and court costs for this—and other actions in this period—may nearly equal the number of actions themselves.

As the movements for peace and the maintenance of the ecology of the earth had blended together, so too had environmental activists and feminists. In early spring of 1980, Grace was one of the planners and presenters for a conference called "Women and Life on Earth," which took place in Amherst, Massachusetts. Hundreds of women from the Northeast attended, and many of them, charged by the fire of that meeting's revelation of the interconnectedness of racism, militarism, the oppression of women, and the tremulous safety of the planet, began immediately afterward to meet in regional and local groups.

Grace Paley, like so many other women, began to turn around in her politics and face the criticism or hostility of men with whom she had worked for years—who resented the feminism of her current actions and refused to struggle with their own consciousness beyond old boundaries. Her heterosexism, for instance, if not homophobia, was recognized and challenged by the many lesbian women who were, more and more often, among her sister workers. As she responded to such challenges with considerable analysis, the social and political distance between Grace—the recovering daddy's girl who had always pleased men and been pleased by them—and the radical feminists she now met began to narrow rapidly.

Smaller groups of women continued to meet, and their desire to demonstrate—literally—what they had learned about the economics and effects of militarism on a global scale grew with their knowledge and understanding. Out of the arguments and revelations of those months and the actions of the next two years, Grace eventually wrote up the Unity Statement, which, because her role was that of scribe, one creator among many, is always printed with the phrase "A collectively written working statement" after its concluding sentence, in place of an authorial attribution. The women did demonstrate what they knew, in November of 1980, in the Women's Pentagon Action.

More than two thousand women went to Washington and surrounded the Pentagon. They wove webs of yarn over the five doors, chanted in their circles, and sang to the armed men who entered and exited, so that for perhaps the first time in their lives, those men were unable to ignore the *meaning* of the presence of women. Hundreds of women were arrested and sent to jail, some for as long as thirty days in federal penitentiaries. Many were treated badly—some even kept in leg irons—a response that offers proof of the anxiety women can produce among powerful men.

In 1982 they returned in the Second Women's Pentagon Action, to roar and hum and chant, to weave their webs, and to hold hands in a dense circle of spirit around the armed men who dispense pain, poison, and death across continents. Grace planted a small sign in the war department's earth, a printed marker that read "The Unknown Woman." (No soldiers in spit-shined boots and white gloves have been sent to guard that spot.) This kind of action, based in magic and women's craft, would not have appealed to Grace Paley in former years. She was not among the witchy women who had hexed Wall Street and Washington in the past, nor had she endorsed the necessity for women to separate from men—at least sometimes— to make policy, to take action, and to keep strong. By the eighties, however, she had become one of those women. The change was neither simple nor easy.

When she returned from China, she was often asked to report on what she had learned about the lives of Chinese women and the situation of lesbian and gay people there. She did not satisfy her questioners on these issues, and on at least one occasion, back home in the Village, she was challenged, accused of having either passed over such matters or not taken them seriously. At first, she offered the standard excuse: people in revolutionary China do not have the time to deal with sexuality—that is a Western luxury; they must struggle with "important" issues. "Do you mean, Grace, that in all of China," one angry young woman demanded, "in *all of China*, you couldn't find even one tiny little lesbian? Come on, Grace!" She did not contradict this metaphoric assessment of her blooming feminist consciousness. She took it in and considered it. Her critics were right, she realized, and she began to make the slow deliberate change that would finally surface in "Listening," written in the early eighties and published as the concluding story of her third collection.

Acknowledgment of the existence of lesbians is absent from Grace Paley's work published before 1985—with two exceptions. In "Northeast Playground," first published in 1967, two of the "unwed mothers on relief," close friends who care for each other's children, are described by the Faith-like narrator as "very handsome dykey women." They are "whores and junkies," mothers of toddlers in daycare and baby daughters they keep pristine "in ribbons and white voile in fine high veneer and chrome imported carriages" at the park (ECLM, 146–47). These two women never let their kids play in the sand and are "disgusted to see them get dirty or wet and g[i]ve them hell when they d[o]" (ECLM, 147). The passage is interesting for its combination of "dykey" with "very handsome" and the description of a rigid mothering style—at odds with that of Faith and her friends in the story cycle—superimposed with hyper-feminine trappings. Though both the context and the description appear to be positive, they draw on twentieth-century stereotypes of lesbians.

In "Dreamer in a Dead Language," first published in 1977 but probably written a few years earlier, Philip Mazzano's disdainful listing of Ricardo's connections reveals his bigotry: "Four old maids in advertising, three Seventh Avenue models, two fairies in TV, one literary dyke..." (LSD, 14). Here, when a negatively portrayed character uses the term "dyke" along with "old maid" and "fairy," we don't necessarily attribute his attitude to either the narrator or, in the case of those readers so inclined, the author.

But in "Faith in a Tree" (even in the final version published in 1974), as in "Northeast Playground," the powerful narrating voice (which is Faith's) is the source of homophobic language and makes mockery of gay men seem acceptable to the reader's eyes and ears. Clever Faith disagrees with soft-hearted Kitty's romantic assessment of the "handsome man in narrow pants" who sits beside Lynn Ballard on a park bench and whispers in her ear. Faith says it's "obvious that he's a weekend queer, talking her into the possibilities of a neighborhood threesome" with "his really true love, the magnificent manager of the supermarket" (ECLM, 86). The man is a "queer"—and a devious creep. In the same story, we are reassured by Faith that two men walking along "leaning toward one another" are "not fairies" but "music lovers inclining toward their transistor" (ECLM, 88).

These examples are a long way from the consciousness of the narrative voice that describes, in "Somewhere Else" (first published in the fall of 1978), the American tourists' yearning "to walk along a street in Shanghai or Canton holding hands with a Chinese person of their own sex, just as the Chinese did—chatting politics, exchanging ideological news" (LSD, 48). We are not told if they also want to do this with an American person of their own sex, but the tone definitely allows for such a possibility, which is certainly not the case in the earlier story. Karl Bissinger, himself gay, explains that "Grace had had no concept of the lesbian, the woman lover, who was born that way and is that way—no concept at all." Grace told him, as they talked about her slowly growing consciousness of heterosexism, that "it takes a long time to learn." About a young friend of theirs, "who was incredibly attractive and poised, well dressed and pretty," he recalls Grace saying, "You know, it wasn't so long ago that I'd have been asking her to dinner with every stray man I knew."

Later the Same Day, published in 1985, publicly presented a leap of consciousness in its author's sexual politics, far from and ahead of that expressed in *Enormous Changes at the Last Minute,* published in 1974. Like her author, Faith begins to take some lessons and some lumps in public after 1970; not only is she attacked by an old friend (Ann in "Friends" [LSD])—accused of having been her parents' spoiled darling—but also her imperfections are revealed in "Zagrowsky Tells," completed in 1984 and published in both *Mother Jones* and *Later the Same Day* in 1985. Grace Paley explains that she had great difficulty composing this story and could finally write it only when she realized that Faith could not be the teller. The author's assignment of identity to the narrator has become central for Paley in recent years. With the arguable exception of "This Is a Story about My Friend George, the Toy Inventor," the last seven stories in *Later the Same Day* are all about telling and listening.

At one point Grace conceived of a series; "Zagrowsky Tells," first published as "Telling," was to be paired with the last story in *Later the Same Day,* called "Listening."[19] Zagrowsky had to tell his story himself, his author realized. When he does, for the first time in the story cycle Paley readers experience the effect of a powerful criticism of Faith by a narrator/character who knows her personally— and Izzy has known Faith a long time. Faith appears peremptory, nosy, and insensitive to the relationship between Izzy and his grandson Emmanuel. Though she is a strong foil for his revelations, she is specifically designated a listener here, as her author was in the period of these later stories and this third collection.

From this critical perspective, Grace Paley's own early imper-fections come into view. In stories written before the late seventies she had included violence against women as mild humor (see "A Woman, Young and Old" [LDM, 29]), the trivialization of rape (see "Enormous Changes" [ECLM, 127—this one also insults old women]), and a subtle anti-Latino linguistic slur (see "An Interest in Life" [LDM, 91]). The small number of such (obviously unconscious in every sense of the word) examples is impressive in the body of Grace Paley's work, especially given her time and place of living and writing, and may be attributed to concerted efforts to grow beyond herself—a constant theme in her lifework. In recent stories, she is more likely to slip some consciousness-raising into the dialogue, as she does in "The Story Hearer," when Faith educates two men in the inner story (Eddie and Jim), one man in the frame (Jack), and readers of both genders throughout, even as she makes Eddie a representative of the limits to our capacity for immediate change:

> At this point the butcher said, What'll you have, young lady?
>
> I refused to tell him.
>
> Jack, to whom, if you remember, I was telling this daylong story, muttered, Oh God, no! You didn't do that again.
>
> I did, I said. It's an insult. You do not say to a woman of my age who looks my age, What'll you have, young lady? I did not answer him. If you say that to someone like me, it really means, What do you want, you pathetic old hag?
>
> Are you getting like that now too? he asked. . . .
>
> Eddie, I said, don't talk like that or I won't tell you what I want.
>
> Whatever you say, honey, but what'll you have? . . .
>
> Did I hear you say City College? asked Eddie as he cut the little chicken's leg out of its socket. Well, when I was a boy, a kid—what we called City College—you know it was C.C.N.Y. then, well, we called it Circumsized Citizens of New York.
>
> Really, said Jim. He looked at me. Did I object? Was I offended?
>
> The fact of male circumcision doesn't insult me, I said. However, I understand that the clipping of clitorises of young girls continues in Morocco to this day.
>
> Jim has a shy side. He took his pork butt and said goodbye. (LSD, 136–38)

Grace had begun to listen to the voices of radical feminists, lesbians, and gay men, and as she had done for immigrant New York Jews, and then for other voices, she created a character to speak with the new voice. In "Listening," named for that necessary exercise and the repeated motif in the text and written late in the period preceding publication of *Later the Same Day*, Grace created her first lesbian character, Cassie. She gave Cassie Faith's loving friendship, a forum for righteous criticism, and the last word. Cassie challenges Faith, not in terms of her personal life—for Faith has a dear lesbian friend, after all—but *as a writer*. Cassie accuses Faith of excluding her—writing out, silencing, erasing her people:

> Listen, Faith, why don't you tell my story? You've told every-body's story but mine. . . . you've just omitted me from the other stories and I was there. In the restaurant and the train, right there. Where is Cassie? Where is *my* life? It's been women and men, women and men, fucking, fucking. Goddamnit, where the hell is my woman and woman, woman-loving life in all this? And it's not even sensible, because we *are* friends, we work together, you even care about me at least as much as you do Ruthy and Louise and Ann. You let them in all the time; it's really strange, why have you left me out of everybody's life? (LSD, 210)

This speech—a readily substantiated, obviously accurate accusation against Grace's own work—may be as startling to the straight reader as it is to Faith. Grace Paley has worked toward acceptance of this narrator on her own terms for years, and great numbers of us are taken by surprise, as we are when Zagrowsky makes racism less than monolithic and Faith's role as a conscience in the community less than clear. By naming Faith a writer here,[20] Grace has brought autobiography to the fore and made it an issue. Whether such an event or conversation ever "really" occurred is irrelevant;[21] what has happened, what is being documented here *as story*, is the calling to account of the writer. She is responsible, as Grace Paley always explains, for the truth of the words she puts out into the world. Though she cannot be held accountable for all of what readers make of her texts, she will always have to answer for her own choices—as Grace Paley said to William Gass some years ago.

Cassie holds Faith accountable. Faith's immediate emotional response is realistic shock, lasting fully twenty minutes, as the two women sit in a silence broken only by Faith's occasionally blurted "My God!" or "Christ Almighty!" (LSD, 210). They are sitting in Faith's car, which she has pulled to the curb, unable to drive, stunned by her friend's accusation. She tries, for about five seconds, to blame Cassie—or "them"—as well as herself, to make this sin of omission mutual. Then, of course, she wants to be forgiven. "Forgive you?" Cassie asks. "You are my friend, I know that, Faith, but I promise you, I won't forgive you. . . . From now on, I'll watch you like a hawk. I do not forgive you" (LSD, 211). We will all be watching now—because we have all been told what Faith and Grace must do. By publishing this story, Grace Paley has publicly committed herself to struggle against heterosexism and homophobia.

As Bob Nichols hoped, she is no longer reluctant to allow her people their politics or to allow deliberately political people in her stories. In fact, even in a story like "Love" (as well as in such obvious cases as "Somewhere Else," "Listening," "Zagrowsky Tells," and "The Expensive Moment"), the hinge upon which the narrator's realization about the nature of loving and "the lover" turns is the friendship broken in disagreement over the Soviet Union, and Faith and Jack "talk over the way the SALT treaty looked more like a floor than a ceiling" before they read a poem, watch tv, and make love (LSD, 7).

Moreover, women in the later stories no longer design their lives around arrangements with men, and loving friendships among women are central. Ruth and Faith, and their guest Xie Feng, who talk about their men and their children in "The Expensive Moment," recognize the flaws in male political pronouncements and personal habits; they fear governmental retribution for the radical acts of impassioned youths; and they know that an assessment of political acuity on the left always includes the environment "nowadays" (LSD, 188). They are the sort of women who, for instance, climbed the fence at Seneca Falls in the summer of 1983. Grace visited there for five days that summer, took part in their actions and deliberations, and climbed the fence with them.

Seneca, New York, is a place where nuclear weapons are assembled and prepared for shipment to Greenham Common, where English women camped for years in protest. North American women created a Women's Peace Encampment beside the army depot there; they set up their tents and wooden walkways, made policy, and took action to support the women of Great Britain in their protest against importing U.S. military poison to England's green and pleasant land.

Saying, typically, that the experience of "Seneca was stories," Grace wrote an essay for *Ms.* magazine in December 1983 describing her visit. She tells how, like the women of the Pentagon actions, Seneca women brought an infusion of ancient magic to their siege; on August 1, 1983, more than twenty-five hundred women marched to the arms depot at Seneca and hung quilts, posters, banners, feathers, beads, pictures, and flowers on the fence. They chanted and hummed, they sang and laughed, and then they climbed the fence. Grace says she knew this would probably be her last shot at such an action; though certainly not *very* old, she thinks she may be *too* old for this sort of thing now. But at the age of sixty-one, she wasn't, so she went over the top, with a little help from her friends, to take the presence of women right up into the faces of the men—and their recruited boys—who had fenced themselves off with their bombs.[22]

Not all of Grace Paley's political actions are in women-only groups these days. She has taken part in antiapartheid demonstrations and marched to demonstrate solidarity with the besieged peoples of Central and South America. She has maintained a relationship with the War Resisters League and continues to support resistance to selective service registration. Since the *intifada* began at the end of 1987, she cofounded the Jewish Women's Committee to End the Occupation of the Left Bank and Gaza and has worked with American and Israeli Jews and in coalition with Palestinians toward radical change in Israeli government policies. Here is yet another example of her continuing development and growth: the woman whose autobiographical speaker idealistically disdained nationhood for Israel in the mid-fifties[23] now seeks a two-state solution to the desperate problem of sovereignty in Palestine and Israel.

In these times of continuing gender wars, even apparently nongendered issues often require action and organization specifically by and for women and children. When Grace traveled to Nicaragua and El Salvador in 1985, she went with a group from MADRE, a friendship organization comprised of North and Central American women; when she visited Israel for the first time in the spring of 1987, she went as a delegate to an International Conference of Women Writers, and much of her work here in the States is done with Jewish American women who support the peace coalitions of Arab and Jewish women in the Middle East. Her determined and increasingly conscious identification with women and her advocacy position have brought Grace the same grief, fear, anxiety, anger, and trouble with (even beloved) men that all other feminist women face.

After years of excusing men, she still makes no demands on them, fictional or nonfictional, that she doesn't make on women, especially herself. She is determined to be responsible for her own consciousness, and in her autobiographical mode, her characters reflect that struggle; what she has learned is also learned by them, male and female. Her most recent work contains such surprises as Faith and Xie Feng's conversation about loving in "The Expensive Moment": "Ah, [Xie Feng] said, do you notice that in time you love the children more and the man less? Faith said Yes! but as soon as she said it, she wanted to run home and find Jack and kiss his pink ears and his last 243 hairs, to call out, Old friend, don't worry, you are loved" (LSD, 194).[24]

What is amazing is that she can pull it off: men still love Grace Paley. Maybe this is a response to textual nurturance; perhaps male readers take the large embrace of her world view for personal mothering. Maybe they believe she will continue to excuse or forgive them as she has in the past. Maybe they simply do not perceive the evolution of her world view as it appears in the stories. Her brother Victor's judgment suggests one reason male readers and critics have rarely become defensive about her fiction. Maintaining that he has never considered her a feminist, and perhaps focusing on the first and even second story collections, he labels her women "sad sacks," who aren't "getting anyplace. They're getting kicked around by men. They seem to be making the same mistakes over and over again. One man leaves them and they move in with another man."

Jess Paley still does not consider Grace a feminist; remembering that she herself denied it, he notes the media-reported party line and observes that she splits off from that line on specific issues. That independence is of course typical of her, and the women's movement itself is by no means definable in one way, but Jess may be thinking of the past, judging Grace by the period when he saw and spoke to her daily. She would hardly proffer a denial of feminism these days.[25] Her daughter Nora and her daughter-in-law Debbie, thoughtful, active women themselves, definitely consider Grace a feminist, though Debbie says that if she had been asked "five years ago [i.e., as late as the early eighties], I might have said no, Grace wouldn't use that word" to define herself.

Sybil Claiborne believes that feminism has wrought the biggest change in Grace's political development, because it influences her "in the *way* she wants to work, the people she wants to work with, the kind of work she wants to do. It's very hard to go back into the old hierarchical, bureaucratic way" of working once you've worked "in a feminist way, and that's colored her way of operating."

In one of her more recently written short prose pieces, published in *365 Reasons Not to Have Another War*, the 1989 War Resisters League Peace Calendar,[26] the first-person narrator accepts her dying mother-in-law's assumption that she "might know something about" what the older woman calls "Women's Lib." That Grace-like narrator easily takes up the position of spokeswoman for the movement, explaining the motives and purpose of feminists with enthusiasm. The mother-in-law is so moved by their dialogue that she stays "up all night thinking" and in the morning announces her realization that "there isn't a thing I've done in my life that I haven't done for some man. Dress up or go out or take a job or quit or go home or leave. Or even be quiet or say something nice, things like that." The dying woman, who is of the same generation as Grace Paley's mother and aunts, gives her blessing to the autobiographical feminist narrator when she says, "You know I was up all night thinking about you and especially those young women. I couldn't stop thinking about what wonderful lives they're going to have."

After *The Little Disturbances of Man* was published in 1959, male writers and critics were delighted with Grace Paley. Saul Bellow included "Goodbye and Good Luck" in his collection called *Great Jewish Stories;*[27] it is the *only* work by a woman he deemed "great." This acceptance was no doubt inspired by her loving portrayal of men—including the ones she calls "rotten"—in those stories, as well as in her occasional willingness to hold women, even young girls, responsible for their treatment at the hands of those men. "Listen, some men love those stories," Grace acknowledges, although "I wrote them thinking, 'These guys are such shits.' " Even if this is not retrospective consciousness, and even if she did indeed think ill of her early fictional men, there is a subtext of tender affection discernible in those stories.[28] That affection is what renders them complex, realistic—"true to life"—even as it makes male readers like and identify with them. "But I was very truthful about the way that they were, and the men heard themselves truthfully. They liked it; the men heard themselves truthfully and they thought it was all right." So it seems.

Having sharpened her analysis of relations between women

and men over the past thirty years and having grown older all the while, Grace has come to suspect that men—or at least older men—"probably don't like me so much anymore." Some of that disaffection, she knows, is generic:

> You know, for men, older women don't exist.... We can really just not be present at all. Women understand this. Women are beginning to understand it later than we used to, because people are younger longer now.[29] And because things *are* better—that is to say—probably in a certain century men wouldn't look at a woman over eighteen. And then maybe one hundred years later, over twenty-five. In many novels you read that a woman "was past her bloom," and then it turns out she's twenty-two! It certainly is true that all young things are blooming; yes, that's true. But people *flower* for years.

Grace thinks that the current level of consciousness in men in the United States is in flux. She credits young men for making efforts to change and is sympathetic: "It's very hard for them, very very hard—for the best of them, it's very hard not to feel attacked." Older men, though, are "so defensive, [even when] they give in in certain areas. They think of themselves, and their own hardships, and they think, well, *I* have had a hard time too. But they know that a woman has a more difficult time of it. They know that about women, but they don't know how to deal with what they know, and they are upset if you make all these connections [showing how the oppression of women is neither separate nor separable from their own behavior]."

This analysis and its effect on both her texts and actions have not shut Grace Paley out of the mainstreams of fiction writing or activist politics, as they might have some twenty years ago. Like so many other female artists and workers, she has benefited from the power and influence of the women's movement. Enormously increased recognition and exceptional rewards have come to her in this past decade, and she understands well that she has risen on the crest of a wave of women. Expressing her gratitude, Grace Paley insists that the difference in audience response is so great that women artists can't even begin to "calculate the power and the happiness of having a constituency . . . having people who will read you and will make you feel that you are speaking to somebody."[30]

In 1980 Grace Paley was elected to the American Academy of Arts and Letters, an honor described by the editors of *Poets and Writers* as "the highest formal recognition of artistic merit in the country." In 1982 *Delta*, a vanguard French journal of contemporary literature and scholarship, devoted an entire issue to Grace Paley, publishing "Lavinia," a Paley bibliography, an interview with her by Kathleen Noda Hulley—guest editor for that issue—and a collection of critical articles.

In 1985 Grace published her third story collection *and* her first book of poems. In spring of the following year, *Later the Same Day* was awarded a PEN/Faulkner Prize for fiction.[31] That winter she also received the Edith Wharton Citation of Merit from the New York State Writers Institute, thus becoming the first State Author of New York.[32] She was selected by a committee of authors and critics: Raymond Carver, Mary Gordon, Alfred Kazin, Robert Towers, and William Kennedy, who, along with New York Governor Mario Cuomo, made the presentation in the state capitol on December 10, 1986. Kennedy, announcing the group's choice for the Wharton Citation, described Grace Paley's luminous, evocative narrative voice as "absolutely singular" among the many in twentieth-century fiction.

In 1987 Grace Paley was awarded the prestigious Senior Fellowship of the Literature Program of the National Endowment for the Arts. The NEA award[33] was designed to "support and honor those who have made a major contribution to American literature over a lifetime of creative endeavor" and is given to "writers, poets, editors and other literary professionals who have expanded the boundaries of this nation's literary heritage." Though Grace is indeed among those who have "expanded the boundaries" of literature in this country, her "lifetime" is probably only about two-thirds used up, and she was somewhat distressed at the sound of all those past tense verbs. She was also "really embarrassed to get all of that money. I wish I'd gotten the Senior Fellowship later, when I'm older."[34] She was surprised too at this sudden run on Grace Paley, typically uncomfortable at becoming a growth stock on the literary market while so many others are still unrecognized. In her discomfort, she does not mention all the years she was overlooked or touted as "an underground success"—because she was a woman writing about women and children, speaking in their voices about what mattered in their days and lives.

She was honored yet again in 1987. In mid-December at a dinner party in the basement of Manhattan's Village Gate, the War Resisters League celebrated Grace Paley's sixty-fifth birthday and its own history with music, dancing, laughing, storytelling, and eating. The fifty-dollar-a-plate dinner, a benefit for the League, had a Russian menu, from sliced pumpernickel and beets to tea with jam cake. These dishes recalled Grace Paley's parents, who fled the czar's prisons, and honored the League's ongoing work toward friendship between the United States and the Soviet Union.

The last "act" of the evening was Grace herself, called onstage to accept a scroll of honor, inscribed with love and gratitude: "To Grace, who made getting arrested a creative act, and going to jail an education." The audience responded to her appearance in the bright nightclub spotlight with a standing ovation. There were cheers, applause, and table pounding; like the crowd in a high school gym, they were rhythmically chanting her name: "Grace, Grace, Grace, Grace." She stood and listened to that outrageous noise for only about twenty seconds, maybe twenty-five, before she yelled into the mike, "Okay! That's enough!"

There was some laughter, but then quiet listening from the audience of three hundred. These were people who had stood with her on the White House lawn and in the Seabrook parking lot, who had climbed the fence with her at Seneca Falls and had picketed local draft boards, who had linked arms with her and had marched against mounted police in neighborhood streets: a coalition of political factions and generations representing the old and new left; liberal, radical, and socialist feminists; gay and lesbian activists; civil rights workers; and members of park and school groups.

She pointed to a child in the audience and said, "There's a person here named Miranda with the same birthday, who's two years old," and then she quickly named others, including her granddaughter Laura, who would soon be eight.[35] She needs to share the honor or, rather, to shed it, to put herself back among the people again. She always needs to talk about the children as well. She said that earlier in the month, when she had spoken to a coalition of activist groups in Boston, she was criticized for talking about children so often, for emphasizing women as caretakers, for accepting that role. She made no apologies: "That's right, I do talk a lot about that. They're right. Well, men should do it too. We should all take care of the children."

She then told the WRL birthday crowd that just lately, "in a cynical or clinical way," she had been thinking about the US–USSR arms pact. Those amiable meetings between Gorbachev and Reagan "released within people a longing for a world without terror.... something was punctured in the American people, something opened up. People were allowed to think without hatred for three or four days," despite the fact that only small gains were made. (After all, she pointed out, within a week Secretary Schultz was talking about a U.S. build-up of conventional weapons.) She spoke directly to the audience, waving her arm to include all the tables in the room: "So, just when you think you can have a nice supper and sit down for twenty minutes, you know, you have to remember, the world still has to be saved—every day."

Then, in the moment of silence she had just created, she abruptly changed direction: "So thanks everybody, and then right away, we're gonna have dancing." Like Emma Goldman, Grace Paley rejects a revolution that won't dance. In a few minutes, even while the musicians were tuning up, she linked arms with a friend, and the two women swung around square-dance style. Her silvery white hair was a hazy cloud in the dim basement, her purple shawl swirled out as she improvised a small buck-and-wing. Photographs of Grace as a young woman remind us that she has been lovely for more than fifty years—the bright eyes and bold smile leap out of her family albums. Like the title of her poetry collection, her natural posture is "leaning forward," an ardent, eager presence.

In the late spring of 1988, Grace Paley retired from teaching at Sarah Lawrence College.[36] Laura Paley might get to see her grandma more often now, and maybe collections of stories and poems will appear more often than every ten or fifteen years. Maybe not. But Grace will continue to shuttle back and forth from country to city, working; she will teach at other schools, taking on single terms as a visiting professor and writer. She will travel to speak and teach in other countries. She will work in committees at PEN and keep her place in the vigils of American Jewish women in New York City who stand in solidarity with Palestinian and Israeli women in coalition.

Her plan, obviously, is not to retire in the usual sense or even to spend much more time writing. Essentially, Grace has "retired" to free herself to work. Long a proponent of hope, always an enemy of despair, Grace Paley is hardly oblivious to the constant and ever more rapid encroachment of disaster in this world. How does she feel about the struggle in these times? Asked before the Gulf War began, "How do you feel about impending disaster?" the famous optimist replied with a smile, "Well, of course I feel gloomy about the end of the world." One continues to work in the face of the end of the world, she says, "because otherwise you kill yourself. . . . you either live every day as though the world will last, or you just quit. If the world isn't going to last, it's not interesting. So you have to live every day as if the world will last."

The value of teaching, then, of organizing?

> Well, I don't know; who knows? [If people] believe what they're learning, then it changes them—and if it changes the people, it can change other things. I actually believe that one group of farmers getting together and having an agreement with, let's say, feed providers—I believe that does change things; I believe that that does make a difference. Lots of people out here [in Vermont] keep saying that farming is over and yes, it's true in a way; cattle farming, dairy farming, is going out. But truck farming, vegetable farming, is coming in. It's not done on a California scale, but they're all making a living at it; they're actually selling the vegetables. It's working—it's beginning to work—selling to restaurants and local places. And those vegetable farmers may have [a lot] to do with developing self-reliance again in the upper valley of Vermont.

Grace Paley believes that lives may be held, preserved, contained in stories, that literature can change the world—maybe even save it—that one's writing "*can* change things, even if you don't always believe that it *will.* There's this great thing that Paul Jacobs said when he was dying—well, he didn't really say it first, it comes from Hillel or Herschel, from one of the great rabbis, one of our smart boys—he said: 'Because you never see the end of your task, neither is it given you to abandon it.' " Since Grace Paley knows that we all "have to remember, the world still has to be saved—every day," there is little chance that she will abandon her task.

Notes

Preface

1. As Susan Koppelman has pointed out, "There is something insidious about Historians and Biographers and the ways in which they make women of achievement seem so different from the rest of us that we are unable to think of ourselves as emulating them. They are not different—at least not in ways that make their lives and achievements something we cannot use for models" (10).

2. When I worry about those limits and their effect on my work, I cheer myself by thinking of the worst example I know: the frustration of Virginia Woolf in writing about the life of Roger Fry, a project she was practically dragooned into accepting. Fry was no longer alive, of course, but she began soon after his death, she had been his good friend, and she knew all of his people quite well. The constraints she felt—some applied deliberately by the very family that had urged the work on her—thoroughly strangled her writing. This project of mine, self-chosen and enormously rewarding, is by no means so constrained.

3. I am aware of the concern of other feminist scholars, reacting to the condescension of traditional critics who minimized and patronized the few women authors they bothered to mention by writing and speaking of one "Emily" or another, and of "Charlotte," "Jane," and "Virginia." The subsequent choice—to write and speak of the women who are our subjects by their full or family names—is made in defense, in the spirit of reparation and homage. That posture is a useful one, especially in the academic world, but it has by no means calcified and is not always necessary. In this book, which offers Grace Paley as a *character* as well as a subject, the use of her

first name—and the first names of others as well—suits the text in both purpose and spirit. Additionally, accepting James Boswell's precedent, I do not intend to address the issue of scholarly objectivity—its elusiveness, its dubious value as an ideal; instead I offer the results of a self-conscious struggle toward an analysis and explication of Grace Paley's lifework.

4. Writers who come after me will write what I have not, saying things like "Arcana did not discuss . . . ," "Arcana's personal relationship with Paley pushed her to editorial decisions which . . . ," and that sort of thing. I'm looking forward to it all.

5. See the Bibliography for Spanier's *Kay Boyle, Artist and Activist*, Hull's "Researching Alice Dunbar-Nelson: A Personal and Literary Perspective," Tate's *Black Women Writers at Work*, and Ascher, DeSalvo, and Ruddick's *Between Women*.

Carolyn Heilbrun's useful *Writing a Woman's Life* was published after I completed all the research and the first draft of this book. Heilbrun deals primarily with novelists and never mentions Grace Paley, but much of what she has written pertains to me, as the biographer, and even occasionally to my subject, as the often-autobiographical fiction writer. Her discussion of Eudora Welty's reluctance/refusal to tell us what we really want to know in *One Writer's Beginnings*, for instance, reminds me of much of the thinking I did while writing this book. Heilbrun's conclusion may be relevant here too. She ends with a brief discussion of "closure" in the lives of women—in and out of fiction—and the life of "the old woman," who "must be glimpsed through all her disguises which seem to preclude her right to be called woman" and who "may well for the first time be woman herself" (131). Here I smile and think about the fact that my book is about a woman who was seventy in 1992, one for whom there is no need for "closure," since her life extends well beyond this text.

Introduction

1. See, for example, Criswell; Gelfant, "Grace Paley"; Kamel; Lyons, "Grace Paley's Jewish Miniatures"; Rody; and Taylor, *Grace Paley*.

2. See, for example, Schliefer; and Taylor, "Documenting Performance Knowledge" and *Grace Paley*.

3. See, for example, DeKoven, "Mrs. Hegel-Shtein's Tears"; Gelfant, "Grace Paley"; Hulley, "Grace Paley's Resistant Form"; Klinkowitz, "Grace Paley"; Schliefer; and Taylor, "Documenting Performance Knowledge" and *Grace Paley*.

4. "Midrash on Happiness," "Conversations," and "The Lion and the Ox." In the summer of 1991, after the manuscript of this book was complete, a new book, *Long Walks and Intimate Talks*, by Grace and her friend Vera

B. Williams appeared; it includes a few new pieces of poetry and prose and Vera has done some new pictures, but it is basically the same text as the 1989 War Resisters League Peace Calendar (see the Bibliography).

5. Actually, by 1985 Grace had also created another character, Ruth Larsen, who often resembles herself. Ruth and Faith are close friends. Since the late seventies, Grace has distributed the most personally autobiographical elements in her narratives between these two characters; perhaps no single character can be said to represent her so definitively now.

6. Forrest L. Ingram cites Franz Kafka, William Faulkner, and Sherwood Anderson as examples of story-cycle authors (14); we might add J. D. Salinger's Glass family stories and suggest that some characters, like both classic and new detectives (e.g., Miss Marple, V. I. Warshawsky, Kinsey Milhone, Sherlock Holmes, and Peter Wimsey), are well understood only when a number of their stories are known.

7. So far, less than a handful of stories seems to have originated outside the neighborhood, so to speak—e.g., "In the Garden." These stories are related to the others most obviously by the familiar "sound" of the narrative voice(s). (At that "sound," readers assume someone from the neighborhood has brought in information or an adventure to tell.)

8. Faith's sister, of course, is Hope, who never became a full character. I have decided not to consider capitalizing on *that*, however, or on the symbolic value of her speedy disappearance from Faith's life in the collected stories, in deference to Grace Paley's exasperated and repeated insistence that she created the siblings Faith, Hope, and Charlie Darwin as a joke.

9. We do so, of course, with the caveat articulated by Thomas C. Caramagno: "As biographers, we hope to detect a pattern in the evidence of our subject's life and work, but what pattern we recognize may depend on our preconceptions of what an artist is, what mentality is, and what a woman's mentality is" (17). Caramagno knows that "true objectivity is impossible because the 'story' [we write] of our subject's life is, to some extent, the result of our having imposed a premature order on the evidence we have gathered, an order that we may fail to remember is fictitious [that is, created by us] itself" (17).

10. Annie Dillard offers a contradictory disapproval of biographical criticism: "Our inquiry into a writer's personal opinions and private visions of things is bankrupt intellectually and nasty as well. Nevertheless, those opinions and that vision are not entirely irrelevant to the production of the work" (151). Grace Paley, less emotional but similarly contradictory, says this about the value of knowing writers' lives: "I don't think there's any value. It's just fun. People like to know; that's all. It can make a person more interesting; it can sell a book. But I don't think it makes a book more interesting to know the life of the writer . . . that has nothing to do with the

text itself. But on the other hand, for young people, it's encouraging" to know the life of the artist. "For instance, when I was in school and studied with Auden, it was wonderful. It was wonderful to know a poet—to really know a poet."

1: The Immigrant Story

1. In Russia, Poland, and other eastern European countries, many Christians "celebrated" Easter with pogroms; mobs of Christians would raid an urban ghetto or a rural shtetl (Jewish village), beating, killing, and raping Jews and vandalizing or destroying their homes, their shops, and, of course, their synagogues. Celebrations of Easter, the holiaay at which Christians emphasize most strongly their belief that Jews are responsible for the crucifixion of Jesus, often encourage mob violence against Jews.

2. Bonnie Lyons, who argues that Jewishness is "thematically central" to Grace Paley's work, says that "*Yiddishkeit*, especially the idealistic, socialist version . . . is the underlying source of values in her work" ("Grace Paley's Jewish Miniatures," 2).

3. A "midrash" is a narrative/commentary, often on the Torah, which deals with ideas and ethics, historically Jewish. The first published text of "Midrash on Happiness" may be found in Gibbons, 151–53.

4. See Arcana, *Our Mothers' Daughters*, chapter 5, for a fuller discussion.

5. "The first story I wrote was a very tiny story about a boy who had to stop taking piano lessons with his teacher. . . . Then I wrote one more story . . . again with a kid in it, about a Spanish superintendant's kid and the other kids on the block—written around the period of big garbage cans and coal heat. A kid by accident rolled a can off and killed somebody, and they were looking for him. It was very simple. Neither of the[se stories] was too successful" (Perry, 42).

6. In these poems, written when she was eight and ten years old, she had already begun to work on the reproduction of conversational speech and dialect and had embraced some of her major themes (family, politics, and social issues).

2: The Story Hearer

1. This may be one of the reasons Grace took so long to make serious criticisms of men and to embrace feminist politics; a solid chunk of her emotional base came from that strong bond with her father.

2. See Arcana, *Our Mothers' Daughters*, chapter 5, for further discussion of this point.

3. Scholars have recently begun to document what North American women's movements noticed thirty years ago. For an overview that includes additional sociocultural analysis, see Schultz.

4. In response to my additional questions about Mira, Jeanne Tenenbaum wrote this poignant—and tender—note: "My aunt Mira died of complications caused by a very rigid form of Parkinson's disease. She was completely unable to function and was finally placed in a home where she remained for about a year. Hers was a very tragic death for she had finally attained vocational status as an x-ray technician and then was felled by this terrible disease. She was a very unhappy person for none of her dreams had come true."

5. Mrs. Pinckney, who worked for Grace and her sister in the early fifties.

3: The Expensive Moment

1. This is an extension of her feelings about little boys when she was much younger; see the previous chapter.

2. Years later, in "The Little Girl," a story with an even more complicated set of ethical problems, Grace created yet another young girl, sexually curious and looking for adventure, who is destroyed by the social realities this early story basically ignores.

3. That phrase is actually used in the text but in quite a different mood from the one suggested by its use as a title. Marvine uses it to describe her daughter Josephine to their family doctor—who delivered the child—as a tough, rambunctious little girl, a lot like her mama. The title was not all that was changed. From the very first sentence, more words, phrases, and paragraphs in that magazine version are not-Paley than Paley. Grace says that when she saw it, she screamed and went right to bed. Like other abused authors, she raged; she had "a nervous collapse." She called the editor to object; he apologized, saying that he hadn't thought she would mind—which is astonishing—and offering to print the story again with her original words. His candid response displays the ignorance and carelessness implicit in his editing. Several "men's magazines" of that era, including *Esquire* when it still printed many sex cartoons and "pin-ups" of nearly naked women, and *Playboy*, which continues the practice, used good fiction and astute journalism as high-quality filler between "girlie" pieces. Such magazines provided space for fiction writers and even paid well—or at least better than "little magazines." This

is still the case with contemporary pornographers; *Playboy* continues to be the best example.

4. These poems and this journal were not found by me or the research librarians with whom I worked.

5. This latter phrase is from yet another story describing a father with coronary disease, "A Conversation with My Father" (ECLM, 161). Both of these stories were written in Isaac's later years, during the late sixties and early seventies.

6. It is interesting to recall that Isaac Goodside was a photographer before becoming a doctor and was a painter and writer when he retired from medicine. Bob Nichols, Grace's second husband, has been both a landscape architect and a writer in their years together.

7. Herschberger's effect on Grace's consciousness may have been instrumental in the text of her singular story "The Floating Truth." See chapter 6 for discussion.

4: A Subject of Childhood

1. Woolf's sister Vanessa Bell, however, a painter and designer who had three children, has often been described in these terms. See Woolf's complete diaries and letters, and Spalding's biography of Bell.

2. See Russ for a discussion of these restrictions.

3. The situation—as always—was really more complex than this. In a recent book of interviews, Grace talks about another element in her decision to write prose fiction. She explains that she wanted to get away from the "literary" influences of poetry as she had always known it: "I mean the reason I began to write stories was that the poems up to then had been too literary, it was really a problem" (Chamberlain, 185).

4. Among the critics who examine and discuss this story are Coppula; DeKoven, "Mrs. Hegel-Shtein's Tears"; Hulley, "Grace Paley's Resistant Form"; Humy; Kamel; Klinkowitz, "Grace Paley"; Mandel; Meier; Neff; Schliefer; and Sorkin, "What Are We, Animals?".

5. See Schliefer, for instance.

5: The Loudest Voice

1. It is also true that she did not receive invitations to join the literary community. Grace Paley—despite her interesting and interested reviews—was not put up for membership in the literary establishment. Indeed, she had at least one classic experience of the other sort: when

Little Disturbances came out in 1959, she attended a literary cocktail party at which she was introduced to Norman Mailer. The great wielder of the phallic pen turned away from his new colleague with one sentence only: "I don't read women writers." (During the Vietnam War, Grace found herself Mailer's ally against the U.S. government; in the eighties, they opposed each other in "the PEN wars," when women members of PEN, including Grace Paley, took that international organization of writers to task for its systematic marginalization of women.)

2. By 1970 Grace had grown comfortable enough with "saying her piece" to wield a megaphone at demonstrations, as she did, for instance, at the Varick Street Draft Induction Center in New York City that spring.

3. The first published version of this story (in *WIN*, August 1968) reads differently. Between 1968 and 1974 Grace altered the text. This is not unusual; she has occasionally published two or three different versions of stories and poems or published what is virtually the same text under two or more different titles.

4. Danny's assessment cannot be far off the mark. In 1987, when the War Resisters League honored Grace on her sixty-fifth birthday, some of the loudest laughs of the evening were in response to verbatim recitations from her appearances in the League's FBI file, now open by law.

5. Grace continued to employ the generic male in her language until very recently; her efforts to correct that long "standard" usage may now be heard in her conversation and read in her fiction. See "The Story Hearer" and "Friends" (LSD) for good examples.

6. See also Gibbons's text, which documents another symposium on social responsibility that Grace took part in nine years later.

7. In dealing with morality and ethics, Grace finds herself with odd bedfellows. Iris Murdoch told the assembled delegates at PEN International's 1988 meeting in London that writers must "defend the ability of ordinary prose to tell the truth," but she then deplored the idea of Women's Studies and Black Studies and even opposed the use of word processors by writers (Fritz, 20–21).

8. Helmut Bonheim discusses four narrative modes present "in most anecdotes": description, report, comment, and "directly quoted speech" (1). He explains that "these four modes are the staple diet of the short story and the novel" (1), and he offers an historical analysis of their use: "In our own age, speech stands high in the esteem of most readers. Description is thought boring except in small doses; comment, [considered] moralistic generalizing, is almost taboo, even where embedded in speech, and even report is preferred in the dress of, or at least heavily interlarded with, speech. . . . Speech seems most neutral, least authorial [as in *authority* and *authoritarian*]. This has not always been so. . . . Many a nineteenth century short story has hardly a word spoken in it" (8–9).

9. Some other examples of the overheard narrator, which Grace has employed more frequently in recent years, are found in "A Conversation with My Father" (ECLM, 167); "The Long-Distance Runner" (ECLM, 189); "Dreamer in a Dead Language" (LSD, 12); "The Story Hearer" (LSD, 134); and "The Expensive Moment" (LSD, 180, 185).

10. Except for the statistically less probable fact that she is a white girl assaulted by a Black man.

11. See, for instance, Bonheim; and especially Klinkowitz, who deals specifically with Grace Paley in these terms in *Literary Subversions* and his *Delta* article.

12. The metafictional quality of Grace Paley's work has increased over time. In the first collection, there are at least two stories in which "stories" are important business. In "The Loudest Voice," the question is, Who should narrate? Who has the right or the responsibility to tell the New Testament story of Jesus' birth? In "The Floating Truth," writing is revealed to be the creation of falsehood. In the second collection, Dennis in "Enormous Changes" is a writer of poetry and song lyrics that are discussed in terms of the appropriateness and effectiveness of content and diction; "Debts" offers an estimate of writers' responsibilities and goals; "Conversation" focuses on the activity of storywriting and contains three characters who are writers (the narrator, the boy, and the girl) and one who is a critic (the father). "The Immigrant Story," like "Ruthy and Edie" in the third collection, presents two versions of one story, disagreement about their veracity, and speculations about their purpose; "The Long-Distance Runner," like the later "Friends," which appeared in *Later the Same Day*, concludes with a statement about writing as the construction of reality. Other examples in *Later the Same Day* include "Love," which mixes the traditionally defined elements of fiction and nonfiction and suggests they cannot be separated or resolved; "Dreamer" focuses on Mr. Darwin's new career as a poet and issues of interpretation and publication/sales; "Somewhere" emphasizes the power dynamics between artist and subject, as does "Zagrowsky," in which its narrator restructures the reader's image of Faith within its notably self-conscious narrative; "Hearer" presents one form of the relationship between audience and storyteller; and "Listening" makes a clear statement about the writer's dual obligations: to listen before telling and to tell the truth.

13. She also resembles the metaphysical poets in her use of science and technology as subject, as in "In Time Which Made a Monkey of Us All" (LDM) and "At That Time, or The History of a Joke" (LSD), or as metaphor, as in "Wants" (ECLM): "He had had a habit throughout the twenty-seven years of making a narrow remark which, like a plumber's snake, could work its way through the ear down the throat,

halfway to my heart. He would then disappear, leaving me choking with equipment" (5).

14. This is a story in which John Keats, "brilliant and tubercular," is imagined among pale green shoots of rice, "working hard in the fields of Shanxi" but still criticized by "the head communard," who laughs at him, saying, "Oh what can ail thee, pale individualist?" (LSD, 182–83). (At around the same time, Bob Nichols was writing William Blake into his fiction as a full character, along with Jack Kerouac, among others.)

6: Enormous Changes

1. The excerpted blurbs on the 1973 edition's cover are from Harvey Swados, who praises Grace's creation of "sexy little girls," and from Philip Roth, who congratulates the author on having an "understanding of loneliness, lust, selfishness and . . . fatigue that is splendidly comic and unladylike."

2. Ultimately, though, both of Grace's children, after transferring from their first colleges, Marlboro and Franconia (which seem to have established an early family foothold in New England), did break their mother's pattern and decide to take degrees; both have also done graduate study in their fields (education and health).

3. A few years later, Grace was able to provide her daughter with a tuition-free education at Sarah Lawrence College, where she had become a member of the writing department faculty. Sarah Lawrence took Nora on probation because her grades and attendance record from high school were so unusual. As her brother would do later at City University of New York, Nora saw to it that she excelled in her first term. Once she had proven to herself—and the college—that she could be a superior student, Nora was free to study as she wished.

4. But, discussing the fact that in this culture for many decades mothering has been defined as the whole purpose of middle-class women's existence after the age of twenty-five or so, she says, "Well, naturally. You lose a job you've had for life. . . . and then nobody's there, nobody's at home with you anymore." She recognizes the grief and confusion women suffer while understanding its real cause: "You know, it's just like menopause—treating that as a psychological disaster. It's a made-up thing—it's just like treating getting older as a disease."

5. The costumes were designed by Lucia Vernarelli, who also illustrated one of Bob's first books with her woodcuts. Lucia is notable here because she is one of the few people who appears in one of Grace Paley's stories under her own name; her family's story is told in "Debts" (which first appeared in 1971 and then in the second collection in 1974). If that

story is as autobiographical as it appears in the scene between the I-narrator and "Lucia," she may have been one of those who encouraged Grace to continue to write family and neighborhood-based stories: "Lucia explained to me that it was probably hard to have family archives or even only stories about outstanding grandparents or uncles when one was sixty or seventy and there was no writer in the family and the children were in the middle of their own lives. She said it was a pity to lose all this inheritance just because of one's own mortality. I said yes, I did understand. . . . I thought about our conversation. . . . It was possible that I did owe something to my own family and the families of my friends. That is, to tell their stories as simply as possible, in order, you might say, to save a few lives" (ECLM, 9–10).

6. Danny Paley says that he has always been certain, despite Grace's disavowal, that "Wants" is absolutely autobiographical.

7. She had rejected the Freudian analysis of women and family life—we may argue that her stories demonstrate that rejection—but hadn't deliberately replaced that increasingly popular perspective with any other.

8. The stories clearly depict "institution" and "experience" as Adrienne Rich defined them in *Of Woman Born: Motherhood as Experience and Institution.*

9. We should remember that Grace Paley herself, first as a young high school graduate and gadabout and then as the young bride of a soldier on active duty, sought work that would take her interest, use her talents, and provide value in the form of social change.

10. Neal Isaacs and Jacqueline Taylor, contemporary scholars working on Grace Paley's stories, agree that this story is the most difficult to analyze or even to discuss. College students insist that they "don't understand" the text, though some do enjoy it while reading. In 1988 Grace Paley herself laughed and said, "Who knows what it's about?"

11. This story was dramatized and taped for a television network showing but is unavailable at present.

12. The change in this title is typical, not only of Grace's playfulness but also of her willingness to foster the active participation of readers in determining the meaning of her texts.

13. This decision is utterly distorted in the feature-length film *Enormous Changes at the Last Minute,* which contains lines from and bits of several Paley stories while dramatizing three of them: "An Interest in Life," "Dreamer in a Dead Language," and "Enormous Changes at the Last Minute." In the film, the pregnant Alexandra and her young lover Dennis walk off into the sunset together (almost literally), implying the perpetuation of the patriarchal nuclear family.

14. Though Grace does make her assume that most married women

enjoy coitus with their husbands: "She didn't want him to fuck her," Jack says of his mother and father, to which Faith replies: "Most people like their husbands to do that" (ECLM, 172). Research of the past twenty or thirty years has suggested that this is, alas, not the case.

15. See Black feminist theory, poetry, and fiction, especially Zora Neale Hurston's *Their Eyes Were Watching God*, in which the now-classic line about the Black woman being "the mule of the world" appears.

16. See Paula Giddings's *When and Where I Enter* or any work by Barbara Smith or bell hooks, for example.

7: An Irrevocable Diameter

1. She has often taught at City University of New York, occasionally at New York University.

2. There are many descriptions of and references to grammar school life, both in the early stories ("The Loudest Voice," "An Interest in Life," "Gloomy Tune") and more recent ones ("Ruthy and Edie," "Friends"); even high school turns up in "A Man Told Me the Story of His Life." College students, classrooms, and teachers have not been Paley subjects, however, except for one (now ironic) snide reference to Sarah Lawrence in "The Floating Truth" and some other brief references in "Enormous Changes at the Last Minute" and "The Long Distance Runner."

3. Earlier stories, written before she became a teacher, also sometimes contain young people—like the estimable Eddie Teitelbaum and his pals, drawn from her Bronx adolescence, and the assorted mothers in "Northeast Playground," drawn from Washington Square Park in the Village and the facts of her own motherhood's maturity.

4. Jane had been teaching at Sarah Lawrence for sixteen years before Grace arrived; she retired in 1986, two years earlier than Grace.

5. Jane dropped out of Vassar after a few years to attend and graduate from the University of Wisconsin at Madison, a source of extremely diverse, not to mention suspect, social and political influences.

6. Jane "moved completely into poetry in about 1970–71."

7. Grace was once asked "if she made a conscious decision *not* to produce the traditional 'well-made story.'" Grace answered, "Well, I didn't know how to write the well-made story. I tried, God knows. I just failed miserably, so I just wrote the way I could. I made honest efforts to write a typical novel, but I failed, I just couldn't do it" (Chamberlain, 19). Like Jane, Grace said that "writing the stories [her own way] loosened my poetry and made it easier" (19).

8. It is also true that in the past decade, as Grace's schedule has

grown more and more hectic, some workshop students have felt shortchanged by her. Some express disappointment in the lack of real contact with her or time to talk with her about their writing. Those who articulate this complaint think she has simply spread herself too thin. This is probably a result of her (stated) policy of almost never refusing requests for her time and work.

9. Similarly, the Women's Pentagon Action(s) used the offices and mailing facilities of the War Resisters League in the late seventies and early eighties.

10. She was reticent here in the same way she had been uncomfortable in her early writing years, because her subject matter (the lives of women and children, the ethnic communities of park and tenement) seemed inappropriate for "literature," seemed, as she had said many times, to be "just this ordinary crap." We have to remember that though Grace Paley was little schooled, the little schooling she did have in "English" and "creative writing" was fostered by traditional scholarship in literature.

11. Others include a one-paragraph polemic on the state of Israel (in "The Used-Boy Raisers," composed in the middle/late fifties), one sentence about women working for peace (in "Living," composed in the early sixties), another single sentence about partisans in the Eisenhower/Stevenson elections (in "Northeast Playground," composed in the mid-sixties), and sporadic references to the sixties "youth culture" (in *Enormous Changes*, composed throughout the sixties and early seventies). The title story of *Enormous Changes* actually contains dialogue in which Dennis stops Alexandra from speaking about the Vietnam War by saying, "Alexandra, you talk a lot, now hush, no politics" (128), and, as if in reply, the text then presents Alexandra querying Dennis about the kind of language and subject one may properly use in poetry (129–30).

12. There is almost no military quality to Corporal Brownstar's life in the early story "A Woman, Young and Old." Military service is fleetingly referred to by the romantic Marvine as life in the "Army of the Republic," and the only slight discomfort of that life is that Browny gets shipped out to Joplin, Missouri.

13. She also wrote "statements," usually in conjunction with other writers; these include "A Call to Resist Illegitimate Authority," written with Paul Goodman for the Support-In-Action Program to back draft resisters in the sixties; "On Soviet Dissidents," written with six other peace activists in 1973; and the "Women's Unity Statement," written in 1982, in collaboration with "about thirty" other women who took part in the two Women's Pentagon Actions. (The first piece was not found for citation purposes; the latter two are in the Bibliography.)

14. First in I-KON (vol. 1, issue 3) and then again in WIN (the December issue).

15. First published in 1955, Heller's first novel was reprinted in 1961 and then saw more than twenty editions by May of 1968, a high point in the rapidly growing antiwar movement.

16. Nonetheless, she was one of those invited, on a date in the sixties no one seems to remember, to join the New York literary branch of concerned citizens at home: Elizabeth Hardwick, Robert Lowell, and Susan Sontag spent an evening with community activists. As Karl Bissinger remembers it, they discussed "the quality of the prose coming out of the peace movement." As Grace recalls, though, the major debate was over the question of whether to *counsel* draft resistance or simply to dispense information to young men facing the draft. "They yelled at us," Grace says. Hardwick and Lowell were against such counseling, as were many liberal supporters of the antiwar movement, possibly because it threatened to carry the same penalty—and the same stigma—as draft refusal itself. Shortly after that evening's discussion, Grace—and many others in the country who had been arguing the question—decided that such action was the right choice. Hence, the national proliferation of movement posters reading "I Counsel Draft Resistance" and the resultant arrests.

17. This was when she was jailed for six days in 1966 for taking part in the sit-down demonstration in the middle of Fifth Avenue, blocking and thus protesting the annual Armed Forces Day Parade. When she was released, she joined the movement to change the intolerable conditions in the old prison.

18. Her late brother-in-law, Sam Tenenbaum, used to say that there wasn't "a street or avenue in New York City worthy of the name if Gracie hasn't lain down on it."

19. Grace was at the War Resisters League's first anti-Vietnam War demonstration in 1963; naturally, she had been with the Village Peace Center when, even before that demonstration, it sponsored a Village meeting about the coming war. In April of 1967, she and her friends were in the protective circle surrounding the young men who committed the first mass draft-card burning; she was also among the War Resisters League members arrested at the draft induction center in December of 1968.

20. As she had protested to Nora, Grace was "a middle-aged lady." In a society that perceives women in terms of sexual body imagery and demands passivity or manipulation as feminine modus operandi, this motherly "little lady" with graying hair, forty-seven years old in 1969, never aroused the rage and hatred that Joan Baez, Jane Fonda, and Vanessa Redgrave had to endure. Grace neither symbolized female sexuality nor threatened patriarchal sexism. Her own "wild" past—however much the FBI might have known about it—was not at issue.

21. John Douglas, Norm Fruchter, and Bob Kramer.

22. She became, then, one of the very small percentage of American women—including those in the military—to do so since 1865.

23. She has incorporated that exchange with the pilot—quoted here from a retelling in personal conversation—into both her essays and her fiction. The most recent incarnations are in a short piece in the 1989 War Resisters League Peace Calendar, called "POW" (opposite the week of June 5), and in *Long Walks* (just past the middle of the unpaginated book).

24. Grace walked and talked with Barbara Deming, comrade in the movement and sister writer; they had a warm friendship that ended with Barbara's death from cancer nearly fifteen years later. See the Bibliography for Grace's introductory essay to Barbara's last book.

8: An Interest in Life

1. Actually, the collected stories were written over the full fifteen years from 1959 to 1974.

2. This statement clearly points to Faith's announced "change" in "Faith in a Tree," near the center of the book.

3. See the Bibliography for a list of selected work.

4. One of whom, in his violent rejection of Mother Church, strongly echoes Jess Paley in his denunciations of Judaism.

5. In the past several years, prompted by the Israeli government's treatment of the Palestinian people, and especially following her first trip to Israel in spring of 1987 and the *intifada* beginning that December, Grace has grown active on Jewish and Israeli/Palestinian issues. She is one of the founders of the Jewish Women's Committee to End the Occupation of Gaza and the West Bank, a group that stands vigil weekly in New York City. Her earlier work, both in the poetry collection and the stories ("Used-Boy Raisers" and "At That Time"), has thus been rendered invalid as a source of accurate information on Grace Paley's current attitudes about Israel and the international structure and situation of the Jewish people. Her work on Middle East issues and her support of the "two-state solution" increased during the U.S. war on Iraq in early 1991 and continues through this period of prolonged U.S. military occupation in the Middle East.

6. Intergenerational exchange was one of her first themes. When thirty-eight-year-old Charles C. Charley finds himself married to Cindy Anne, a high school student, in "An Irrevocable Diameter" (written in the late fifties), he explains that "one acquires important knowledge in the dwelling place of another generation," though he believes that "in six or seven years," when Cindy has grown up, he and she "will be strangers" (LDM, 123).

7. This is not true in the early "In Time Which Made a Monkey of Us All," which ends on a sober—even grim—note, but the story does contain this theme in a transspecies version: the "child" is Itzik, a monkey in Teitelbaum's Zoo, the family pet shop. Eddie Teitelbaum suggests that his father has raped a chimpanzee at the city zoo and that "Itzikel" is his half-brother. Eddie is literally his brother's keeper.

8. Her race/color is not described but only assumed—Grace Paley is not immune to the ingrained white narrative assumption of a character's being white, Black only when labeled so.

9. Debbie Weissman came from a more conservative background than her young husband did. She had known, she says, only "parents who had no politics of any sort or were right-wing," and she had had "to sneak to demonstrations" in her teens. For her, "it was sort of nifty to meet an older person who had this view of the world." Debbie met Grace one morning after she had stayed overnight at the Eleventh Street apartment: "I woke up in the morning and there was this little woman, and Danny was talking to her like she was his mother but he kept calling her Grace. And I couldn't figure out who she was; where I grew up nobody called their mother by her name. It's very funny." Debbie had never heard of Grace before meeting her: "I didn't know she existed. I only found out she was a writer after I'd met both her and Danny, because one day I was in a bookstore with a friend who held up a copy of *Little Disturbances* and asked, 'Is this the Grace you met?'"

10. Bob's novels reflect and draw from all his travel during this period, but especially the journeys to Chile and China, which he and Grace would visit in 1974. See the Bibliography.

11. By 1987, when their friend George Denison, himself a well-known writer (*The Lives of Children*) and activist, died, Grace was called by reporters for statements—"quotes" they could use in their obituary articles and radio coverage of Denison's important work. Bob, who had been much closer to George for many years, was not queried.

12. In his article "Chile: The Left before the Coup," published in March 1974, we find what might be the original of that now immortal noodle factory (8), of such interest to the Western travelers in his own quartet of novels and a center of controversy for the travelers from the United States in Grace's later "Somewhere Else" (LSD).

13. For example, the series of picture posters "Would you burn a child," etc.

14. She says she "really got a lot done there that time," and she took another residency there in 1974 but was not so successful on the second occasion; little work came out of that period. She has not taken any other writers' residencies.

15. As Grace deliberately depicted him in "A Conversation with My Father," first published in 1971 in *New American Review,* he was a classicist who had come to resist even the *idea* of change—social, personal, or aesthetic.

16. When Karl Bissinger accompanied Grace to visit her father in his last years, he had a conversation with the old man in which Dr. Goodside whispered to Karl when Grace was out of the room, "Have you any influence with that girl? Can you keep her from doing these crazy things she's always doing?" Karl, who had accompanied "that girl" on some of her "crazy" missions, just said, "No sir, I don't. And I can't."

17. On the spring day Isaac Goodside died, Grace was officiating at the first Women's Studies/Women's Literature event ever organized at Sarah Lawrence College. She got a phone call at midday, telling her that her father was dying. She left immediately—Jane Cooper took over her duties at school—and arrived in time to spend a few hours with him before he died.

18. And Faith's. When Grace published *Enormous Changes,* she prefaced the stories with this paragraph: "Everyone in this book is imagined into life except the father. No matter what story he has to live in, he's my father, I. Goodside, M.D., artist, and storyteller. G.P." There are three stories in which Isaac Goodside will be readily recognized as a model—or at least a major inspiration—even without this directional signal from the author: Mr. Darwin in "Faith in the Afternoon," Alexandra's father in "Enormous Changes at the Last Minute," and the father of the writer-narrator in "A Conversation with My Father." There are three other stories in which less notable fathers might also be modeled after Isaac: Jack Raftery in "Distance," the title character in "The Burdened Man," and Jack's father in "The Immigrant Story."

9: A Woman, Young and Old

1. A few years earlier, she had been overlooked entirely. When an action she organized and directed in a distinctly Gandhian mode of nonviolent civil disobedience (at a draft induction center) was severely criticized in print, despite her obvious presence and obvious leadership, the "blame" for her strategy was assigned to a man, a prominent colleague who had taken part in the event. (See *WIN,* May 1, 1970, pp. 6–8.)

2. *Woman Hating* came out in 1974, like Grace's *Enormous Changes* (for which Andrea had read the manuscript and helped Grace put the stories together), and its dedication reads, "For Grace Paley, and in Memory of Emma Goldman." Within the next few years, Andrea and

Grace became estranged, however, in a complex of personal/political conflict.

3. Noam Chomsky, Dave Dellinger, Daniel Berrigan, David McReynolds, and Sidney Peck; there were no other women.

4. In an interesting current version of this scenario, similar critics (also connected with the War Resisters League) recently castigated Olive Bowers—another female U.S. peace activist who had solicited contributions to support her trip as delegate to a peace conference—for what they called "chasing dissidents" while she was in the Soviet Union (Benn, 6).

5. All of these men (but none of the women, except perhaps as wives) received publicity in the United States as leading intellectuals, writers, and scientists who were silenced in the Soviet Union.

6. Within the texts themselves, Faith—like Grace—is ultimately identified overtly as both a writer and an activist.

7. At Loyola University of Chicago in March 1987, when asked by her audience if she had ever consider writing a novel, she said, "No. Yes. I don't know. Well, I might. I mean I have considered it, and I might again."

8. Some critics would move the date up to Edgar Allan Poe's definitive, prescriptive analyses of the form; others would go back literally thousands of years, finding "the story" at the root of all narrative prose. For my purpose here, Irving will serve.

9. National magazines with wide readership had popularized the genre; thousands of stories were published every year. This situation continued until well into the twentieth century, with the mid-century erosion of large-format, slick magazines and their replacement by "little magazines" and academic journals as the predominant publishers of short fiction.

10. Unless, in such forms as science fiction and fantasy, or even formulaic detective fictions or romances, they have made clear that they are doing just that—pretending.

11. Certainly "well-made" stories are still being written, just as some contemporary films have wrapped-up endings and some recently designed buildings contain no large open spaces—or the illusion of them—to mitigate their density and ponderousness. But these are now recognized as "traditional" structures and considered, in most genres, romantic, if not retrograde, in their insistence on the illusion of finality and closure.

12. Thirty-one of the forty-five collected stories feature a first-person narrator; at least twenty-two of these are arguably autobiographical.

13. None of the first collection of stories is short enough to be considered here; Grace was more conventional then, and so was the short story genre. "Living," "Northeast Playground," "Politics," "Debts," and "Wants" in *Enormous Changes* might qualify; all are less than three pages

long. *Later the Same Day* contains "At That Time, or The History of a Joke," which is also less than three pages, and "In This Country, But in Another Language, My Aunt Refuses to Marry the Men Everyone Wants Her To," "A Man Told Me the Story of His Life," "This is a Story about My Friend George, the Toy Inventor," and "Mother," which are all less than two pages long. These are not fragments; they are complete stories.

14. Though the name is not printed *as* initials, the title letters of the organization stand for Playwrights/Poets, Essayists/Editors, and Novelists. Given the critical history of the short story in English, we should not be surprised that they never thought to make it PENS, to include writers of short fiction. Notwithstanding that exclusion, Grace Paley joined the organization six months before her friend and Sarah Lawrence colleague Muriel Rukeyser began her 1975–76 term as president of PEN.

15. This committee was founded by Grace and Meredith Tax (author of *Rivington Street* and *Union Square*) in 1986, when PEN women realized that the organization's conservative leadership—the president was Norman Mailer—was never going to act on its marginalization of women and people of color in the membership or its trivialization of issues important to them, unless strongly pressed to do so. The Women's Committee has since applied and maintained the necessary pressure.

16. Cited by Karen Peterson (8). Even critics who think they are treating her work seriously can slip into trivializing language, as do Robert B. Shaw, who refers to her poetry as "perky" (38), and Minako Baba, who concludes an otherwise appropriately scholarly article by referring to the stories as a "delightful brand of sociological art" (54).

17. Now that Grace has retired from, and Esther has been fired by, Sarah Lawrence College, and now that Grace, like Esther, has become an active supporter of peace movements in the Middle East, these groups overlap in different directions, but the point remains.

18. The roles of reader and writer are often reversed. Jane tells about the time in the early seventies that she was in residence at the McDowell Colony in New Hampshire and drove over to see Grace and Bob in Vermont. She had with her the poetry she was working on and some older pieces, along with an essay detailing her development in skill and consciousness as a (woman) poet. She took this assortment of pieces over to Grace "so I could show them to her and say, 'Do you think these are okay? And what should I do with this essay now that it's gotten so huge?' " Grace, who rarely reads through a full text at one sitting, disappeared for two hours and came back to say, "I read the whole thing. Jane, don't you see? You've got your book." Grace, Jane says, "had the vision to see that all these parts put together would make a book." (The book is *Maps and Windows*.)

10: Goodbye and Good Luck

1. As did her writing. See "In a Vermont Jury Room" in *Sevendays*, the poetry in "Love," the first story in *Later the Same Day*, and the "Vermont Poems" section of *Leaning Forward*.

2. Nora's presence, and her Vermont politics, must have been instrumental in her mother's growing interest in the rural countryside, the people of the New England mountains, and ecological issues. Nora was, even earlier than Grace, strongly attuned to the need for such work, like the Women and Life on Earth Conference and the Women's Pentagon Actions. She introduced Grace, and maybe even Bob, to the folks who had voted in their town meeting to impeach Richard Nixon before most of the rest of the country had fully recognized his abuses of the presidency.

3. Two long trips to Puerto Rico in 1976 and 1977, both made between school terms because Grace was teaching full-time, were also relatively private excursions. They went, she says, because Bob was working with Puerto Rican people on the Lower East Side ("Puerto Rico is a very important part of New York"), because she was able to write there, and because it was "a warm place." But she hardly became a tourist on the beach or a writer in luxurious isolation. What she learned on those trips became part of her international analysis and appeared in her writing; written into one of her *Sevendays* columns is a story about Faith and Richard visiting the Darwins at the Children of Judea, just after Faith has returned from a conference in Puerto Rico on the bilingual child and public education. The whole piece is a discussion of the colonial relationship between Puerto Rico and the United States and the ignorance of U.S. citizens about that relationship (February 28, 1977, p. 15). See also the stories "In the Garden" and "Somewhere Else" in *Later the Same Day*.

4. First published in 1978 in the *New Yorker* and later included in *Later the Same Day*.

5. In fact, Bob's quartet, his novel in four parts, is attributed to Joe in the text of Grace's story: "He was, when not in China, writing a novel, a utopia, a speculative fiction in which the self-reliant small necessary technology of noodle-making was one short chapter" (LSD, 51).

6. As in "A Conversation with My Father," in which the stories within the title story contain many of the same ideas as the story's outer framework (the painful dialogue between parent and child, their conflicting world views, the elder's refusal or inability to change, the younger's rejection of the elder), the two stories that are combined in "Somewhere Else" amplify our understanding by becoming one story.

7. This situation is reminiscent of an experience Bob Nichols had several years earlier. He had designed a vest-pocket park for an uptown

neighborhood and was present at the ground-breaking celebration. The playground installation, its bare wood and metal fittings considered *de rigueur* in rapidly gentrifying white neighborhoods, was accepted somewhat cynically by the local Black organizers. One of those women said to him, "Very nice, Mr. Nichols. I guess if it'd been downtown you'd have painted it."

8. This is typical of her pacing; the events that inspired the China episodes in this story took place in May 1974, and the story first appeared in October 1978.

9. Alternating with Noam Chomsky.

10. Both Bob and Nora recall the camp as a small village, which she compares with the women's peace camps at Greenham Common in England and at Seneca, New York.

11. The Clamshell Alliance, which Nora Paley helped organize, caused the proliferation of such small affinity groups as Ompomponoosic and WAND, which Grace and Bob joined. Created in 1976, the Alliance represents a growing percentage of New England's populace and remains active; the Seabrook struggle has advanced, often in court.

12. The Russian text translates as USA–USSR DISARM!; the U.S. English banner read NO NUCLEAR WEAPONS/NO NUCLEAR POWER/ USA OR USSR.

13. WRL's chairwoman Norma Becker (who had been with Grace in Washington the night she met Nora on the Pentagon steps), Jerry Coffin, Scott Herrick, Pat Lacefield, David McReynolds, Craig Simpson, and Steve Sumerford.

14. Grace, Karl Bissinger, Gail Bederman, Cathy Carson, Ralph DiGia, Ed Hedemann, Warren Hoskins, Linnea Capps Lacefield, Karen Malpede, Glenn Pontier, and Van Zwisohn.

15. The picture was taken by Karl, who worked for years as a portrait and magazine photographer, during which he took some now-famous shots of literary figures, including Paul Bowles and Colette.

16. Quoted by Sybil Claiborne in *Climbing Fences*, n.p.

17. Jane shared the spotlight that night with another poet, Louis O. Coxe.

18. An apt reading; the poems are in *Scaffolding*.

19. The theme is present in several of the other stories in that collection as well, like "Friends," in which the characters are telling each other and the reader alternate versions of their mutual past, present, and future throughout the text. This issue continues to be of great importance to Grace Paley (see the Endor and Thiers interview).

20. As she has elsewhere; see "Debts," "The Long-Distance Runner," "Dreamer in a Dead Language," and "Love."

21. The depth and extent of Grace Paley's friendship with specific women who are lesbians is not the point here. Her increasing sensitivity to lesbian and gay issues is manifest in her other writings as well. See, for instance, her essay "Thinking about Barbara Deming."

22. As always in a country where women are the figureheads of the anti-ERA forces, some women are opposed to the Seneca camp and demonstration(s), but, as Grace wrote, they were not impervious to the work of their sisters. One local woman, a counterpicket of sorts who had been wearing a t-shirt that said "Nuke the bitches 'til they glow," removed the last three words of her slogan, "reserving further action for deeper thought" ("Seneca Stories," 56).

23. See "The Used-Boy Raisers," (LDM, 131–32). Those who know Grace only as the writer of the early stories occasionally turn up now, condemning her as a "diasporist" for the opinion stated by Faith in that story.

24. This new perspective—conflicted as it is—is also reflected in Faith's pointed description of her partner's assessments of women on the street in "Midrash" (Gibbons), and the selfish pride of the young father in "Anxiety" (LSD).

25. His comments, however, suggest something about her response to the North American women's movement as it gathered strength for this second wave over twenty years ago. Some women, who still judge her by her older work, insist that Grace is not a feminist; this mirrors the situation of those Jews who have read only her earliest story collection and consider her "merely" a diasporist.

26. Called "Conversations" and printed on the page opposite the second week of March.

27. First published in 1963.

28. See, for instance, Ginny's runaway husband in "An Interest in Life" and the self-centered Peter in "The Pale Pink Roast," both in *The Little Disturbances of Man.*

29. She talks about a conversation she had with her friend Vera B. Williams, the artist with whom she collaborated on the 1989 War Resisters League Peace Calendar. Grace and Vera arranged and analyzed the same kinds of experiences that are described in Doris Lessing's *The Summer before the Dark*, in which women deliberately alter their appearance and posture/gesture to manipulate male response.

30. From her speech in acceptance of the Edith Wharton Citation of Merit, the State Authorship of New York.

31. The prize carried a $1,000 stipend.

32. She received a $10,000 honorarium for those two years of service to her home state. Her term of office ended in December 1988.

33. The award carried with it $40,000, great esteem, honor, and fame.

34. On the other hand, she is grateful for "all of that money," which will be very useful because, having lived a financially marginal life as an unpaid mother and part-time office worker and teacher with consistently small salaries, "I'm not gonna have a big pension."

35. When Debbie gave birth to Laura, Grace was thrilled. "It's just like falling in love," she told Sybil Claiborne. "It's amazing! I never thought I'd feel this way again."

36. Yet another sort of public esteem has recently been conferred on her: Allan Gurganus, the acclaimed author of *Oldest Living Confederate Widow Tells All*, recently donated $25,000 of that novel's phenomenal earnings to found a scholarship at Sarah Lawrence in honor of Grace Paley, who was his first writing teacher.

Bibliography

Abel, Elizabeth, ed. *Writing and Sexual Difference*. Chicago: University of Chicago Press, 1982.

Adams, Phoebe. Review of *Enormous Changes*. *Atlantic*, April 1974, 120.

Allen, Bruce. Review of *Enormous Changes*. *Library Journal* 99 (March 1, 1974): 678.

Allen, Walter. *The Short Story in English*. Oxford: Clarendon Press, 1981.

Annan, Gabriele. Review of *Enormous Changes*. *Times Literary Supplement*, February 14, 1975.

Arcana, Judith. "Grace Paley and 'Friends.' " In *Women's Friendship Stories*, ed. Susan Koppelman. Tulsa: University of Oklahoma Press, 1991.

———. *Our Mothers' Daughters*. Berkeley: Shameless Hussy Press, 1979.

———. "Truth in Mothering: Grace Paley's Stories." In *Narrating Mothers*, ed. Brenda O. Daly and Maureen Reddy. Knoxville: University of Tennessee Press, 1991.

Ascher, Carol, Louise DeSalvo, and Sara Ruddick. *Between Women: Biographers, Novelists, Critics, Teachers and Artists Write about Their Work on Women*. Boston: Beacon, 1984.

Aspesi, Natalia. "Grace Paley l'indomabile." *La Repubblica*, November 19, 1987, Cultura 1. (Translation by Suzanne S. Gossett.)

Avery, Evelyn. "Oh My 'Mischpocha'! Some Jewish Women Writers from Antin to Kaplan View the Family." *Studies in American Jewish Literature* 5 (1986): 44–53.

Baba, Minako. "Faith Darwin as Writer-Heroine: A Study of Grace Paley's Short Stories." *Studies in American Jewish Literature* 7 (Spring 1988): 40–54.

Baumbach, Jonathan. "Life-Size." Review of *Enormous Changes. Partisan Review* 42, no. 2 (1975): 303–6.

———. *Writers as Teachers/Teachers as Writers*. New York: Holt, Rinehart and Winston, 1970.

Bendow, Burton. "Voices in the Metropolis." Review of *Enormous Changes. Nation*, May 11, 1974, 597–98.

Benn, Ruth. "Eugene to Moscow: Making the Connections." *The Nonviolent Activist*, December 1988, 6–8.

Benstock, Shari, ed. *Feminist Issues in Literary Scholarship*. Bloomington: Indiana University Press, 1987.

Blake, Harry. "Grace Paley, a Plea for English Writing." *Delta* 14 (May 1982): 73–80.

Blake, Nancy. "Grace Paley's Quiet Laughter." *Revue française d'etudes americaines* 4 (October 1977): 55–58.

Blake, Patricia. "Little Disturbances of Woman." *Time*, April 15, 1985, 98.

Boethel, Martha. "An Interview with Grace Paley." *Texas Observer*, October 11, 1985, 15–16.

———. "Writing to Save the World." *Texas Observer*, October 11, 1985, 1, 14–15.

Bonetti, Kay. *An Interview with Grace Paley*. Audiotape 6102. Columbia, Mo.: American Audio Prose Library, 1986.

Bonheim, Helmut. *The Narrative Modes: Techniques of the Short Story*. Cambridge: D. S. Brewer, 1982.

Boswell, James. *The Life of Samuel Johnson*. Abridged edition, ed. Bergen Evans. New York: Modern Library, 1965.

Bresnahan, Roger J. " 'Borne Back Ceaselessly into the Past': The Autobiographical Fiction of Sherwood Anderson." *Midwestern Miscellany* 9 (1981): 54–60.

Broner, E. M. "The Dirty Ladies: Earthy Writings of Contemporary American Women—Paley, Jong, Schor and Lerman." *Regionalism and the Female Imagination* 4, no. 3 (1979): 34–43.

———. "Grace and Faith." Review of *Later the Same Day*, by Grace Paley. *Women's Review of Books* 2 (September 1985): 7–8.

Bruce, Melissa. "*Enormous Changes at the Last Minute:* A Subversive Song Book." *Delta* 14 (May 1982): 97–114.

Calinescu, Matei. "Ways of Looking at Fiction." *Bucknell Review* 25, no. 2 (1980): 155–70.

Caramagno, Thomas C. "Manic-Depressive Psychosis and Critical Approaches to Virginia Woolf." *PMLA* 103 (January 1988): 10–23.

Cevoli, Cathy. "These Four Women Could Save Your Life." *Mademoiselle*, January 1983, 104–7.

Chamberlain, Mary, ed. *Writing Lives: Conversations between Women Writers*. London: Virago, 1988.

Chambers, Ross. *Story and Situation: Narrative Seduction and the Power of Fiction*. Minneapolis: University of Minnesota Press, 1984.

Christ, Carol P. *Diving Deep and Surfacing: Women Writers on Spiritual Quest*. Boston: Beacon, 1980.

Claiborne, Sybil, ed. *Climbing Fences*. New York: War Resisters League, 1987.

Clemons, Walter. "The Twists of Life." *Newsweek*, March 11, 1974.

Cohen, Sarah Blacher. "Jewish Literary Comediennes." In *Comic Relief: Humor in Contemporary American Literature*, ed. Sarah Blacher Cohen. Urbana: University of Illinois Press, 1978.

Conway, Celeste, et al. "Grace Paley Interview." *Columbia: A Magazine of Poetry and Prose* 2 (1978): 29–39.

Cooper, Jane. *Maps and Windows*. New York: Collier Books, 1974.

———. *Scaffolding*. London: Anvil Press Poetry, 1984.

Coppula, Kathleen A. "Not for Literary Reasons: The Fiction of Grace Paley." *Mid-American Review* 7, no. 1 (1986): 63–72.

Cousineau, Diane. "The Desire of Woman, the Presence of Men." *Delta* 14 (May 1982): 55–66.

Crain, Jane Larkin. " 'Ordinary' Lives." Review of *Enormous Changes. Commentary*, July 1974, 92–93.

Crawford, John. "Archetypal Patterns in Grace Paley's 'Runner.' " *Notes on Contemporary Literature* 11 (September 1981): 10–12.

Criswell, Jeanne Salladé. "Cynthia Ozick and Grace Paley: Diverse Visions in Jewish and Women's Literature." In *Since Flannery O'Connor: Essays on the Contemporary American Short Story*, ed. Loren Logsdon and Charles W. Mayer. Macomb: Western Illinois University Press, 1987.

Darnton, Nina. "Taking Risks: The Writer as Effective Teacher." *New York Times*, special education section, April 13, 1986, 65–67.

Davidson, Cathy, and E. M. Broner, eds. *The Lost Tradition: Mothers and Daughters in Literature*. New York: Frederick Ungar, 1980.

DeKoven, Marianne. "Later and Elsewhere." Review of *Later the Same Day. Partisan Review* 53, no. 2 (1986): 315–18.

———. "Mrs. Hegel-Shtein's Tears." *Partisan Review* 48, no. 2 (1981): 217–23.

Dillard, Annie. *Living by Fiction*. New York: Harper and Row, 1982.

Doherty, Gail, and Paul Doherty. "Paperback Harvest." *America* 133 (October 1975): 234–47.

Draine, Betsy. "Women as 'Major Authors': The Horizon of Expectations." Typescript, 1987.

Ellmann, Richard. *Oscar Wilde*. New York: Knopf, 1988.

Endor, Karen, and Naomi Thiers. "We're Talking to Each Other More and More: An Interview with Grace Paley." *off our backs*, April 1988, 4–5.

Federman, Raymond. "Self/Voice/Performance in Contemporary Writing." In *Coherence*, ed. Don Wellman. Braintree, Mass.: O. Ars/Alpine Press, 1981.

Feinstein, Elaine. "Getting Through." *New Statesman*, February 14, 1975.

Fletcher, Janet, Francine Fralkoff, Anneliese Schwarzer, and Judith Sutton. "The Best Books of 1985." *Library Journal* 111 (January 1986): 49.

Flynn, Elizabeth A., and Patrocinio P. Schweickart, eds. *Gender and Reading*. Baltimore: Johns Hopkins University Press, 1986.

Foley, Barbara. *Telling the Truth: The Theory and Practice of Documentary Fiction*. Ithaca: Cornell University Press, 1986.

Friebert, Stuart. "Kinswomen." Review of *Leaning Forward*, by Grace Paley, and *Shelter*, by Laura Jensen. *Field* 34 (Spring 1986): 93–102.

Friedman, Maya. "An Interview with Grace Paley." *Story Quarterly* 13 (1981): 32–39.

Fritz, Leah. "A Gathering of Women Writers." *Women's Review of Books* 5 (September 1988): 20–21.

Frye, Joanne. *Living Stories, Telling Lives: Women and the Novel in Contemporary Experience*. Ann Arbor: University of Michigan Press, 1986.

——. "The Politics of Reading: Feminism, the Novel, and the Coercions of 'Truth.' " Typescript, 1987.

Gardiner, Judith Kegan. "On Female Identity and Writing by Women." In *Writing and Sexual Difference*, ed. Elizabeth Abel. Chicago: University of Chicago Press, 1982.

Gelfant, Blanche H. "Grace Paley: A Portrait in Collage." In *Women Writing in America*, by Blanche H. Gelfant.

——. *Women Writing in America: Voices in Collage*. Hanover, N.H.: University Press of New England, 1984.

Gibbons, Reginald, ed. *The Writer in Our World*. Boston: Atlantic Monthly Press, 1986.

Giddings, Paula. *When and Where I Enter: The Impact of Black Women on Race and Sex in America*. New York: Bantam, 1985.

Gilbert, Celia. "Grace Paley's New Poems." Review of *Leaning Forward*. *Sojourner*, April 1986, 41.

Gilbert, Sandra M., and Susan Gubar. *No Man's Land: The Place of the Woman Writer in the Twentieth Century*. New Haven: Yale University Press, 1988.

Girgus, Sam B. *The New Covenant: Jewish Writers and the American Idea*. Chapel Hill: University of North Carolina Press, 1984.

Gold, Donna. "Separating Fact from Fiction Isn't Always Easy, Says Paley." *Maine Sunday Telegram* (Portland edition), April 2, 1989, 27A.

Gold, Ivan. "On Having Grace Paley Once More among Us." *Commonweal*, October 25, 1968, 111–12.

Gubar, Susan. " 'The Blank Page' and Female Creativity." In *Writing and Sexual Difference*, ed. Elizabeth Abel. Chicago: University of Chicago Press, 1982.

Harrington, Stephanie. "The Passionate Rebels." *Vogue*, May 1969, 146–51, 218.

Harris, Lis. Review of *Enormous Changes*. *New York Times Book Review*, March 17, 1974.

Harris, Robert R. "Pacifists with Their Dukes Up." *New York Times Book Review*, April 14, 1985.

Healey, Robert C. "Enter a New Storyteller." *New York Herald*, April 26, 1959.

Heilbrun, Carolyn G. "A Response to *Writing and Sexual Difference.*" In *Writing and Sexual Difference*, ed. Elizabeth Abel. Chicago: University of Chicago Press, 1982.

———. "Women's Biographies of Women." Review of seven biographies. *Review* 2 (1980): 337–45.

———. *Writing a Woman's Life*. New York: W. W. Norton, 1988.

Hellerstein, Kathryn. "Yiddish Voices in American English." In *The State of the Language*, ed. Leonard Michaels and Christopher Ricks. Berkeley: University of California Press, 1980.

Hendricks, Fredric Jefferson. "*Accent*, 1940–1960: The History of a Little Magazine." Ph.D. diss., University of Illinois at Urbana-Champaign, 1984.

Hull, Gloria T. "Researching Alice Dunbar-Nelson: A Personal and Literary Perspective." In *All the Women Are White*, ed. Gloria T. Hull et al.

Hull, Gloria T., Patricia Bell-Scott, and Barbara Smith, eds. *All the Women Are White, All the Blacks Are Men, But Some of Us Are Brave*. Old Westbury: Feminist Press, 1982.

Hulley, Kathleen. "Grace Paley's Resistant Form." *Delta* 14 (May 1982): 3–18.

———. "Interview with Grace Paley." *Delta* 14 (May 1982): 19–40.

Hulley, Kathleen, ed. *Grace Paley*. Special issue of *Delta: Revue du Centre d'Etude et de Recherches sur les Ecrivains du Sud aux Etats-Unis* 14 (May 1982).

Humy, Nicholas Peter. "A Different Responsibility: Form and Technique in Grace Paley's 'Conversation With My Father.' " *Delta* 14 (May 1982): 87–96.

Hurston, Zora Neale. *Their Eyes Were Watching God.* Urbana: University of Illinois Press, 1978.

Iannone, Carol. "A Dissent on Grace Paley." *Commentary,* August 1985, 54–58.

Ingram, Forrest L. *Representative Short Story Cycles of the Twentieth Century: Studies in a Literary Genre.* The Hague: Mouton, 1971.

"International Symposium on the Short Story." *Kenyon Review* 30 (1968): 443–90.

Isaacs, Neal D. *Grace Paley: A Study of the Short Fiction.* Boston: G. K. Hall/Twayne Series, 1990.

Jacobs, Rita D. Review of *Later the Same Day. World Literature Today* 60 (Spring 1986): 310–11.

Jones, Nancy Baker. *On Solid Ground: The Emergence of the Self-Created Woman in Contemporary American Literature.* Ph.D. diss., University of Texas at Austin, 1986.

Kamel, Rose. "To Aggravate the Conscience: Grace Paley's Loud Voice." *Journal of Ethnic Studies* 11 (Fall 1983): 29–49.

Kapelovitz, Abby P. "Mother Images in American-Jewish Fiction." Ph.D. diss., University of Denver, 1985.

Kapp, Isa. "Husbands and Heroines." Review of *Enormous Changes. New Leader* 57 (June 24, 1974): 17–18.

Kaye/Kantrowitz, Melanie, and Irena Klepfisz. "An Interview with Grace Paley." *The Tribe of Dina.* Special double issue of *Sinister Wisdom* 29/30 (1986): 289–96.

Kennedy, William. "Be Reasonable—Unless You're a Writer." *New York Times Book Review,* January 25, 1987, 3.

Kingston, Maxine Hong. *The Woman Warrior.* New York: Knopf, 1976.

Klinkowitz, Jerome. "Fiction: From the 1950s to the Present." *American Literary Scholarship* (1979): 275–309.

———. "Grace Paley: The Sociology of Metafiction." *Delta* 14 (May 1982): 81–86.

———. *Literary Subversions: New American Fiction and the Practice of Criticism.* Carbondale: Southern Illinois University Press, 1985.

Koppelman, Susan. Review of *Between Women* [by Carol Ascher, Louise DeSalvo, and Sara Ruddick]. *Women Studies Review* 8 (January/February 1986): 10–12.

Langer, Elinor. *Josephine Herbst: The Story She Could Never Tell.* New York: Warner Books, 1984.

LaSalle, Peter. "Short Stories: The Survival of the Species—Hearing Whispers of Poetry." *Commonweal,* June 21, 1985, 376.

Lidoff, Joan. "Clearing Her Throat: An Interview with Grace Paley." *Shenandoah* 32, no. 3 (1981): 3–26.

———. "Fluid Boundaries: Women Reading Women Writing." Typescript, n.d.

Lyons, Bonnie. "Grace Paley's Jewish Miniatures." Typescript, 1988.

———. "Tillie Olsen: The Writer as a Jewish Woman." *Studies in American Jewish Literature* 5 (1986).

McCaffrey, Larry, and Sinda Gregory. *Alive and Writing: Interviews with American Authors of the 1980s.* Urbana: University of Illinois Press, 1987.

MacManus, Patricia. "Laughter from Tears." *New York Times Book Review,* April 19, 1959, 28–29.

McMurran, Kristin. "Even Admiring Peers Worry that Grace Paley Writes Too Little and Protests Too Much." *People Magazine,* February 26, 1979, 22–23.

McReynolds, David. "Anti-Draft Week: N.Y. I, II, III." *WIN,* May 1, 1970, 6–8.

Mandel, Dena. "Keeping Up with Faith: Grace Paley's Sturdy American Jewess." *Studies in American Jewish Literature* 3 (1983): 85–98.

Marchant, Peter, and Earl Ingersoll, eds. "A Conversation with Grace Paley." *Massachusetts Review* 26 (Winter 1985): 606–14.

Marcus, Jane. *Virginia Woolf and the Languages of Patriarchy.* Bloomington: Indiana University Press, 1987.

Martin, Wendy. "The Satire and Moral Vision of Mary McCarthy." In *Comic Relief: Humor in Contemporary American Literature,* ed. Sarah Blacher Cohen. Urbana: University of Illinois Press, 1978.

Maslin, Janet. "Film: 3 Paley Stories." *New York Times,* April 11, 1985.

May, Charles, ed. *Short Story Theories.* Athens: Ohio University Press, 1976.

Meier, Joyce. "The Subversion of the Father in the Tales of Grace Paley." *Delta* 14 (May 1982): 115–28.

Mellors, John. "Americans and Others." Review of *Little Disturbances. The Listener,* May 22, 1975, 685–86.

Merriam, Eve. Review of *Later the Same Day. Ms.,* April 1985, 13–14.

Michaels, Leonard. "Conversation with Grace Paley." *Threepenny Review* 3 (Fall 1980): 4–6.

Mickelson, Anne Z. *Reaching Out: Sensitivity and Order in Recent American Fiction by Women.* Metuchen, N.J.: Scarecrow Press, 1979.

Midwood, Barton. "Short Visits with Five Writers and One Friend." *Esquire,* November 1970, 150–53.

Miller, Jane. *Women Writing about Men.* New York: Pantheon, 1986.

Morley, Hilda. "Some Notes on Grace Paley While Reading Dante: The Voice of Others." *Delta* 14 (May 1982): 67–72.

Murray, Michele. Review of *Enormous Changes. New Republic,* March 16, 1974, 27.

Neff, D. S. " 'Extraordinary Means': Healers and Healing in 'A Conversation with My Father.' " *Literature and Medicine* 2 (1983/84): 118–24.

Neubauer, Carol E. "Developing Ties to the Past: Photography and Other Sources of Information in Maxine Hong Kingston's *ChinaMen.*" *MELUS* 10, no. 4 (1983): 17–36.

Newton, Judith, and Deborah Rosenfelt, eds. *Feminist Criticism and Social Change: Sex, Class and Race in Literature and Culture.* New York: Methuen, 1985.

Nichols, Marianna da Vinci. "Women on Women: The Looking Glass Novel." *Denver Quarterly* 11 (Autumn 1976): 1–13.

Nichols, Robert. *Arrival.* New York: New Directions, 1977.

———. "Bob Nichols' China Diary." *WIN,* February 27, 1975, 7–11; April 3, 1975, 5–9; July 24, 1975, 8–10; August 7, 1975, 6–11.

———. "Chilean Diary Revisited." *WIN,* November 22, 1973, 7–8.

———. "Chile—The Left before the Coup." *WIN,* March 21, 1974, 7–9.

———. *Clara Remembered.* Brooklyn: Musty Bone, 1989.

———. *Exile.* New York: New Directions, 1980.

———. *The Expressway: A Street Play. WIN,* August 17, 1968, 10–29.

———. *Garh City.* New York: New Directions, 1978.

———. *The Harditts in Sawna.* New York: New Directions, 1979.

———. "Lessons of Chile." *WIN,* October 3, 1974, 4–7.

———. "A Play for Peace: Regional Actions." *WIN,* February 15, 1972, 26–27.

———. *Slow Newsreel of Man Riding Train.* San Francisco: City Lights Books, 1962.

———. "Who'll Stop the Rain: Three Poems by Robert Nichols." *WIN,* October 15, 1972, 18–19.

Nichols, Robert, with Grace Paley. "Chilean Diary." *WIN,* May 17, 1973, 6–8; May 24, 1973, 10–12; May 31, 1973, 9–10; June 7, 1973, 12–13.

Nichols, Robert, with Lucia Vernarelli. *Address to the Smaller Animals.* Thetford, Vt.: Penny Each Press, 1976.

Novak, William. "The Uses of Fiction: To Reveal and to Heal." Review of *Enormous Changes. America* 130 (June 8, 1974): 459–60.

Nyren, Dorothy. Review of *Little Disturbances. Library Journal* 84 (April 1959): 1280.

Olsen, Tillie. "A Biographical Interpretation of 'Life in the Iron Mills.' " In *Life in the Iron Mills by Rebecca Harding Davis.* Old Westbury, N.Y.: Feminist Press, 1972.

Orloff, Kossia. "Grace Paley's *Enormous Changes at the Last Minute:* Bonding among Women—Release from Bondage." Typescript, n.d.

"Pacifist Mission to Moscow." *War Resisters League Action Special.* New York: War Resisters League, n.d.

Packer, Nancy H. Review of *Enormous Changes*. *Studies in Short Fiction* 12 (Winter 1975): 34–35.

Paley, Grace. "Conversations." *SevenDays*, February 28, 1977, 15.

———. "Conversations in Moscow." *WIN*, May 23, 1974, 4–12.

———. "Cop Tales." *SevenDays*, April 1980, 24.

———. "Digging a Shelter and a Grave." Review of *The Nuclear Age*, by Tim O'Brien. *New York Times Book Review*, November 17, 1985, 7.

———. *Enormous Changes at the Last Minute*. New York: Dell, 1975.

———. "Essay on Dogs." *WIN*, January 17, 1980, 22.

———. " ' . . . i guess it must have been someone else.' " *WIN*, May 15, 1977, 30–33.

———. "In a Vermont Jury Room." *SevenDays*, May 9, 1977, 51.

———. *Later the Same Day*. New York: Farrar Straus Giroux, 1985.

———. *Leaning Forward*. Penobscot: Granite Press, 1985.

———. "The Lion and the Ox." *SevenDays*, March, 28, 1977, 36.

———. *The Little Disturbances of Man: Stories of Women and Men at Love*. New York: Doubleday, 1959.

———. "Living on Karen Silkwood Drive." *SevenDays*, June 6, 1977, 11–12.

———. "Midrash on Happiness." In *The Writer in Our World*, ed. Reginald Gibbons. Boston: Atlantic Monthly Press, 1986.

———. "Mom." *Esquire*, December 1975, 85–86. (Later published as "Other Mothers," *Feminist Studies* 4 [June 1978]: 166–69.)

———. "Peace Movement Meets with PRG in Paris." *WIN*, April 24, 1975, 4–5.

———. *Poems*. Notebook manuscript by Grace Goodside. Danny Paley/Jeanne Tenenbaum Collection, Bronx/New York City.

———. Preface to *A Dream Compels Us: Voices of Salvadoran Women*. Philadelphia: South End Press, 1989.

———. Preface to *Jewish Women's Call for Peace: A Handbook for Jewish Women on the Israeli/Palestinian Conflict*. Ithaca: Firebrand Press, 1990.

———. Preface to *The Shalom Seders: Three Haggadahs Compiled by New Jewish Agenda*, ed. Arthur Waskow. New York: Menorah/Public Resource Center, 1984.

———. "Report from the DRV." Edited speech transcript. *WIN*, September 9, 1969, 4–11.

———. "The Sad Story About the Six Boys About to Be Drafted in Brooklyn." *WIN*, December 12, 1967, 18.

———. "The Seneca Stories: Tales from the Women's Peace Encampment." *Ms.*, December 1983, 54–62, 108.

———. "Some Notes on Teaching: Probably Spoken." In *Writers as Teachers/Teachers as Writers*, ed. Jonathan Baumbach. New York: Holt, Rinehart and Winston, 1970.

——. Speech of Acceptance and Thanks. Presented at the celebration of the presentation of the first Edith Wharton Citation of Merit (State Authorship Conferred), Albany, December 10, 1986. Audio tape transcript, Danny Paley Collection, Brooklyn Heights/New York City.

——. "Thinking about Barbara Deming." In *Prisons That Could Not Hold*, by Barbara Deming. San Francisco: Spinsters Ink, 1985.

——. "Upstaging Time: A Celebration of Life in Progress." *Lear's*, January 2, 1989, 85–93.

——. "We Were Strong Enough to Kill the Parents in Vietnam. Does That Make Us Good Enough to Raise the Orphans?" *Ms.*, September 1975, 69–70, 95–96.

Paley, Grace, with Noam Chomsky et al. "On Soviet Dissidents." *WIN*, November 22, 1973, 15.

Paley, Grace, with other members of the Women's Pentagon Action. "Women's Pentagon Action Unity Statement." New York: Women's Pentagon Action in conjunction with the War Resisters League, April 1982.

Paley, Grace, with Vera B. Williams. *Long Walks and Intimate Talks*. New York: Feminist Press, 1991.

——. *365 Reasons Not to Have Another War: 1989 Peace Calendar*. New York and Philadelphia: War Resisters League and New Society Publishers, 1988.

Park, Clara Claiborne. "Faith, Grace and Love." *Hudson Review* 38 (Autumn 1985): 481–88.

Pattee, Fred Lewis. *The Development of the American Short Story: An Historical Survey*. New York: Harper, 1923.

Peden, William. *The American Short Story: Continuity and Change, 1940–1975*. New York: Houghton Mifflin, 1975.

Perry, Ruth. "Grace Paley." In *Women Writers Talking*, ed. Janet Todd. New York: Holmes and Meier, 1983.

Peterson, Karen. "What Is Feminist Writing and Why Do We Need Feminist Publishing?" *National Newsletter of the Feminist Writers Guild* 8 (Winter 1985–86).

Phillips, Robert. Review of *Enormous Changes*. *Commonweal*, November 1, 1974, 116–18.

Rabinowitz, Dorothy. Review of *Enormous Changes*. *Saturday Review/ World*, March 23, 1974, 44.

Rainwater, Catherine, and William J. Scheick, eds. *Contemporary American Women Writers: Narrative Strategies*. Lexington: University of Kentucky Press, 1985.

Raphael, Marc L. "Female Humanity: American Jewish Women Writers Speak Out." *Judaism* 30 (Spring 1981): 212–24.

Ratner, Rochelle. Review of *Leaning Forward*. *Library Journal* 111 (February 1986): 83.

Reeve, Benjamin. "Eccentric Constellations." *Harper's*, June 1974, 96.

Reid, Ian. *The Short Story*. London: Methuen, 1977.

Remmick, David. "Grace Paley, Voice from the Village." *Washington Post*, April 14, 1985.

Review of *Later the Same Day*. *Publishers Weekly*, March 19, 1986.

Review of *Little Disturbances*. *Kirkus Reviews* 27 (February 15, 1959): 152.

Review of *Little Disturbances*. *New Yorker*, June 27, 1959, 86.

Rich, Adrienne. *Blood, Bread and Poetry*. New York: W. W. Norton, 1986.

———. *Of Women Born: Motherhood as Experience and Institution*. New York: W. W. Norton, 1979.

———. *On Lies, Secrets and Silence*. New York: W. W. Norton, 1979.

Rody, Caroline. "The 'Schlemiel' and Grace Paley: An American Female Reinvention of a Yiddish Fool." Presented at the "Jewish American Women Writers: Translating the Eastern European Experience" Panel, Women in America Conference, Georgetown University, April 8, 1989.

Rosenblith, Murray. "Occupation at Seabrook October 1979." *WIN*, October 25, 1979, 4–9.

Rosenfelt, Deborah. "From the Thirties: Tillie Olsen and the Radical Tradition." In *Feminist Criticism and Social Change: Sex, Class and Race in Literature and Culture*, ed. Judith Newton and Deborah Rosenfelt. New York: Methuen, 1985.

Roth, Philip. *Reading Myself and Others*. New York: Farrar Straus and Giroux, 1975.

Ruddick, Sara. "Maternal Thinking." *Feminist Studies* 6 (Summer 1980): 342–67.

———. *Maternal Thinking: Toward a Politics of Peace*. Boston: Beacon, 1989.

Russ, Joanna. *How to Suppress Women's Writing*. Austin: University of Texas Press, 1983.

Saal, Rollene W. "Four New Faces in Fiction." *Saturday Review*, April 11, 1959, 38.

Sale, Roger. "Fooling Around, and Serious Business." Review of various books and authors. *Hudson Review* 27 (Winter 1974/75): 623–35.

Satz, Martha. "Looking at Disparities: An Interview with Grace Paley." *Southwest Review* 72 (Autumn 1987): 478–89.

Schilb, John. "The Politics of the 'Author-Function' in Contemporary Feminist Criticism." Typescript, 1987.

Schliefer, Ronald. "Grace Paley: Chaste Compactness." In *Contemporary*

American Women Writers: Narrative Strategies, ed. Catherine Rainwater and William J. Scheick. Lexington: University of Kentucky Press, 1985.

Schram, Peninnah. "One Generation Tells Another: The Transmission of Jewish Values through Storytelling." *Literature in Performance* 4, no. 2 (1984): 33–45.

Schultz, Debra. *Risk, Resiliency, and Resistance: Current Research on Adolescent Girls/Survey for the Ms. Foundation Funding Initiative for Girls.* New York: National Council for Research on Women, 1991.

Schwartz, Helen J. "Grace Paley." In *American Women Writers*, vol. 3, ed. Lina Mainiero. New York: Frederick Ungar, 1981.

Shapiro, Harriet. "Grace Paley: 'Art Is on the Side of the Underdog.' " *Ms.*, May 1974, 43–45. (Includes review of *Enormous Changes.*)

Shapiro, Nora. "Handcrafted Fictions." *Newsweek*, April 15, 1985, 91.

Shaw, Robert B. "Brief Reviews." Review of *Leaning Forward. Poetry* 148 (April 1986): 36–48.

Shulman, Alix Kates. "The Children's Hour." *Village Voice Literary Supplement*, June 1985, 9–10.

Silesky, Barry, et al. "A Conversation." *Another Chicago Magazine* No. 14 (1985): 100–114.

Slawson, Judy. "Grace Paley: Changing Subject Matter with a Changing Passionate and Committed Life." *Villager*, May 18, 1978, 13.

Smith, Sidonie. *A Poetics of Women's Autobiography.* Bloomington: Indiana University Press, 1987.

Sorkin, Adam J. "Grace Paley." In *Twentieth Century American Jewish Fiction Writers.* Vol. 28 of *Dictionary of Literary Biography*, ed. Daniel Walden. Detroit: Gale, 1984.

———. " 'What Are We, Animals?': Grace Paley's World of Talk and Laughter." *Studies in American Jewish Literature* 2 (1982): 144–54.

Spalding, Frances. *Vanessa Bell.* New York: Harcourt Brace Jovanovich, 1985.

Spanier, Sandra Whipple. *Kay Boyle, Artist and Activist.* Carbondale: Southern Illinois University Press, 1986.

Sternburg, Janet. *The Writer on Her Work.* New York: W. W. Norton, 1980.

Sternhell, Carol. Review of *Later the Same Day. Nation*, June 15, 1985, 739–41.

Stevick, Philip, ed. *The American Short Story, 1900–1945: A Critical History.* Boston: Twayne, 1984.

Suleiman, Susan Rubin. "Writing and Motherhood." In *The (M)Other Tongue: Essays in Feminist Psychoanalytic Interpretation*, ed. Shirley Nelson Garner, Claire Kahane, and Madelon Sprengnether. Ithaca: Cornell University Press, 1985.

"Symposium on Fiction." *Shenandoah* 27 (Winter 1976): 3–31.

Taliaferro, Frances. Review of *Later the Same Day*. *Washington Post*, April 28, 1985.

Tate, Claudia. *Black Women Writers at Work*. New York: Continuum, 1986.

Taylor, Jacqueline. "Documenting Performance Knowledge: Two Narrative Techniques in Grace Paley's Fiction." *Southern Speech Communication Journal* 53 (Fall 1987): 65–79.

———. *Grace Paley: Illuminating the Dark Lives*. Austin: University of Texas Press, 1990.

———. "Grace Paley on Storytelling and Story Hearing." *Literature in Performance* 7 (April 1987): 46–58.

Towers, Robert. "Moveable Types." Review of *Later the Same Day*. *New York Review of Books*, August 15, 1985, 26–29.

Tyler, Anne. "Mothers in the City." Review of *Later the Same Day*. *New Republic*, April 29, 1985, 38–39.

Vidal, Gore. "American Plastic: The Matter of Fiction." *New York Review of Books*, July 15, 1976, 31–39.

Weaver, Gordon, ed. *The American Short Story, 1945–1980: A Critical History*. Boston: Twayne, 1983.

Welty, Eudora. *One Writer's Beginnings*. New York: Warner Books, 1983.

———. "The Reading and Writing of Short Stories." In *Short Story Theories*, ed. Charles May. Athens: Ohio University Press, 1976.

Winegarten, Renee. "Paley's Comet." Review of *Enormous Changes*. *Midstream* 20 (December 1974): 65–67.

Wisse, Ruth R. *The Schlemiel as Modern Hero*. Chicago: University of Chicago Press, 1971.

"Women Protest at PEN Conference." *New Directions for Women* No. 3/4 (1986): 1, 16.

Wood, Michael. "Flirting with Disintegration." Review of *Enormous Changes*. *New York Review of Books*, March 21, 1974, 19–22.

Woolf, Virginia. *The Diary of Virginia Woolf*. 5 vols. Edited by Anne Olivier Bell and Andrew McNeillie. New York: Harcourt Brace Jovanovich, 1977–84.

———. *The Letters of Virginia Woolf*. 6 vols. Edited by Nigel Nicolson and Joanne Troutmann. New York: Harcourt Brace Jovanovich, 1975–80.

———. *Orlando*. New York: Harcourt, Brace, 1956.

———. *Roger Fry*. New York: Harcourt Brace Jovanovich, 1968.

———. *A Room of One's Own*. New York: Harcourt, Brace and World, 1929.

———. *Three Guineas*. New York: Harcourt, Brace and World, 1938.

———. *A Writer's Diary*. New York: Harcourt Brace Jovanovich, 1954.

Yudkin, Leon Israel. *Jewish Writing and Identity in the Twentieth Century*. New York: St. Martin, 1982.

Index

Note on the Author

Judith Arcana is the director of the Union Institute Center for Women and a professor of literature and women's studies in Union's Graduate School. She is the author of *Our Mothers' Daughters*, *Every Mother's Son*, *Celebrating Nelly*, and many articles, essays, and speeches about women's issues, including abortion, mother-blaming, ethnic and racial stereotypes, and Jewish women. A poet and story writer as well, her work has appeared recently in *Bridges*, *Sojourner*, and the anthology *Word of Mouth*, vol. 2.